Small Museums

A GUIDE TO THE SMALL MUSEUMS OF BRITAIN

Christine Redington

I.B.Tauris *Publishers*
LONDON · NEW YORK

Published in 2002 by I.B.Tauris & Co Ltd,
6 Salem Road, London W2 4BU
175 Fifth Avenue, New York NY 10010
www.ibtauris.com

In the United States of America and in Canada distributed by Palgrave
Macmillan a division of St. Martin's Press, 175 Fifth Avenue, New York
NY 10010

ISBN 1 86064 623 9

A full CIP record for this book is available from the British Library
A full CIP record for this book is available from the Library of Congress

Library of Congress catalog card: available

Set in Monotype Bembo and VAG Rounded by Ewan Smith, London
Printed and bound in Great Britain by MPG Books Ltd, Bodmin

Contents

Photography Credits

All photographs, unless otherwise stated, have been provided by and are the copyright of the individual museums.

COVER: Veilleuse by Jacob Petit of Paris, mid 19th century (Bramah Tea and Coffee Museum, London). Turkey Red export label c. 1929 (Colour Museum, Bradford). Banjo-playing busker, automaton by Gustave Vichy, Paris (Keith Harding's Mechanical Music Museum, Gloucestershire). A pair of Scottish silver coursing presentation collars, 1830 (Leeds Castle Dog Collar Museum, Leeds).

SOUTH WEST: The Barometer World features Philip Collins.

SOUTH EAST: Milk Delivery Box courtesy of the Dairy Council. Jane Austin's House courtesy of the Jane Austen Memorial Trust. Dog Collar Museum courtesy of the Leeds Castle Foundation. Ellen Terry's House courtesy of the National Trust.

LONDON: Twinings in the Strand photograph by Christine Redington.

EASTERN REGION: Prickwillow Drainage Engine Museum photograph by Christine Redington. Castle Point Transport Museum photograph by Dr J.A. Waite. Fakenham Gas Museum photograph by Christine Redington. Museum of the Broads photograph by Raymond Jeckells.

EAST CENTRAL: Vina Cooke Museum features Vina Cooke.

NORTH EAST: Museum of Victorian science features Tony Swift.

SCOTLAND: Bank of Scotland Museum courtesy of the Governor and Company of the Bank of Scotland. Russell Collection courtesy of the University of Edinburgh. Museum of Piping photograph by Christine Redington. Orkney Wireless Museum features James Thomson.

NORTH WEST: Windermere Steam Boat Museum photograph features the Wet Dock and is courtesy of the Windermere Steam Boat Museum.

WEST CENTRAL: Kelsmcott Museum photograph by Hilary Came. Museum of the Jewellery Quarter courtesy of Birmingham Museum and Art Gallery.

Maps drawn by Christine Redington (not to scale).

Acknowledgements

My thanks to all those museum curators and volunteers who took the time to fill in questionnaires about their museums, send photographs and a range of information, which made this book possible. Thanks also to Philippa Brewster for her enthusiasm and editorial help and to Deborah Susman and Ewan Smith for the preparation of the book. My thanks also to Dr Lester Crook for his initial support and help with the original proposal for this book. Finally my grateful thanks to Frances for her encouragement, support and help during the research and preparation of the book.

Key to Symbols

❄ Open in the winter
✸ Open in the summer

Admission charge
① £1–3 adult ticket
② £3–6
③ £6 upwards

Ⓟ Parking at the museum
🅿 Parking possible nearby
♿ Accessible for the disabled
🅆🅒 Toilets
☕ Café
✕ Restaurant
⚠ Shop
🎥 Photography possible
👪 Enjoyable for the family

Introduction

What kind of museums?

Odd, quirky, fascinating, bizarre and just plain interesting: the selection of small museums listed in this book have just those things to offer the visitor. The museums hold particular and selective collections such as lawnmowers, costumes, shells or collars for dogs. It also contains museums that are centred on a specific theme – for instance, the 18th-century novelist Jane Austen, the explorer Captain James Cook or a subject such as shipwrecks.

Visiting these museums can take you on a tour of the history of Britain. In Cornwall a tin mine at Geevor and a china clay mine at Wheal Martyn reveal the industrial past. Museums with particular collections are often there because the town was the base for this industry in the past. Birmingham has a jewellery museum, while Stockport in Greater Manchester has a museum about hat-making. In Macclesfield, Cheshire, are two museums concerned with silk-making and weaving and in Honiton in Devon is a collection of lace.

The book is intended as a helpful companion on your travels around Britain and is divided into areas such as the South West or North East. On the maps of each area, the underlined towns or villages indicate a museum mentioned in the following text.

Definition of a small museum

This is not as obvious as it appears. The basic difference between large and small museums is often one of funding. Major museums in London, such as the Science Museum, have government funding. The museums also tend to be in large buildings, to contain a number of different exhibits and to be well staffed. They are widely publicised and therefore well known, and receive thousands of visitors.

In contrast, a small museum may receive no subsidy or funding. In some cases the museum may cover quite a lot of acres but could still be considered small in the definition offered by this book. The publicity may not be as good or wide-reaching as that of some of the major museum buildings, and the number of visitors can be quite limited.

Museum buildings

The buildings are often very interesting in themselves, being old restored houses or industrial structures. The Drainage Museum in Prickwillow near Ely is a converted pumping-engine house, while the Slate Museum in Llanberis, North Wales, consists of all the various buildings of a slate-mine. In Dumfries, Scotland, the Aviation Museum is in the airfield's original control tower.

Why visit small museums?

What makes these museums so interesting is that they are often run by the collectors of the exhibits themselves. John and Judy Stimson's collection can be seen at the Museum of the Home in Pembrokeshire, Wales, and like many museum proprietors, they are knowledgeable, dedicated enthusiasts. Entering a small museum can often be a revelation, for not only are you suddenly faced with a fascinating collection but if you ask questions you can be given a wealth of first-hand information and sometimes demonstrations of how the particular items work. For instance, in the Museum of Entertainment near Spalding, Lincolnshire, you are given a guided tour and demonstration of the exhibits by someone who was a friend of the original collector and who helped to restore some of the organs, old gramophones and other items. Volunteers not only take the money at the door, but often help in restoring items in the museum. At the Martello Tower in St Osyth's, Essex, an enthusiast restores the recovered parts of wartime aeroplanes in the workshop on the first floor and the smell of various oils pervades the atmosphere.

Your contribution

This has to be a selection of museums, since if all the museums in the country were included it would be impossible to pick the book up, let alone carry it around with you. There are many rural museums and museums that tell the history of their town or village. As you visit some of the museums included in the book, you may find yourself searching out others. If you find one that really should be included, then do write to us and let us know. The address is: Small Museums Book, I.B. Tauris & Co Ltd, 6 Salem Road, London W2 4BU. Remember, this book on small museums is about collections or themes.

A warning!

The factors that make small museums so interesting also make them vulnerable. Times and dates of opening can alter. Museums can, alas, close down. The inevitable delay between the research and publication of this book means that some factors might have changed. If you have trouble contacting a museum then do telephone the local Tourist Office. For visitors not familiar with our telephone system, dial 192 to ask for a telephone number. *If you are travelling any distance to a museum, please, please contact them first to avoid disappointment.*

Introduction

1. South West

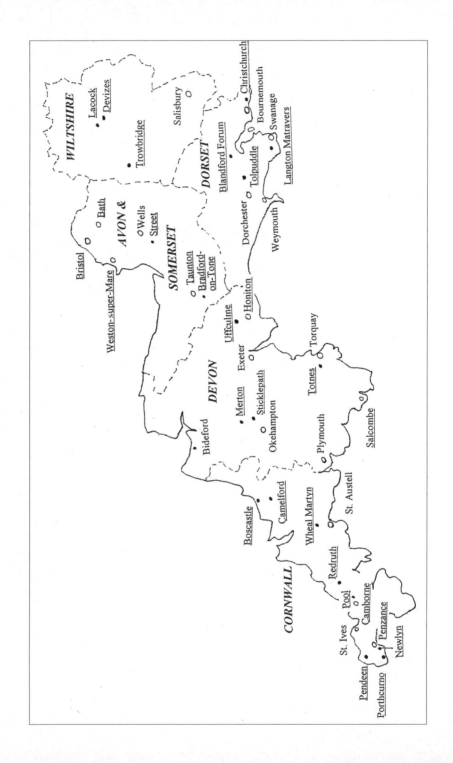

Avon and Somerset

BATH
The Book Museum ❄ ✳
Manvers Street, Bath, Avon & Somerset BA1 1JW

TEL: 01225 466000 FAX: 01225 482122

COLLECTION: For the book lover, this museum illustrates the history of bookbinding from Roman times to the modern day. Until the invention of cloth binding (hardback) in the 19th century, books were usually sold in paper wrappers. The owner would then take the book to a bookbinder. On display is a large collection of bookbinding tools and a number of engraved brass blocks for making designs on the front and back covers. In addition the museum houses first editions of the novelists Jane Austen and Charles Dickens and such authors as the British prime minister Benjamin Disraeli (1868 & 1874–80), and the 17th-century diarist Samuel Pepys. The collection also includes Winston Churchill, Sir Arthur Conan Doyle and Jan Morris.

BUILDING: The museum is in a basement, down a flight of stairs, and therefore has no access for wheelchairs. It is a former sorting office of the General Post Office.

OPENING TIMES: *All year*, Monday to Friday: 9am–1pm & 2pm–5pm, Saturdays: 9.30am–1pm. (Closed Sunday.)

ADMISSION CHARGES: ①

🅿 ♿ 🎥

DIRECTIONS: Manvers Street is near the Bath bus and railway stations.

BATH
Bath Postal Museum ❄ ✳
8 Broad Street, Bath, Avon & Somerset BA1 5LJ

TEL: 01225 460333

E-MAIL: info@bathpostalmuseum.co.uk

WEBSITE: www.bathpostalmuseum.org

COLLECTION: The organised postal system for ordinary people was introduced in the British Isles in about 1650. Until 1839 cost depended on distance but in 1840 cost started to be based on weight. The museum explains the postal service's history and displays such things as the Clay Tablets, an Act of Parliament in the time of Cromwell initiating 'The Post', the interior of a Victorian Post Office and an enlarged copy of the Penny Black stamp. There is the first wall letterbox of 1857, a model train showing the 'pick-up' and 'delivery' system and letter balances. Films on video show the postal services past and present. There are also special displays. A library is available for research by appointment only.

BUILDING: The building from where the first postage stamp, the famous Penny Black, was sent on 2 May 1840.

OPENING TIMES: *All year*, Monday to Saturday: 11am–5pm. (Closed Sunday.)

ADMISSION CHARGES: ①

🅿️ ♿ 🆆🅲 ☕ ⚠️ 📹 👫

DIRECTIONS: Walk north up Manvers Sreet, away from the station. Turn left down Cheap Street and first right, walk up past the art gallery and at the fork turn left into Broad Street. The museum is on the left.

BRADFORD-ON-TONE
Sheppey's Cider Farm Centre ❄️ ✳️

Three Bridges, Bradford-on-Tone, Taunton, Avon & Somerset TA4 1ER

TEL: 01823 461233 FAX: 01823 461712

COLLECTION: Winner of 200 awards for its quality ciders, Sheppey's Cider Farm Centre offers a range of activities such as cider sampling. The Cider Farm has 370 acres with 42 acres of cider apples. The museum houses cider-making equipment and other antique agricultural equipment. A video shows the cider-maker's year.

BUILDING: Former cowsheds, one-storey brick buildings, approximately 1910, with some new additions. The licensed tea-room is open only from May to October: 9.00am–4.30pm.

OPENING TIMES: *All year*, Monday to Saturday: 8.30am–6.00pm, Sunday (Easter to Christmas only): 12.00 noon–2.00pm.

ADMISSION CHARGES: ①

🅿️ ♿ 🆆🅲 ✕ ⚠️ 📹 👫

DIRECTIONS: On the A38 midway between Taunton and Wellington.

BRISTOL
Harvey's Wine Museum ❄️ ✳️

12 Denmark Street, Bristol, Avon & Somerset BS1 5DQ

TEL: 0117 927 5039 FAX: 0117 927 5001

E-MAIL: alun.cox@adsweu.com

COLLECTION: Everything to do with drinking wine is featured in the museum, and there are display boards about the history of wine and methods of production. Important items in the museum include the Russell 'Amen' Glass, a trumpet wine glass with a diamond-point inscription of two verses of the Jacobite national anthem (Jacobites were the supporters of the Scottish Stuart dynasty, who laid claim to the throne of Britain). Silver neck-labels for bottles and an enamel neck-label from the Battersea factory are on display, plus sack jugs from 1565 (sack was a white wine from Spain and the Canaries). Early wine bottles from 1600 to 1800, corkscrews and wine-making equipment feature

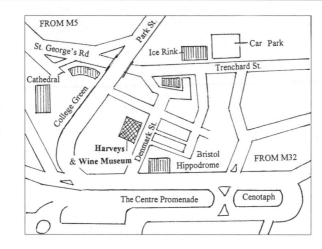

Harvey's Wine Museum, Bristol

amongst wine-coolers and an early 18th-century glass punch-bowl. Tastings are offered for parties.

BUILDING: The collection is in the cellar spaces with connecting tunnels, dating from 1220 to 1780, with two large spaces available for lectures and receptions. The museum is all on one level, but access is difficult for the disabled.

OPENING TIMES: *All year*, Monday to Friday: 10am–6.00pm, Saturday: 10am–5.00pm. Closed Sundays & bank holidays.

ADMISSION CHARGES: ②

🅿 ♿ 🚾 ☕ ⚠ 📷

DIRECTIONS: See map.

BRISTOL
University of Bristol Theatre Collection ❋ ✽

Department of Drama, Cantocks Close, Bristol, Avon & Somerset BS8 1UP

TEL: 0117 928 7836 FAX: 0117 928 7832

E-MAIL: theatre-collection@bris.ac.uk

WEBSITE: www.bris.ac.uk/Depts/Drama

COLLECTION: For those seriously interested in theatre. The collection, founded in 1951, aims to inform the visitor on theatre history and practice. It holds over 5,000 set and costume designs, set models, portraits and some props and costumes. The archives of the London and Bristol Old Vic Theatres are also in the collection. Temporary exhibitions on themes such as 'Shakespeare' and 'Theatre and the Sea' are held regularly.

BUILDING: Housed in an old printing works, which dates from about 1900. The entrance to the museum is at 21 Park Row.

Avon and Somerset

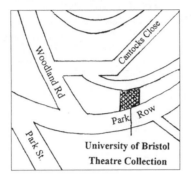

University of Bristol Theatre Collection, Bristol

University of Bristol Theatre Collection

OPENING TIMES: *All year*, Monday to Friday: 9.15am–4.45pm. (Closed Saturday & Sunday.) Closed Christmas and bank holidays. An appointment is recommended.

ADMISSION CHARGES: Free

🅿 ♿ 🚻 📷

DIRECTIONS: See map.

STREET
The Shoe Museum ❄ ✹

C. & J. Clark Ltd, Street, Avon & Somerset BA16 0YA

TEL: 01458 842320 FAX: 01458 843110

COLLECTION: The history of shoemakers C. & J. Clark, founded in 1825 by Cynus Clark, features as part of the displays. The early ways of making shoes are explained by the tools and photographs of the out-workers, who made the shoes in their own homes until the second half of the 19th century. The out-workers came to be paid every week, bringing their completed shoes and collecting materials for the next week's work. Machines for sole-cutting and sewing and many other tasks took over and some of these, dating from 1860 to 1920, are on display. Shoes from Roman times to 1950 form part of the collection and include a satin-lace boudoir bootee made for a member of the royal family.

BUILDING: The museum is mainly in the 1829 building originally built by Cynus Clark for making rugs, mops and chamois leather.

OPENING TIMES: *All year*, Monday to Friday: 10am–4.45pm, Saturday: 10am–5pm, Sunday: 11am–5pm.

ADMISSION CHARGES: Free ·

🅿 📷 ⛹

DIRECTIONS: Street is south of Wells. The museum is signposted in Street.

TAUNTON
Somerset Cricket Museum ✴

7 Priory Avenue, Taunton, Avon & Somerset TA1 1XX

TEL: 01823 275893

COLLECTION: Ian Botham's bat has its home in the museum. Other heroes of cricket are remembered by photographs and prints, even a school blazer. Caps of the 18 first-class counties feature alongside a display of ceramic miniature cricket bags. The business side is remembered by a printing press for score cards and occasional bat-making demonstrations. There is an extensive research library.

BUILDING: The museum is housed in the 'Priory Barn', dating from the late 15th and early 16th centuries. Possibly the gate-house for the Priory, it has been altered many times since the dissolution of the monasteries in 1539. Café, toilets and shop are in the adjacent County Cricket Club.

OPENING TIMES: *April to the end of October*, Monday to Friday: 10am–4pm. (During 1st-class cricket matches, entrance is available only to cricket spectators.)

ADMISSION CHARGES: ①

Ⓟ ♿ 🆆🅲 ∪ ⚠ 🍴 👪

DIRECTIONS: South of Taunton railway station at the County Cricket Ground.

WESTON-SUPER-MARE
The Helicopter Museum ❄ ✴

The Heliport, Locking Moor Road, Weston-super-Mare, Avon & Somerset BS22 8PL

TEL: 01934 635227 FAX: 01934 822400

E-MAIL: office@helimuseum.ffnet.co.uk

WEBSITE: www.helicoptermuseum

COLLECTION: A unique collection of helicopters, this museum is the only one of its kind in the UK. Originally a private collection, it has grown to include more than 50 full-size aircraft. Using words, pictures, models, documents and artefacts, the museum traces the history of the helicopter from Leonardo da Vinci's design of 1489 to today. Different helicopter manufacturers and the role of the helicopter are also shown.

BUILDING: On part of the original 1936 Weston Airport, there are two display halls and a helicopter restoration area under cover.

OPENING TIMES: *April to October*, daily: 10am–6pm. *November to March*, Wednesday to Sunday: 10am–4pm. (Closed Monday & Tuesday.) Closed 25 & 26 December & 1 January.

ADMISSION CHARGES: ②

Ⓟ ♿ 🆆🅲 ∪ ⚠ 🍴 👪

DIRECTIONS: Follow the propeller signs! The museum is on the A368/A371, just three miles from Weston-super-Mare seafront and close to junction 21 of the M5.

Avon and Somerset

Cornwall

BOSCASTLE
The Museum of Witchcraft ✳

The Harbour, Boscastle, Cornwall PL35 OAE

TEL: 01840 250111

E-MAIL: Museumofwitchcraft@compuserve.com

COLLECTION: Being up to date with witchcraft means that the museum holds a large press-cuttings file of events this century. The more traditional images of witchcraft, many from 16th- and 17th-century woodcuts, are on display, or held in the archive. Other elements of the witches' world are curses, charms and spells and the expertise of healing herbalists. A crystal ball and two cups for tealeaf readings, plus broomsticks, a cauldron and a black-handled knife, all help to tell the tale of witchcraft from the Stone Age Druids to the present day.

BUILDING: Divided into 'interest areas', such as ritual magic and spells and charms. Toilets and a café are next door to the museum.

OPENING TIMES: *Easter to end of October*, Monday to Saturday: 10.30am–6.00pm, Sunday: 11.30am–6.00pm.

ADMISSION CHARGES: ①

🅿 🆆 ⚠ 🖼 ⛄

DIRECTIONS: Boscastle is on the north coast of Cornwall, north of Camelford. Park in the main village car-park and walk towards the harbour. The museum is easy to find.

CAMELFORD
British Cycling Museum ❄ ✳

The Old Station, Camelford, Cornwall PL32 9TZ

TEL/FAX: 01840 212811

COLLECTION: From pennyfarthings to a quadracycle, over 400 bicycles are on display in the Main Exhibition Hall. There are displays of puncture repairing and oil, carbide, candle and battery cycle-lamps. Cycling pictures, cycling medals and even ceramic cycling items all help to tell the story of bicycles and their riders, from 1818 to today. There is also an extensive library of books.

BUILDING: A Victorian railway station.

OPENING TIMES: *All year*, Sunday to Thursday: 10am–5pm. (Closed Friday & Saturday.)

ADMISSION CHARGES: ①

🅿 ♿ 🆆 ⚠ 🖼 ⛄

DIRECTIONS: One mile north of Camelford on the B3266 Boscastle road, near a cross-roads.

A test for
witchcraft,
Museum of
Witchcraft,
Boscastle

NEWLYN
The Pilchard Works ✳

Tolcarne, Newlyn, Penzance, Cornwall NR18 5QH

TEL: 01736 332112 FAX: 01736 332442

E-MAIL: pilchardco@aol.com

COLLECTION: Both a working salt pilchard factory and a museum. Screw presses, still used in the packing season, are in the Press Room along with Britain's only pilchard net-making machine, 1870. Pictures, photographs and text outline 400 years of Cornish salt pilchard production. The factory has been exporting its traditional products for over 90 years.

BUILDING: Two restored granite buildings, built in 1874.

OPENING TIMES: *Easter to end of October*, Monday to Friday: 10am–6pm. (Closed Saturday & Sunday.)

ADMISSION CHARGES: ①

🅿 🚾 ♿ 📷 🚻

DIRECTIONS: Newlyn is south of Penzance. The Pilchard Works lies just behind the harbour on the other side of the river to The Coombe which leads to the A30. It is near the Meadery.

PENDEEN
Geevor Tin Mine ❄ ✳

Pendeen, Penzance, Cornwall TR19 7EW

TEL: 01736 788662 FAX: 01736 786059

Cornwall

British Cycling
Museum,
Camelford

E-MAIL: geevor@uhonline.co.uk

COLLECTION: There are 18 areas to explore, showing the machinery and harsh conditions of the place. Once a working mine extracting tin ore, it closed in 1990. The main underground area is flooded, but visitors can explore one underground mine. A library and archive are available to view by appointment.

BUILDING: Largest preserved mine site in the United Kingdom. Wheelchair access is limited to certain areas of the site.

OPENING TIMES: *January to end of March*, Monday to Friday: 10am–4pm. (Closed Saturday & Sunday.) *April to end of October*, Sunday to Friday & Saturdays of bank holidays: 10am–5pm. (Closed normal Saturdays.) Closed November & December.

ADMISSION CHARGES: ②

Ⓟ ♿ 🚾 ♿ ⚠ 🚼 ⛹

DIRECTIONS: Beside the B3306, from St Just to St Ives at Pendeen. Or follow signs on A3071 from Penzance.

PENZANCE
Cornwall Geological Museum ✳

Alverton Street, Penzance, Cornwall TR18 2QR

TEL: 01736 332400

WEBSITE: www.geological.nildram.co.uk

COLLECTION: Predominantly Cornish rocks, fossils and minerals but some from around the world. Archive information is available on early geology and geologists such as Davy, Carne and Henwood.

BUILDING: Purpose-built in 1866 on three floors. The museum occupies the west wing of the largest granite-built building in the UK.

OPENING TIMES: *April to October*, Monday to Saturday: 10am–4.30pm. (Closed Sunday.) The museum could be open at some times during the winter. Check before visiting.

ADMISSION CHARGES: ①

Ⓟ ♿ ⓌⒸ ⚠ 📷 👫

DIRECTIONS: From the town centre go up the main street past the statue of Humphrey Davey and through the traffic lights. There is a granite municipal building on the right. The museum is in the west wing, or left-hand side, of this building and the entrance is round the side.

PENZANCE
The National Lighthouse Museum ✳

Trinity House National Lighthouse Centre, Wharf Road, Penzance, Cornwall TR18 4BN

TEL: 01736 360077

WEBSITE: www.trinityhouse.co.uk

COLLECTION: Touching and operating some of the exhibits are ways of appreciating the craftsmanship of those who made them. This is Victorian engineering at its best. Lights from many different lighthouses are on display, including an automatic gaslit light, a 160-year-old Occulting Optic, which cut off at regular intervals. Also on show is the only known hyper-radial lens, which is the largest lens ever made. Other equipment is all ex-service and the whole makes up probably the largest collection of lighthouse equipment in the world. There is a video and a reconstructed lighthouse room containing the original curved furniture. Outside are coloured buoys.

BUILDING: A 100-year-old Grade II listed building. Originally Trinity House Workshop, where the granite blocks for constructing the Wolf Rock Tower were cut. Eighty per cent of the museum is accessible by wheelchair, but there is no disabled toilet.

OPENING TIMES: *Easter to end of October*, Sunday to Friday: 10.30am–4.30pm. (Closed Saturday.)

ADMISSION CHARGES: ①

Ⓟ ♿ ⓌⒸ ⚠ 📷 👫

DIRECTIONS: Wharf Road runs by the harbour, from the railway station. The museum is on the right just before the bend, which becomes Battery Road.

POOL
Camborne School of Mines Geological Museum and Art Gallery ❄ ✳

Pool, Redruth, Cornwall TR15 3SE

TEL: 01209 714866

Cornwall

Assay Laboratory, Camborne School of Mines Geological Museum and Art Gallery

E-MAIL: Reception@csm.ex.ac.uk

WEBSITE: www.ex.ac.uk/CSM

COLLECTION: A 'tunnel of discovery' of teaching displays is under the balcony, but the best geological specimens are in the central area. On show are gems and ornamental stones, minerals of ancient Egypt, and fossils and minerals from America and Africa, plus a host of other items from crystals to oxides and the Cornish collection from famous mining areas.

BUILDING: Purpose-built in 1975. One main room on the ground floor is accessible by wheelchair, the upper floor and gallery are not.

OPENING TIME: *All year*, Monday to Friday: 10am–4pm. (Closed Saturday & Sunday.)

ADMISSION CHARGES: Free

Ⓟ ♿ WC Ⓢ 🚻

DIRECTIONS: From the M5 take the A30 (via Okehampton and Bodmin) to Cornwall. Take the turn off after Redruth, marked Camborne/Pool A3047, and keep bearing left until you reach a set of traffic lights. Turn left at these. CSM is about 300 yards along the A3047 on the left hand side of the road, on the campus of Cornwall College (avoid entrance to Cornwall College immediately before the main gates). CSM is clearly visible from the road.

POOL
Cornish Mines and Engines ✳

Pool, nr. Redruth, Cornwall

TEL/FAX: 01209 315027

COLLECTION: There are two Cornish beam engine houses, with their engines intact.

South West

The beam engines' characteristic was the cut-off of steam injection before the stroke was complete in order to allow the steam to do work by expanding. These engines were used all over the world for heavy pumping work. The 1887 winder originally raised ore and men from 1,600 feet below the ground. The pumping engine is massive. The Cornwall Industrial Discovery Centre explains the life and the machines of the industrial age.

BUILDING: Dates from early 1900. Safeways café is only two minutes away.

OPENING TIMES: *March to end of October*, daily: 11am–5pm.

ADMISSION CHARGES: ②

ⓟ ♿ WC ⚠ 📷 ∰

DIRECTIONS: From the A30 take the Pool exit; turn left at the traffic lights, follow the A3047. The Pumping Engine House and the Discovery Centre are two minutes from Safeways. The Engine House is on the other side of the Redruth to Camborne road.

PORTHCURNO
Museum of Submarine Technology ❄ ✳

Porthcurno, Penzance, Cornwall TR19 6JX

TEL/FAX: 01736 810966

WEBSITE: www.porthcurno.org.uk

COLLECTION: Once the world's largest international cable station, Porthcurno now houses an array of brass and mahogany instruments from the days of cable telegraphy. It has working early railway and landline telegraphs, early and World War II wireless and much more. The display tells the history of Porthcurno's vital role in the establishment and growth of Britain's communications network. The museum holds an extensive telegraph and communications archive, by appointment only.

BUILDING: One external building and underground tunnels, built into the granite cliffs during World War II to protect the Telegraph Station. Food is available at Cable Station Inn, opposite the museum.

OPENING TIMES: *Easter to end of October*, daily: 10am–5pm. *Winter*, Sunday–Tuesday, 10am–5pm. (Closed Wednesday to Saturday.)

ADMISSION CHARGES: ②

ⓟ ♿ WC ⚠ 📷 ∰

DIRECTIONS: Take the A30, Penzance to Land's End road, turn left at signpost to St Buryan, then follow signs to Porthcurno (and signs for Minack Theatre). Park at the cove.

REDRUTH
Tolgus Tin Mill ❄ ✳

New Portreath Road, Redruth, Cornwall TR16 4HN

TEL: 01209 215185

COLLECTION: Rescued by the Trevithick Trust from a semi-derelict condition, the Tolgus

Stamping Mill and Steamworks is now run by the Trust. Equipment, ranging from 1860 to 1960, has been restored and can be seen running. Visitors walk under cover to the various parts of the mill, such as the Sand House or Second and First Frame House, learning about the process as they go. Water wheels, dipper wheels and shaking tables are on display.

BUILDING: The importance of this only remaining tin streaming mill in Cornwall can be judged by the fact it is now a scheduled ancient monument. It is level walking with access by wheelchair, but there are no other disabled facilities. Toilets and café are available at Cornish Goldsmith site, adjoining the mill.

OPENING TIMES: *All year*, Monday to Friday: 9.30am–5.30pm, Sunday: 10.am–4.30pm. Saturday openings in July and August only. *Winter*, Sunday to Wednesday: 10am–4pm. (Closed Thursday to Saturday.) Check opening times before visiting. Closed 22 December–2 January.

ADMISSION CHARGES: ①

🅿 ♿ ⚠ 📷 👫

DIRECTIONS: On the B3300 Redruth to Portreath road at the Cornish Gold Centre site, or follow signs from the A30 Redruth interchange.

WHEAL MARTYN
Wheal Martyn China Clay Heritage Centre ✳

Wheal Martyn, Carthew, St Austell, Cornwall PL26 8XG

TEL/FAX: 01726 850562

E-MAIL: enquiries@whealmartyn.com

WEBSITE: www.wheal-martyn.com

COLLECTION: Occupying two old china clay works, the museum gives an insight into this industry. A video introduces the Historic Trail and. A walk through the Clay Works themselves reveals a 35-feet-diameter water wheel and a modern working clay-pit. Exhibitions display tools of the industry, the 1899 locomotive Lee Moor No. 1 and geological specimens. Cornwall's contribution to the production of fine china in Britain is explained in a special exhibition.

BUILDING: A 26-acre site, with two trails included in the entrance price. Limited wheelchair access but there is a disabled toilet and Braille for the reception exhibition.

OPENING TIMES: *April to end of October*, Sunday to Friday: 10am–6pm. (Closed Saturday.)

ADMISSION CHARGES: ②

🅿 ♿ 🚾 ♿ ⚠ 📷 👫

DIRECTIONS: On B3274 from St Austell to Stenalees.

Devon

HONITON
Allhallows Museum (lace) ✳

High Street, Honiton, Devon EX14 8PE

TEL: 01404 44966 FAX: 01404 46591

E-MAIL: dyateshoniton@msh.com WEBSITE: www.honitonlace.com

COLLECTION: The museum displays items of local history from prehistoric times, but one of the most important is its collection of lace. Lace has been made in the town since 1560 and the industry spread through east Devon and into west Dorset. Known as Honiton lace, it is a high-quality lace and was much in demand during the 17th and 18th centuries for collars and cuffs and costume edgings. The name Honiton lace is now a generic term for the particular techniques and designs involved. The Norman Gallery contains a comprehensive exhibition drawn from the museum's lace collection and shows lace from 1630 onwards. In the Nichol Gallery the history of the industry and its tools are displayed. Demonstrations of Honiton lace-making take place in the museum throughout June, July and August, with occasional demonstrations during September and October.

BUILDING: The buildings are part of the former Allhallows Chapel, dating from the 13th century, and a former school dining hall, dating from the 18th century. Only part of the museum, the lace collection is suitable for a wheelchair. There is a stair-lift to the upper area.

OPENING TIMES: *April to October*, Monday to Friday: 10am–5pm, Saturday: 10am–1.50pm. (Closed Sunday.)

ADMISSION CHARGES: ①

🅿 ♿ ⚠ 🎥 👫

DIRECTIONS: The entrance to the museum is on the High Street next to St Paul's church in the town centre.

MERTON
Barometer World and Museum ❊ ✳

Quicksilver Barn, Merton, Okehampton, Devon EX20 3DS

TEL: 01805 603443 FAX: 01805 603344

E-MAIL: enquiries@barometerworld.co.uk

COLLECTION: From scientific instrument to something many homes regularly tapped to check the weather, the history of the barometer is revealed in this museum. Probably the largest collection of English barometers on public display in the world, it ranges from a tiny barometer no bigger than a 10p piece to traditional mercury and aneroid baro-

Barometer World and Museum, Merton

meters, barographs and a barometer once owned by William Wordsworth. The collection was gathered by Edwin Banfield. There is an activity sheet for children.

BUILDING: Housed in one room, part of the larger Barometer World premises, which restores and sells barometers.

OPENING TIMES: *All year*, Monday to Saturday: 9am–5pm. (Closed Sunday & bank holidays.) Opening hours in January may vary, museum probably closed.

ADMISSION CHARGES: ①

Ⓟ ♿ WC ⚠ 🚻

DIRECTIONS: Barometer World, Merton, is 20 yards off the A386, which runs through Merton from Great Torrington to Hatherleigh. Clearly signposted in the village.

SALCOMBE
Salcombe Maritime Museum ✳

Market Street, Salcombe, Devon TQ8 8DE

TEL: (Tourist Information Centre) 01548 843927

COLLECTION: Shipwrecks have provided treasures from the sea-bed in this maritime museum. Also on display are shipwrights' tools, models of ships and paintings of locally built fruit schooners. These boats raced home from the Bahamas or Mediterranean with fresh citrus and exotic fruits for the 19th-century British market. Some displays are changed every year. There is a young sailors' corner for children.

BUILDING: Erected in 1893 as the local council offices. It now houses the town Information Centre with the museum on the ground floor. Toilets are available at the car-park. The museum is all on one level but there is no disabled toilet.

OPENING TIMES: *Easter to end of October*, daily: 10.30am–12.30pm & 2.30pm–4.30pm.

ADMISSION CHARGES: ①

🅿 ♿ ⚠ 📷 👫

DIRECTIONS: Salcombe is on the south coast of Devon. The museum is close to the main street and displays a prominent banner, 'Maritime Museum', when open.

STICKLEPATH
Finch Foundry ✳

Sticklepath, Okehampton, Devon EX20 2NW

TEL: 01837 840046

COLLECTION: Sickles, scythes and shovels were produced at this 19th-century forge, for agriculture and mining. Historic water-powered machinery, massive tilt-hammers and a grinding-stone remind the visitor of how busy and noisy this forge used to be. The forge is now owned by the National Trust.

BUILDING: Old forge building in the middle of the picturesque village of Sticklepath. The car park is narrow and unsuitable for coaches.

OPENING TIMES: *Beginning of April to end of October*, Monday & Wednesday to Sunday: 11.00am–5.30pm. (Closed Tuesday.)

ADMISSION CHARGES: ①

Ⓟ 🆆🅲 ⛴ ⚠ 📷 👫

DIRECTIONS: Finch Foundry is four miles east of Okehampton, on the A382.

TOTNES
Devonshire Collection of Period Costume ✳

Bogan House, High Street, Totnes, Devon TQ9 5NP

TEL: 01803 862857

COLLECTION: Many of the costumes were worn by individuals who lived locally. Bridgit D'Oyly Carte was one of the contributors. The collection ranges from the mid-18th century to the present day and includes accessories and children's clothing. An annual exhibition explores different themes such as 'Holidays 1920s and 1930s' or 'The Rise and Fall of the Bustle 1865–1890'.

BUILDING: A medieval house, last major modernisation in 1550 for William Bogan, merchant and mayor of Totnes. Toilets in nearby car-park.

OPENING TIMES: *May (Spring Bank Holiday) to end of September*, Monday to Friday: 11am–5pm. (Closed Saturday and Sunday.) By appointment at other times.

ADMISSION CHARGES: ①

🅿 ⚠ 👫

DIRECTIONS: Totnes is west of Torquay. The museum is in the centre of town, facing the market square.

UFFCULME
Coldharbour Mill Wool Museum ❄ ✳

Uffculme, nr. Cullompton, Devon EX15 3EE

TEL: 01884 840960 FAX: 01884 840858

E-MAIL: info@coldharbourmill.org.uk

WEBSITE: www.coldharbourmill.org.uk

COLLECTION: A unique piece of social and industrial history, Coldharbour Mill is work-ing again. It had been spinning wool and worsted yarn for 200 years but closed in 1981. It reopened in 1982 and the steam engine, which powered the mill, is in full working order and powered up on 'Steam-up' days. Old machines can be seen in action and newly spun wool is wound up on bobbins. Visitors are taken on a guided tour of the mill and shown all the stages that a sheep's fleece goes through to make knitting wool.

BUILDING: One of the country's most complete heritage sites, dating from 1797, with the building and machinery still intact. There is a four-storey building, a combing shed and various rooms around the mill-yard re-creating a dye-house and cottage industry weaver's workshop.

OPENING TIMES: *April to October*, daily: 10.30am–5pm. Last tour 4pm. *November to March*, Monday to Friday: telephone for times of tours. (Closed Saturday & Sunday.)

ADMISSION CHARGES: ②

Ⓟ ♿ WC ✕ ⚠ 🎦 ⛹

DIRECTIONS: Coldharbour Mill is two miles from junction 27 of the M5. Follow the signs to Willand (B3181) then brown signs to the Working Wool Museum at Uffculme.

Dorset

BLANDFORD FORUM
Calvacade of Costume ❄ ✳

Lime Tree House, The Plocks, Blandford Forum, Dorset DT11 7AA

TEL: 01258 453006

COLLECTION: When Betty Penny began collecting costumes to help her amateur dram-atics, she had no idea how they were to take over her life. They were used in a Calvacade of Costume entertainment for charity. The costumes were worn and a commentary and music accompanied the parade. This was so successful that the Calvacade was performed all over the country. Eventually, with the help of a very generous donation, Betty Penny bought Lime Tree House so that the costumes could be properly displayed and looked after. They date from the 1730s to the 1960s and help to provide a history of clothing and accessories. Costumes by Norman Hartnell feature. There are rooms displaying underwear and lace, fans, jewellery, parasols, gloves, books, pictures and a display of handmade Dorset buttons, and a collection of dolls dressed in costume from the 15th to the mid-20th centuries will interest children.

BUILDING: A Georgian house, built around 1760 after the great fire of 1731. It is a Grade II listed building. There is a lecture room. Access by wheelchair on the ground floor only. Disabled toilets are on this level.

OPENING TIMES: *Easter to October*, Thursday to Monday: 11am–5pm. *October to Easter*, Thursday to Monday: 11am–4pm. Last admission half an hour before closing. (Closed Tuesday & Wednesday.) Closed 17 December to mid-February.

ADMISSION CHARGES: ①

🅿️ ♿ wc ♻ ⚠️ 👬

DIRECTIONS: Blandford Forum is on the A354 Puddletown (near Dorchester), Salisbury road. From the town centre, the marketplace, go north, following the one-way system up Salisbury Street and take the first right into The Plocks. Lime Tree House is 50 yards along on the right.

BLANDFORD FORUM
Royal Signals Museum ❄ ✳

Blandford, Dorset DT11 8RH

TEL: 01258 482248 FAX: 01258 482084

E-MAIL: royalsignalsmuseum@mail.army.org.uk

WEBSITE: www.royalsignals.army.org.uk/museum/

COLLECTION: From the coloured smoke used by the Romans to radio signals, communications on the battlefield have often made a vital difference to the outcome of the fighting. This museum tells the story of the men and women of the Royal Engineers Signals Service and the Royal Corps of Signals, from the Crimean War to the Falklands and the Gulf wars. Also depicted are the stories of other groups involved in communications, such as the Auxiliary Territorial Service (ATS). There are interactive 'hands-on' displays for younger visitors and special events throughout the year, such as Dorset Air Day.

BUILDING: The museum is within the boundaries of the camp of the Royal Corps of Signals. Visitors have to pass through a security checkpoint. Book in advance if you want to make getting in easy and quick.

OPENING TIMES: *April to October*, Monday to Friday: 10am–5pm, Saturday & Sunday: 10am–4pm. *November to March*, Monday to Friday: 10am–5pm. (Closed Saturday & Sunday.)

ADMISSION CHARGES: ②

Ⓟ ♿ wc ✗ ⚠️ 🎥 👬

DIRECTIONS: The museum is clearly signed from the A354 Blandford bypass. Military signs direct the visitor to the museum and the camp.

CHRISTCHURCH
Museum of Electricity ✳

The Old Power Station, Bargates, Christchurch, Dorset BH23 1QE

TEL: 01202 480467 FAX: 01202 480468

WEBSITE: www.christchurch.gov.uk

COLLECTION: The Edwardian generating station houses a unique collection of electrical generating and distribution equipment. The centrepoint of the collection is a restored 1914 Bournemouth tram. There is also a collection of 19th- and 20th-century domestic appliances and electricity service vehicles, including the Sinclair C5 (a very small electric car invented in the 1980s by Clive Sinclair.) Regular demonstrations are given by museum stewards to illustrate experiments carried out by Michael Faraday and his contemporaries. Ask at the desk before taking photographs.

BUILDING: The Christchurch Generating Station, dating from 1903. No lift to first-floor exhibits. Stewards will help. There is a disabled toilet.

OPENING TIMES: *Easter to end of September,* Monday to Friday: 12 noon–4.30pm. (Closed Saturday & Sunday.)

ADMISSION CHARGES: ①

Ⓟ ♿ 🚾 ⚠ 📷 👫

DIRECTIONS: Take the A338 Ringwood to Bournemouth road. Exit on to the B3073 and follow the signs to Christchurch Town Centre. After crossing the railway bridge look for the museum signs on your left. The entrance is opposite the 'Castle Ironmongers' shop. By foot, the museum is in Bargates, close to Christchurch town centre. Leave the High Street via the pedestrian underpass.

LANGTON MATRAVERS
The Museum of the Purbeck Stone Industry ✳

Langton Matravers, Swanage, Dorset

TEL: 01929 423168

WEBSITE: www.langton.mcmail.com

COLLECTION: Cut and polished since Roman times, Purbeck marble can be seen in most English cathedrals as well as in most of the churches of Purbeck. It is the topmost layer of the various 'beds' of stone. A complete picture of the ways in which the local stone was quarried and used can be found in the museum. The geology is explained and there are displays of apprentice pieces, plus stonemasons' tools, photographs and a reconstruction of a section of underground quarry.

BUILDING: Housed in a barn-like building, which was originally a coach-house and stables belonging to the huge rectory.

OPENING TIMES: *April to October,* Monday to Saturday: 10am–12 noon & 2pm–4pm. Other times by appointment.

South West

ADMISSION CHARGES: ①

Ⓟ ♿ 📷

DIRECTIONS: From the A351, Wareham to Corfe Castle village, take the B3069 at the end of Corfe Castle to Kingston and Langton Matravers. The museum is in St George's Close beside the Parish Church of St George.

TOLPUDDLE
Tolpuddle Martyr Museum ❋ ✳

Tolpuddle, Dorchester, Dorset DT2 7EH

TEL: 01305 848237

WEBSITE: www.tolpuddlemartyrs.org.uk

COLLECTION: Famous for having contributed to the birth of the trade union movement, the six Tolpuddle Martyrs are celebrated in this museum. Their story is told from arrest to deportation to triumphant return as free men. The museum has undergone a major refurbishment and has interactive multi-media screens, which help to explain all aspects of the martyrs' struggles and the background to their story.

BUILDING: The museum has evolved from the library of the Tolpuddle Memorial Cottages built in 1934. There is a disabled toilet.

OPENING TIMES: *April to October*, Tuesday to Saturday: 10am–5.30pm, Sunday: 11am–5.30pm. (Closed Monday.) *November to March*, Tuesday to Saturday: 10am–4pm, Sunday: 11am–4pm. (Closed Monday.)

ADMISSION CHARGES: Free

Ⓟ ♿ 🚻 🅰 📷 🚻

DIRECTIONS: Tolpuddle is six miles east of Dorchester on the A35.

Wiltshire

DEVIZES
Kennet & Avon Canal Trust Museum ❋ ✳

Devizes Wharf, Couch Lane, Devizes, Wiltshire SN10 1EB

TEL: 0130 721279 FAX: 0130 727870

COLLECTION: From 1780 to 1990, the story of the waterway is told by the use of maps, documents, working models, photographs, artefacts and an interactive, computer-based touch-screen. The visitor will find out about the way the canal was used and the promoters, surveyors and navvies and engineers who built it. Life on the waterway is also described, introducing boatmen and lock-keepers.

BUILDING: An old warehouse. Wheelchair-users will need to make advance arrangements to visit the museum.

OPENING TIMES: *All year*, daily: 10am–5pm (4pm in winter).

ADMISSION CHARGES: ①

Ⓟ ♿ 🚾 ⚠ 🖼 ♨

DIRECTIONS: Devizes Wharf is well signposted within Devizes.

LACOCK
Fox Talbot Museum ❋ ✳

Lacock Abbey Estate, Lacock, Chippenham, Wiltshire SN15 2LG

TEL: 01249 730459   FAX: 01373 830472

E-MAIL: M.W.Gray@bath.ac.uk

COLLECTION: Fox Talbot was a mathematician, physicist, classicist, a man of many talents, and his life and work are celebrated in this museum. He lived from 1800 to 1877 and spent some time as resident of the Abbey. Perhaps one of his most famous contributions is the invention of the positive/negative process in September 1840. He became known as the father of modern photography. The Abbey and the village belong to the National Trust.

BUILDING: The museum is inside a 16th-century barn at the entrance to Lacock Abbey. The Upper Gallery area is devoted to exhibitions by contemporary and 19th-century photographers. Toilets and pub in village.

OPENING TIMES: *March to October*, daily: 11am–5pm, *November to February*, Saturday & Sunday: 11am–4pm. (Closed Monday to Friday.) Closed weekends at Christmas and New Year.

ADMISSION CHARGES: ②

Ⓟ ♿ 🚾 ⚠

DIRECTIONS: three miles south of Chippenham, just east of the A350.

TROWBRIDGE
Trowbridge Museum (working cloth mill) ❋ ✳

The Shires, Court Street, Trowbridge, Wiltshire BA14 8AT

TEL: 01225 751339

COLLECTION: Working machinery still produces cloth, which is sold in the shop. The museum is on the spinning-floor of this building, which was the last mill left in the town. The museum also has a weaver's cottage, a tailor's shop and a draper's shop. There are other collections to do with the history of the town, such as the Whitaker Collection, which tells the story of a local family over 200 years and includes a reconstruction of a medieval castle.

BUILDING: All the displays are on one floor in the museum. The museum itself is in the middle of the Shires. Park in the shopping centre car-park.

OPENING TIMES: *All year*, Tuesday to Friday: 10am–4pm, Saturday: 10am–5pm. (Closed Sunday and Monday.)

ADMISSION CHARGES: Free

🅿 ♿ 🅆🅲 Ⓢ 🎥 👫

DIRECTIONS: Trowbridge is on the A361 Frome to Devizes road. See map.

**Trowbridge
Museum,
Trowbridge**

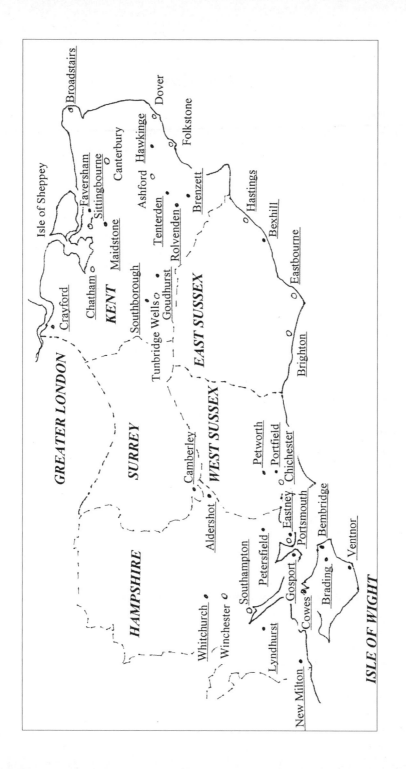

Hampshire

ALDERSHOT
The Museum of the Army Physical Training Corps ❈ ❋

Army School of Physical Training, Fox Lines, Queens Avenue, Aldershot,
Hampshire GU11 2LB

TEL: 01252 347168 FAX: 01252 340785

WEBSITE: www.aptc.org.uk

COLLECTION: During the Indian Mutiny and the Crimean war, in the 19th century, it
became clear that the British soldiers were very unfit. In 1860 Major Frederick Ham-
mersley took twelve sergeants from different regiments to train them as fitness instructors.
The first army gymnasium was built in Aldershot in 1866. On display at the museum are
pictures of the training and the equipment from 1860 to the present day. The history of
the instructors during World Wars I and II is described and on show are the international
honours won by members of the Corps in a range of sports, and even a silver replica of
the Fox gymnasium still in use today.

BUILDING: An ex-gymnasium, built in 1893. There is a Naffi (army cafeteria) adjacent
to the museum. Limited facilities and access for the disabled.

OPENING TIMES: *All year*, Monday to Thursday: 9am–4.30pm, Friday: 9am–12.30pm.
(Closed Saturday & Sunday.) Open other times by appointment. Closed during August,
Easter and Christmas.

ADMISSION CHARGES: Free

🅿 🆆🅲 ♿ 🚻

DIRECTIONS: From M3, leave at junction 4, take the A331 and immediately follow signs
for the A325 (Farnborough, Aldershot, Farnham). Pass over the motorway, follow the
A325 for two miles and at Queens roundabout (Forte Crest Hotel on left) turn left. At
next roundabout (St Albans) take fourth exit, at next roundabout bear right into Queens
Avenue. Pass Stadium on left, take next turning on left and park in car-park on right.
There is no charge for the car-park.

ALDERSHOT
The Parachute Regiment and Airborne Forces Museum ❈ ❋

Browning Barracks, Aldershot, Hampshire GU11 2BU

TEL: 01252 349619

COLLECTION: From the original briefing models of early operations to displays of
weapons and equipment from the Falklands campaign, the museum tells how the air-
borne forces have been involved in operations over the last 50 years. There is an extensive
collection of medals, uniforms and other items of war.

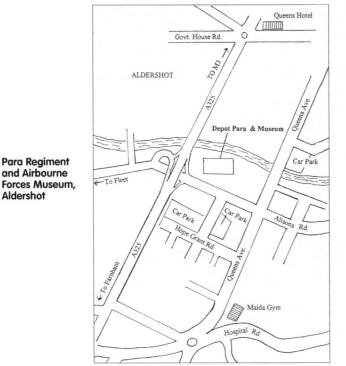

Para Regiment and Airbourne Forces Museum, Aldershot

BUILDING: Opened in 1969 at its present location in an active army barracks. The museum was originally established in 1947 in an officers' mess.

OPENING TIMES: *All year*, daily: 10am–4.30pm (last admission 3.45pm), weekends: 10am–4pm.

ADMISSION CHARGES: ①

Ⓟ ♿ 🅦🅒 ⚠ 👫

DIRECTIONS: See map.

ASHURST
National Dairy Council Museum ✳

Longdown Activity Farm, Longdown, Ashurst, nr. Southampton, Hampshire
SO40 4IH

TEL: 023 8029 3326 FAX: 023 8029 3376

E-MAIL: annette@longdown.uk.com

COLLECTION: The museum is in the middle of a modern activity farm, which offers visitors the chance to get involved with work on the farm and with the animals. As a

Milk delivery box
vehicle, National
Dairy Council
Museum, Ashurst

contrast to the modern-day milking machines currently used at the farm, the museum's collection of historical dairying exhibits offers a unique history lesson. There are butter pats, butter churns, a churn delivery vehicle of the 1890s and milk delivery box vehicle of 1910–24, plus many more exhibits from the 19th and 20th centuries.

BUILDING: Old converted farm buildings, three main rooms. Most areas are accessible by wheelchair. There is a picnic and play area and a kiosk selling hot and cold drinks and snacks.

OPENING TIMES: *1 June–29 October*, daily: 10am–5pm. (Check exact opening and closing dates if visiting near beginning of June or end of October.)

ADMISSION CHARGES: ②

Ⓟ ♿ WC ⚠ 📷 ♟

DIRECTIONS: Leave the M27 at junction 3 for the M275 and Totton. Pick up the A35 to Lyndhurst just outside Totton. Cross the A326 and shortly afterwards turn left to the Longdown area and the activity farm.

CHAWTON
Jane Austen's House ❄ ✳

Chawton, nr. Alton, Hampshire GU34 1SD
TEL/FAX: 01420 83262
WEBSITE: www.janeaustenmuseum.org.uk
COLLECTION: Famous for her novels such as *Sense and Sensibility* and *Pride and Prejudice*, Jane Austen (1775–1817) lived in the house with her mother and sister Cassandra from 1809 until her death. The rooms display family mementoes and documentary material such as copies of letters written by Jane Austen. There are portraits of the family, including one of Jane, and several silhouettes. Her two brothers, Frank and Charles, are remembered in various memorabilia. There is also a costume display of Regency clothes. There is a bookshop within the museum.
BUILDING: A red-brick 17th-century house. Ground floor, garden and outbuildings accessible by wheelchair. No lift to 1st floor. Teashop and pub nearby.
OPENING TIMES: *1 March to 30 November*, daily: 11am–4pm. *December, January, February*, Saturday & Sundays: 11am–4pm. Closed Christmas Day & Boxing Day.
ADMISSION CHARGES: ②

🅿 ♿ 🚾 ⚠

DIRECTIONS: From the M25 exit at junction 10 on to the A3 Guilford bypass and take the A31 Farnham and Alton bypass. Turn off at the A31/A32 junction roundabout. The museum is signposted off the roundabout at the junction of the A31 (Winchester) with the A32 (Fareham) roads. The car-park is opposite the museum.

EASTNEY
Eastney Beam Engine House ❄ ✳

Henderson Road, Eastney, Portsmouth, Hampshire PO4 9JF
TEL: 023 9282 7261 FAX: 023 9287 5276
E-MAIL: espendlove@portsmouthcc.gov.uk
WEBSITE: www.portsmouthmuseums.co.uk
COLLECTION: Restored and in running order, the beam engines became part of an industrial museum in 1978. One of the main attractions is a pair of James Watt beam engines, still in their original Victorian engine house (for information on beam engines see entry: Cornish Mines and Engines, Pool, Cornwall). When the museum is open, one of these engines is in steam. There are a variety of other pumping engines on display, many in runnning order.
BUILDING: The steam engine house, opened in 1887.
OPENING TIMES: The last complete weekend (Saturday & Sunday) in every month. *April to September*: 1pm–5.30pm, *October to March*: 1pm–5pm.
ADMISSION CHARGES: ①

Hampshire

Jane Austen's
House,
Chawton

🅿 ♦♦

DIRECTIONS: Eastney is south of Portsmouth and west of Southsea, on the coast. The museum is just behind the Esplanade and near the Marina.

GOSPORT
Royal Navy Submarine Museum ❄ ✸

Haslar Jetty Road, Gosport, Hampshire PO12 2AS

TEL: 02392 510354 or 765250 FAX: 02392 511349/589985

E-MAIL: rnsubs@rnsubmus.co.uk WEBSITE: www.rnsubmus.co.uk

COLLECTION: Here is the chance to go on board a real submarine, the HMS *Alliance*, which is permanently moored at the museum, and to discover how submarines work. The history of the submarine to the present day is told in displays and equipment, one example being an articulated diving-suit. Many hands-on exhibits, such as a diving-bell, help the visitor experience the reality of life under the water. There are model submarines and even a totem pole given by a Native American tribe to the submarine HMS *Totem*.

BUILDING: At the southern end of Gosport's Millennium Promenade, the museum is seeking to develop the site with the help of lottery funding. Partial access only for wheelchairs. There is a waterfront picnic area and a cafeteria.

OPENING TIMES: *All year*, daily, except 24 December to 1 January inclusive. *April to October*: 10am–5.30pm. *November to March*: 10am–4.30pm (last tour of the submarine HMS *Alliance* one hour before closing).

ADMISSION CHARGES: ②

🅿 🆆🅲 ☂ ⚠ 📷 ♦♦

DIRECTIONS: There is a frequent ferry service between Gosport and Portsmouth Harbour station. From Gosport Ferry follow the Millennium Promenade (approximately 10 mins) to the museum. By road leave the M27 at junction 11. Follow the A32 (look out for brown signs for Gosport Historic Waterfront).

LYNDHURST
New Forest Museum ❊ ❋

Main Car-Park, High Street, Lyndhurst, Hampshire SO43 7NY

TEL: 01703 283914

COLLECTION: A chance to experience four seasons of the New Forest in one audio-visual show, giving a sense of the beauty of the place. Exhibits explaining charcoal burning, tree-felling for timber to build a 17th-century galleon, the wildlife of the forest, the ponies and some of its human characters all help to increase visitors' knowledge and understanding of the New Forest. There is an extensive reference library open Monday to Friday 10am–4pm, free of charge.

BUILDING: Opened in 1988, there is one large exhibition area. The car-park, in front of the museum, is run by the local council and there is a charge. There are public toilets near the museum.

OPENING TIMES: *All year*, daily (except Christmas Day): 10am–6pm (last entrance into museum at 5pm).

ADMISSION CHARGES: ①

Ⓟ ♿ 🅆🅒 ⚠ 📷 👫

DIRECTIONS: Lyndhurst is at the crossroad of the A35 Bournemouth to Southampton road and the A337 Lymington to Cadman road. The museum is next to the large car-park behind the main street.

NEW MILTON
The Sammy Miller Museum (motorbikes) ❊ ❋

Bashley Farm, Bashley Cross Roads, New Milton, Hampshire BH25 5SZ

TEL: 01425 620777 FAX: 01425 619696

COLLECTION: Many of these motorcycles are extremely rare, and all are restored. There are prototypes such as the McCandless Prototype Norton Twin and Japanese Road Racers, plus a 1936 Indian Four, an AJS V4 and Broughs, Triumphs and Ariels. Sammy Miller is still winning motorcycle competitions although he is in his late forties, and sometimes he shows his motorcycles at race circuits throughout Europe. Over 200 motorcycles are on display, as well as a reconstruction of a typical 1925 motorcycle workshop and trophies, plaques, photographs and posters.

BUILDING: Set within an attractive courtyard with a tea-room, candle shop and craft shop. The buildings are 100 years old.

OPENING TIMES: *All year*, daily: 9.30am–4.30pm.

Hampshire

ADMISSION CHARGES: ②

Ⓟ ♿ 🆆 🗑 ⚠ 📹 👫

DIRECTIONS: The museum is south west of Lyndhurst on the B3055 from Hinton to Lymington road. It is on the south side of the road on the corner of Steam Lane.

PETERSFIELD
The Bear Museum (teddy bears) ❄ ❋

38 Dragon Street, Petersfield, Hampshire GU31 4JJ

TEL: 01730 265108

E-MAIL: judy@bearmuseum.freeserve.co.uk WEBSITE: www.bearmuseum.co.uk

COLLECTION: Starting her collection of teddy bears in 1981, Judy Sparrow found the collection grew so rapidly that she opened the museum in 1984. There are bears dating from 1905 to the present day, including Albert, a 1910 Steiff bear, 1930s English bears made by Merrythought and bears made by the Chad Valley Company. Amongst the displays are a bear's house and a teddy bears' picnic.

BUILDING: An 18th-century house, which is a listed historic building.

OPENING TIMES: *All year*, Tuesday to Saturday: 10am–4.30pm. (Closed Sunday & Monday.)

ADMISSION CHARGES: Free

🅿 🆆 ⚠ 👫

DIRECTIONS: The museum lies on the old London to Portsmouth road through Petersfield. Parking is available in the town centre and the museum is signposted from there.

PORTSMOUTH
Charles Dickens Birthplace Museum ❄ ❋

393 Old Commercial Road, Portsmouth, Hampshire PO1 4QL

TEL: 023 9282 7261 FAX: 023 9287 5276

E-MAIL: espendlove@portsmouthcc.gov.uk

WEBSITE: www.portsmouthmuseums.co.uk

COLLECTION: This small terraced house is where Dickens was born in 1812. This prodigious writer produced 20 major novels including *Oliver Twist* and *Little Dorrit*, plus a large amount of journalism. Reminders of Dickens' writing career, such as an inkwell and paper-knife, are on display, as well as the couch on which he died in his house in Kent. The museum is decorated in the Regency style and furnished in a manner that Charles Dickens' parents might have chosen. There are portraits of Dickens' family and an exhibition, which features information on Dickens and a small collection of memorabilia. Regular readings from Dickens' work are held during the summer months.

BUILDING: Built in 1805. There are three furnished rooms to view: the parlour, dining room and the bedroom where Dickens was born.

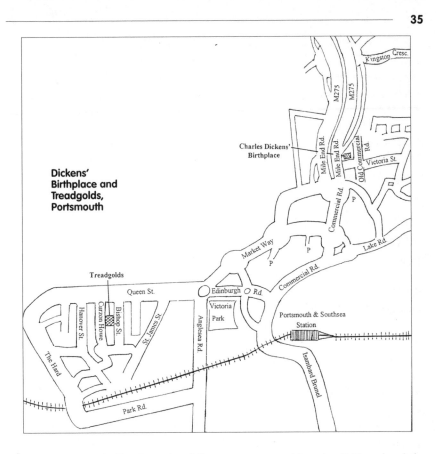

Dickens' Birthplace and Treadgolds, Portsmouth

OPENING TIMES: *April to September*, daily: 10am–5.30pm. *November & December*, daily: 10am–5pm. (Closed Christmas to March.) Last ticket sold 30 minutes before closing time. Open on Dickens' birthday, 7 February: 10am–5pm.

ADMISSION CHARGES: ①

🅿 🚾 ♿

DIRECTIONS: See map.

PORTSMOUTH
W. M. Treadgold Industrial Heritage Museum (iron and steel merchants) ✳

Bishop Street, Portsmouth, Hampshire PO1 3DA

TEL: 023 9282 4745 FAX: 023 9283 7310

WEBSITE: www.hants.gov.uk/museum/treadgold/

COLLECTION: Established in 1809 as a smithy and ironmongers, Treadgolds also sold equipment, tool and metal supplies. The latter were sold to craftsmen such as smiths,

Hampshire

shipwrights, wheelwrights and coopers. The company traded until 1988, the business remaining relatively untouched by the 20th century. Opening as a museum in 1995, the shop, stockroom, forges and general metalworking shop, office, stable and cart-store are all here to see. Machines, tools and artefacts are on display. There is a refurbished tenement to view.

BUILDING: Original building containing the shop, forge, stable and tenement were originally leased for Treadgold's business until 1860. William Treadgold aquired the whole site in 1865 and demolished most of the tenements to build the forge and stable. Access by wheelchair is possible, but there are no facilities for the disabled.

OPENING TIMES: *April to end of September*, Wednesday & Thursday: 10am–4pm (Closed Friday to Tuesday.)

ADMISSION CHARGES: Free

P &. ⚠ 📷 ♯♯♯

DIRECTIONS: See map.

SOUTHAMPTON
Southampton Maritime Museum ❊ ✸
Woolhouse, Town Quay, Southampton

TEL: 023 8063 5904

E-MAIL: a.arnott@southampton.gov.uk

WEBSITE: www.southampton.gov.uk

COLLECTION: The real story of the *Titanic* is told through original artefacts and the voices of local people whose lives were affected by the tragedy. Information about the docks and the shipping companies that used them is on display, plus ship models. There is a large reserve collection of material on shipbuilding, liner ephemera and furniture. Although the museum is small, Southampton's maritime collections are the largest of any non-national museum. Viewing of collections not in museum by appointment.

BUILDING: A 15th-century wool warehouse built by the monks of Beaulieu. It was used as a prison during the Napoleonic period and is now a scheduled ancient monument. Only the ground floor is accessible by wheelchair. Photography allowed by arrangement. There is a special children's area.

OPENING TIMES: *All year*, Tuesday to Sunday: 10am–5pm. (Closed Monday.) Closed some public holidays, Christmas, Boxing Day and New Year.

ADMISSION CHARGES: Free

P &. ⚠ ♯♯♯

DIRECTIONS: The museum is opposite the Town Quay.

WHITCHURCH
Whitchurch Silk Mill ❄ ✳

28 Winchester Street, Whitchurch, Hampshire RG28 7AL

TEL: 01256 892065

COLLECTION: Producing high-quality fabrics from the finest silk yarns, the mill's skilled weavers work on the original machinery. There are winding and warping machines from around 1890 and twelve power looms from 1890 to 1950. Originally powered by the water wheel, some of the early looms are now run on electricity.

BUILDING: A Grade II listed building, the textile watermill was built around 1800 on the River Test and has been weaving silk since the 1820s. There is a riverside garden.

OPENING TIMES: *All year*, Tuesday to Sunday & Bank Holiday Mondays: 10.30am–5pm (last admission 4.15pm). (Closed Monday.)

ADMISSION CHARGES: ①

Ⓟ 🚻 ⅃ ⚠ 🎥 ♁

DIRECTIONS: The Silk Mill is south of Whitchurch, half-way between Winchester and Newbury (the A34). Follow the signs from the A34.

Isle of Wight

BEMBRIDGE
Maritime Museum (Isle of Wight shipwreck centre) ✳

Sherborne Street, Bembridge, Isle of Wight

TEL: 01983 872223 or 873125

COLLECTION: Deep-sea diver Martin Woodward started salvage diving around the Isle of Wight in 1968 and kept many artefacts found on wrecks. It was always his ambition to open a museum and displayed in the galleries are the result of his collecting. Ships' bells, a figurehead, a large copper cooking pot all come from SS *Mendi*. Spanish pieces of eight, canonballs and ships' crockery are all from local wrecks. There is an area that displays divers' equipment and salvaged material from further away, such as Nan King porcelain recovered from the South China Sea in 1985. The sad tale of the submarine HMS *Swordfish* is revealed. It disappeared in 1940, and Martin Woodward discovered the wreck in 1983 some miles off St Catherine's Point.

BUILDING: Providence House was built in the mid-1800s and was once a bakery and shop. It ceased trading in 1973 and became semi-derelict. It was refurbished and opened as a museum in 1977/78. Only the ground floor is accessible by wheelchair. There is a café opposite the museum.

OPENING TIMES: *March to October*, daily: 10am–5pm.

ADMISSION CHARGES: ①

⊞ ⚠ 📷 ♨

DIRECTIONS: Bembridge is on the east coast on the B3395 Sandown to St Helens road. The museum lies behind the B3395, towards the beach.

BRADING
The Lilliput Antique Doll and Toy Museum ❋ ✳

High Street, Brading, Isle of Wight PO36 0DJ

TEL: 01983 407231

COLLECTION: A wooden doll presented to the ex-premier of Russia Nikita Khrushchev forms part of this collection, as do a bisque doll given by Queen Victoria to an estate employee's daughter and an 1885 Steiner doll from France. In addition there are steam trains, tin cars and vans, a range of dolls' houses and much more.

BUILDING: 17th-century cottages, six rooms. There is also a collector's shop.

OPENING TIMES: *All year*, daily (except Christmas Day): 10am–5pm.

ADMISSION CHARGES: ①

⊞ ⚠ 📷 ♨

DIRECTIONS: Brading is on the A3055 Ryde to Sandown road. The museum is on this road in the village opposite the church.

COWES
Cowes Maritime Museum ❋ ✳

Branch Library, Beckford Road, Cowes, Isle of Wight PO31 7SG

TEL: 01983 293341

COLLECTION: The displays record the maritime history of the Isle of Wight and Cowes in particular. Three Uffa Fox-designed dingies are exhibited, including Prince Philip's *Coweslip*. There is a large archive of J. Samuel White's shipyard.

BUILDING: A room in the Cowes Library. The library is in a former Wesleyan chapel. The room is accessible by wheelchair but there are no other facilities for the disabled.

OPENING TIMES: *All year*, Monday to Wednesday: 9.30am–6pm & Friday to Saturday: 9.30am–4pm. (Closed Thursday & Sunday.)

ADMISSION CHARGES: Free

⊞ ♿ 📷

DIRECTIONS: The library is behind the coast road and south of the castle.

VENTNOR
Museum of Smuggling History ✳

Botanic Garden, Ventnor, Isle of Wight PO38 1UL

TEL: 01983 853677

COLLECTION: Wool, brandy, silks, tobacco, tea, gold, watches, diamonds and drugs, all have been smuggled into the country. This museum shows how goods were smuggled, some of the personalities involved and the events over a 700-year period.

BUILDING: The small reception building in the Botanic Garden car-park is deceptive, for the museum is actually housed in extensive underground vaults in three large galleries. Toilets and a cafeteria are nearby. The Botanic Garden consists of 22 acres.

OPENING TIMES: *April to September*, daily: 10am–5pm.

ADMISSION CHARGES: ①

🅿 ⓢ 📽 ⅲ

DIRECTIONS: On the A3055, one mile west of Ventnor, car-park for Botanic Garden.

Kent

BRENZETT
Brenzett Aeronautical Museum ✳

Ivychurch Road, Brenzett, Romney Marsh, Kent TN9 0EE

TEL: 01797 344747

COLLECTION: This is a unique collection of wartime equipment and memorablilia found at aircraft crash sites. Amongst the exhibits are a Canberra bomber, a Vampire trainer and a Dakota cockpit, plus a 'Dam Buster' bomb.

BUILDING: Once home to the Women's Land Army as a hostel during World War II, the museum buildings still have the women's 'graffiti' in evidence. The airfield was built during the war and first used in 1943.

OPENING TIMES: *April, Good Friday, Easter weekend, Easter Monday*. Then every Saturday and Sunday including bank holidays to the end of October: 11am–5.30pm. Plus: *July, August to end of September*, Wednesday, Thursday and Friday: 11am–5.30pm. (Closed Monday & Tuesday.)

ADMISSION CHARGES: ①

🅟 ♿ 🆆🅲 ⓢ 📽 ⅲ

DIRECTIONS: Brenzett is south of Ashford on the A259 Rye to New Romney road.

BROADSTAIRS
Crampton Tower Museum ✳

Rear of Post Office, High Street, Broadstairs, Kent CT10 2AB

TEL: 01843 862078 or 864446

COLLECTION: Commemorating the work of Thomas Russell Crampton (1816–88), a notable Victorian civil engineer. He designed and built locomotives and railways in East Kent and also in Izmir, Belgium and France. In addition he built the Berlin waterworks, the Broadstairs gasworks, bridges and many other structures. Working drawings, models and patents are displayed in the museum plus items from the Thanet Electric Tramways. BUILDING: A flint-built tower, which was part of the first Broadstairs public water supply, built in 1859 by Thomas Russell Crampton. OPENING TIMES: *Easter to mid-October*, Monday, Tuesday, Thursday, Friday and bank holiday Sundays: 2.30pm–5pm (Closed Wednesday, Saturday and Sunday). ADMISSION CHARGES: ①

🅿 ⓐ 📹

DIRECTIONS: The museum is on the High Street, opposite Broadstairs station.

CHATHAM
Kent Police Museum ❄ ✳

Chatham Historic Dockyard, Dock Road, Chatham, Kent ME4 4TE

TEL: (World Naval Base) 01634 403260

WEBSITE: www.worldnavalbase.org.uk

COLLECTION: Truncheons and leg-irons, uniforms and badges, even guns are on display. The museum tells the history of Kent Constabulary from 1857 and shows many artefacts from the period.

BUILDING: The old boilerhouse in Chatham Historic Dockyard, which also houses the World Naval Base and the Historical Society Museum.

OPENING TIMES: *April and May*, Wednesday, Thursday: 12 noon–4pm, Sunday: 1pm–5pm. *June to November*, plus Saturday: 12 noon–4pm. *February*, Wednesday & Sunday, 1pm–5pm. Closed December and January.

ADMISSION CHARGES: Free

Ⓟ ♿ ⓐ 📹 🚻

DIRECTIONS: The Historic Dockyard is signposted from junctions 1 and 3 of the M2 and junction 6 of the M20. It is on the A231 Dock Road.

CRAYFORD
David Evans World Of Silk ❄ ✳

Bourne Industrial Park, Bourne Road, Crayford, Kent DA1 4BP

TEL: 01322 559401 FAX: 01322 556420

E-MAIL: retail@davidevans.co.uk

COLLECTION: David Evans (1791–1874) bought the Crayford site in 1843 and went into silk production. The museum tells the story of the origin of silk in China in 2640 BC and explains the life cycle of the silk worm. Working machinery, archive photographs and a video presentation provide information on how the factory functioned in the past and continues to operate today. The process includes weaving the silk, dyeing, hand-block printing and modern screen-printing methods. This is a working factory and guided tours are available if pre-booked.

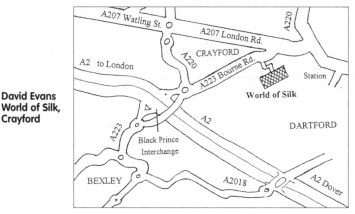

**David Evans
World of Silk,
Crayford**

BUILDING: The silk factory itself.

OPENING TIMES: *All year*, Monday to Saturday: 9.30am–5pm. (Closed Sunday.)

ADMISSION CHARGES: ①

Ⓟ ♿ 🚾 ⊽ ⚠ 👪

DIRECTIONS: Turn off the A2 at the Black Horse interchange. See map for museum.

FAVERSHAM
Chart Gunpowder Mill ✳

Westbrook Walk, off Stonebridge Way, Faversham, Kent

TEL: (Fleur de Lis Heritage Centre) 01795 534542 FAX: 01795 533261

E-MAIL: Faversham@btinternet.com

WEBSITE: www.faversham.org

COLLECTION: Rescued from the jaws of the bulldozer in 1967, this gunpowder mill has been restored by the Faversham Society. It is the oldest gunpowder mill in the world and was the centre of the nation's explosives industry for 400 years. On display is the machinery used in the process of gunpowder manufacture. A new computer-based 'explosives experience' is to be added.

BUILDING: One very large shed, with a thick blast wall at one end.

OPENING TIMES: *Easter to end of October*, Saturday, Sunday and bank holidays: 2pm–5pm.

ADMISSION CHARGES: Free

Ⓟ 🚾 ⚠ 📷 👪

DIRECTIONS: From the M2 take the Faversham turning, left into the A2, turn right into the B2040, then half a kilometre later, turn left. See map (p. 42).

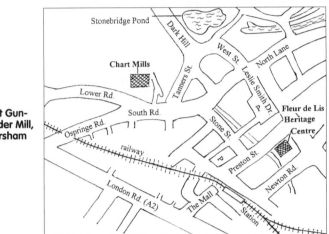

Chart Gun-
powder Mill,
Faversham

GOUDHURST
Finchcocks (The Living Museum of Music) ✳

Goudhurst, Kent TN17 1HH

TEL: 01580 211702 FAX: 01580 211007

E-MAIL: finchcocks@argonet.co.uk

WEBSITE: www.argonet.co.uk/finchcocks

COLLECTION: Some 90 historical keyboard instruments fill the eight oak-panelled rooms. A 1785 beautifully painted harpsichord by Joachim Antunes of Lisbon and an 1815 fortepiano by Johann Fritz, Vienna, feature amongst chamber organs, virginals, harpsichords, clavichords and a range of early pianos. A number of the instruments have been fully restored. Richard Burnett, a leading exponent of the early piano, acquired Finchcocks in 1970 and it is his collection that is housed there. Finchcocks is now a musical centre of international repute and many events take place in the house. There is also a collection of musical pictures and prints.

BUILDING: An early Georgian manor in an unspoilt setting. The house is noted for its brickwork and little of the building has been altered over time. There are 13 acres of grounds and parkland.

OPENING TIMES: *Easter Sunday to the end of September*, Sunday and Bank Holiday Monday: 2pm–6pm. *August*, also Wednesday & Thursday: 2pm–6pm.

ADMISSION CHARGES: ③

Ⓟ&♿🚻⌂✕♿📷

Viennese
fortepiano by
Conrad Graf,
1826,
Finchcocks,
Goudhurst

DIRECTIONS: Finchcocks is on the A262 Lamberhurst to Biddenden road, west of Goudhurst.

HAWKINGE
Kent Battle of Britain Museum ✳

Aerodrome Road, Hawkinge, nr. Folkestone, Kent CT18 7AG
TEL: 01303 893140
COLLECTION: Spitfires, Hurricanes and Messerschmitts, all full-size replicas, immediately set the atmosphere. The stories of the young pilots of World War II, on both sides, are told by means of diaries and photographs. A collection of RAF uniforms, flying kits, weapons and airfield vehicles create a picture of the life of a pilot and and an airfield. There is a small display from World War I.
BUILDING: The site of the former RAF station, which was used during the famous Battle of Britain. The museum is housed within the original 1940 airfield buildings, some of which still bear the scars of war. There is no café but drinks and snacks are available in the shop. There are no disabled toilets.
OPENING TIMES: *Easter Friday to the end of September,* seven days a week: 10am–5pm (last

Dog Collar
Museum,
Maidstone

admission one hour before closing).

ADMISSION CHARGES: ①

Ⓟ ♿ 🚾 ♿ ♟

DIRECTIONS: From the M20 exit for Folkestone on to the A260, signposted Canterbury. Hawkinge is situated on the A260 between Folkestone and Canterbury. The museum is one mile along Aerodrome Road, Hawkinge.

MAIDSTONE
Dog Collar Museum ❄ ✳

Leeds Castle, Maidstone, Kent ME17 1PL

TEL: 01622 765400 (24-hour) 01622 880362 FAX: 01622 767838

COLLECTION: These are collars for dogs, not clergymen. Collars with spikes to protect the neck of the hunting dog from the teeth of bears and wolves, collars of leather with applied brass ornament and valuable collars of silver are on display at the museum. This comprehensive collection was presented by Mrs Gertrude Hunt in memory of her husband, John Hunt, a distinguished medievalist. The collars date from the 15th and 16th centuries.

BUILDING: A former coach-house and early 20th-century squash court in the gatehouse. The fabric of the buildings dates from the 13th century. The museum is within Leeds Castle and has no separate entrance fee. A café and restaurant are situated in Leeds Castle grounds.

OPENING TIMES: *1 March to 31 October*, daily: 11am –5pm. *1 November to 28 February*, daily: 10.15am–3pm.

ADMISSION CHARGES: ③

Ⓟ &. 🚾 ♿ ✕ ⚠ ⛹

DIRECTIONS: Exit from the M20 on junction 8. Leeds Castle is signposted from there (about five minutes from the junction). The castle is between the A20 and the B2163, just south of the M20. The Dog Collar Museum is in the Gate Tower.

MAIDSTONE
The Tyrwhitt-Drake Museum of Carriages ✲ ✳

Archbishops' Stables, Mill Street, Maidstone, Kent ME15 6YE

TEL: 01622 754497

COLLECTION: Realising that the motor-car was forcing horse-drawn carriages off the road, Sir Garrard Tyrwhitt-Drake began collecting carriages. The result was the first collection of its kind in Britain and is viewed as the finest in Europe. Queen Victoria's state landau is on display along with barouches, broughams, the mail phaeton and gigs.

BUILDING: Fourteenth-century archbishop's stables, now a historical monument. The museum is on two floors; only the ground floor is accessible by wheelchair. There is no disabled toilet.

OPENING TIMES: *All year*, Monday to Saturday: 10am–5.15pm (last admission 4.30pm). Sunday: 11am–4pm.

ADMISSION CHARGES: ①

🅿 &. ⚠ 📷 ⛹

DIRECTIONS: See map.

Tyrwhitt-Drake Museum of Carriages, Maidstone

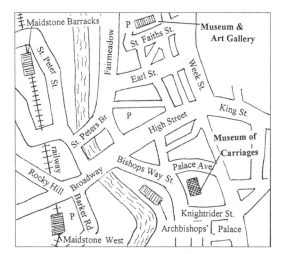

ROLVENDEN
Motor Museum ❄ ✹

Falstaff Antiques, 63 High Street, Rolvenden, Kent TN17 4LP

TEL: 01580 241234

COLLECTION: A unique collection of Morgan three-wheel cars, dating from 1913 to 1935, and the only known Humber Tri-car of 1904. Also on display are motorcycles, bicycles, a 1936 Bampton caravan and a selection of automobilia.

BUILDING: Falstaff Antiques shop. The museum is part of the shop. Due to the size of the museum, there is no space for parties of children.

OPENING TIMES: *All year*, Monday to Saturday: 10am–6pm. (Closed most Sundays.)

ADMISSION CHARGES: ①

P WC ⚠ 🎥

DIRECTIONS: Rolvenden is three miles from Tenterden towards Hastings on the A28. Travelling from Tenterden to Hastings, the shop is on the left in Rolvenden, just after the right turn to Tunbridge Wells.

SITTINGBOURNE
Dolphin Yard Sailing Barge Museum ✹

Crown Quay Lane, Sittingbourne, Kent ME10 3SN

TEL: 01795 423215

WEBSITE: www.kentaccess.org.uk.artmuse/dolphin

COLLECTION: This is the only surviving barge repair yard and it is a working museum with barges undergoing repair. There is a boatyard and basin, barge blocks, a sail loft, shipwright's shop and a forge. On display in the museum is a large collection of ship-wrights', blacksmiths' and riggers' tools, plus models, plans and photographs. In the sail loft is a corner explaining the sailmaker's craft; the rest is taken up with the history and development of the barge.

BUILDING: The derelict Charles Burley Bargeyard was rescued by the Society for Spritsail Barge Research, and appointed trustees began the work of restoring the yard and putting it back into operation in 1968. There is a picnic area and a nature trail.

OPENING TIMES: *Easter to end of October*, Sundays and bank holidays only: 11am–5pm.

ADMISSION CHARGES: ①

P ♿ WC ⚠ 🎥 ⛲

DIRECTIONS: Signposted off the A2 in Sittingbourne, which is the High Street. St Michaels Road off the High Street. The signpost for Dolphin Yard reads to Crown Quay Lane. Dolphin Yard is behind the railway station.

SOUTHBOROUGH
Salomons Museum ❈ ✳

David Salomons Estate, Broomhill Rd, Southborough, Tunbridge Wells,
Kent TN3 0TG

TEL: 01892 515152 FAX: 01892 539102

E-MAIL: enquiries@salomons.org.uk WEBSITE: www.salomons.org.uk

COLLECTION: Two remarkable men, Sir David Salomons (1797-1873) and Sir David
Lionel Salomons (1851-1925) lived at this house. Sir David bought a small villa in 1829
and set about converting it into a large country house. During his life he fought to secure
equal rights with other Englishmen for Jews, Roman Catholics and Quakers. Sir David
Lionel Salomons, Sir David's nephew, was a man of science and an accomplished photographer. There are two rooms for displaying memorablilia of the Salomons family. One
of the main attractions is a monthly guided tour of these rooms and the Victorian Science
Theatre, which houses one of the finest Welte player pipe organs ever installed in Britain.
BUILDING: The house was built by the two Salomons. David Lionel helped in the design
of the stable complex, which had space for 21 horses. Work began on the Science Theatre
in 1894; it was probably used for lectures but is a fine example of a Victorian theatre. The
house is now a conference and training centre. Sunday lunches are available in the conference centre.

OPENING TIMES: *All year*, the Memento Rooms: Monday, Wednesday and Friday: 2pm–
5pm. Guided tours by prior arrangement. Historical guided tours: once a month at 12
noon and 2.30pm (check for dates).

ADMISSION CHARGES: Memento Rooms: Free. A small donation of £2 is requested to
be put towards the Welte Organ Restoration Fund. Tour: ①

Ⓟ & Ⓦ🅲 ⌨

DIRECTIONS: Through Tunbridge Wells to Southborough and to the end of the village
with shops on your right. At traffic lights turn left into Speldhurst Road and drive to
the end of the houses on your right. Then turn left into Broomhill Road.

TENTERDEN
The Colonel Stephens Railway Museum ✳

Tenterden Town Station, Station Road, Tenterden, Kent TN30 6HE

TEL: (general enquiries Town Station and Kent and East Sussex Railway) 01580 765155

COLLECTION: Colonel Stephens built and ran the Kent and East Sussex Railway and 17
other independent railways. The hub of all these activities, his office, has been reconstructed for the museum with all the original furniture, pictures and paperwork arranged
as it was in 1928. A carriage compartment of the early 1900s sets the atmosphere of the
railways. On display are details of Colonel Stephens' military career and the smallest five-
ton, standard-gauge locomotive in the country.

Ellen Terry
Memorial
Museum,
Tenterden

BUILDING: Built by the Ministry of Supply during 1939–40, it is a larger version of the World War I Nissen hut. The premises have undergone some reconstruction. The small museum is in part of the building. Café, toilets and shop are available at the adjacent station.

OPENING TIMES: *April to October*, weekends and bank holidays: 1pm–5pm. *June to September*, plus Tuesday, Wednesday and Thursday: 1pm–5pm. (Closed Monday and Friday.)

ADMISSION CHARGES: ①

Ⓟ ♿ Ⓦⓒ 🎥

DIRECTIONS: From the M20 take junction 9 (Ashford) and then follow the A28 to Tenterden, which is about twelve miles south west of Ashford. The museum is adjacent to Tenterden railway station, which is just off the High Street.

TENTERDEN
Ellen Terry Memorial Museum ✳

Smallhythe Place, Tenterden, Kent TN30 7NG

TEL: 01580 762334

COLLECTION: A legend in English theatre, actress Ellen Terry (1847–1928) was part of the theatre family that produced John Gielgud. She chose Smallhythe Place as her home from 1899 until her death. Displays of her magnificent Lyceum Theatre costumes, photographs and gifts from great actors such as Henry Irving and friends such as George Bernard Shaw and Albert Seymour set the scene. The Barn Theatre is also open to view, courtesy of the Barn Theatre Society, but can be closed some days at short notice.

BUILDING: Once the harbour master's house, built around 1514, this charming half-timbered house, set in a cottage garden, is a National Trust property. Parking is in a lay-by. Not easy for a wheelchair as there are many different levels. A restaurant and picnic area (not NT) are available 500m away at Tenterden Vineyard Park.

OPENING TIMES: *1 April to 31 October*, daily, except Thursday and Friday: 1.30pm–6pm. (Last admission 5.30pm.) Barn Theatre: 1.30pm–5pm.

ADMISSION CHARGES: ②

🅿 🆆🅲 ⛹

DIRECTIONS: two miles south of Tenterden on the east side of the road to Rye.

Surrey

DEEPCUT
Royal Logistic Corps Museum ✲ ✵

The Princess Royal Barracks, The Royal Logistic Corps, Deepcut, Camberley, Surrey GU16 6RW

TEL: 01252 340871

COLLECTION: A Northern Ireland bomb disposal scene, plus many other events and places, have been created as tableaux to bring the work of the army to life. The work of the regiment feeding the troops under difficult circumstances, keeping the postal services operating and many other tasks are explained. Over the last 500 years the soldier has been transported and supplied with arms and equipment. The museum tells this story by means of a darkened display hall and dramatic lighting and many displays, paintings and photographs. A large archive of documents and photographs is available to view by appointment.

BUILDING: Built in 1995 to display the large collection.

OPENING TIMES: *All year*, Monday to Friday: 10am–4pm, Saturday: 10am–3pm. (Closed Sunday & bank holidays.) Closed for public holidays.

ADMISSION CHARGES: Free

Ⓟ 🆆🅲 ♿ ☕ ⛹

DIRECTIONS: Leave the M3 at junction 3 and take the A30 to Camberley. From Camberley turn left on to the B3015. Deepcut and the museum are off the B3015, north of the Basingstoke Canal.

East Sussex

BEXHILL-ON-SEA
Bexhill Museum of Costume and Social History ✳

Manor Gardens, Upper Sea Road, Old Town, Bexhill-on-Sea, East Sussex TN40 1RL

TEL: 01424 210045

COLLECTION: Dressed models display costumes from medieval to Victorian times. There are special collections of dolls, lace and embroidery. Memorabilia and a late 19th- to 20th-century kitchen and schoolroom give a feeling of history.

BUILDING: Part of Lord Delaware's stable block. A flintstone building. Toilets and a café nearby.

OPENING TIMES: *Easter to October*, daily: 10.30am–5pm, Saturday & Sunday: 2pm–5pm. (Last entry half an hour before closing.) (Open for party bookings only during the winter.)

ADMISSION CHARGES: ①

ⓟ ♿ Ⓢ

DIRECTIONS: See map.

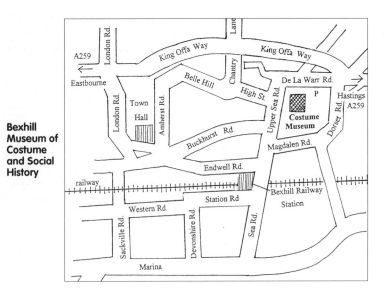

Bexhill Museum of Costume and Social History

BRIGHTON
Brighton Fishing Museum ❊ ✳
201 Kings Road Arches, Brighton, East Sussex BN1 1NB

TEL/FAX: 01273 723064

COLLECTION: A look at the fishing industry of Brighton and the area. There are six decommissioned fishing boats outside, which children can climb into. One of the first films ever made in the UK (1896) is shown on video.

BUILDING: Two arches on Brighton beach. Toilets and café are nearby.

OPENING TIMES: *All year*, daily: 9am–5pm.

ADMISSION CHARGES: Free

🅿 ♿ ⚠ 📷 🚻

DIRECTIONS: The Lower Esplanade.

EASTBOURNE
Museum of the Royal National Lifeboat Institution ❊ ✳
King Edward Parade, Eastbourne, East Sussex BN21 4BY

TEL: 01323 730717

COLLECTION: To explain the history of the Eastbourne lifeboats there are models and memorabilia. Many lifeboat rescues are described by means of photographs. Eastbourne had its first lifeboat in 1822, which was privately owned, two years before the Royal National Lifeboat Institution was founded. It was the wreck of the East Indiamen ship the *Thames* that led Member of Parliament John Fuller to have the lifeboat built.

BUILDING: An old boat-house, built in 1898. On ground level and very small.

OPENING TIMES: *March, April & October to December*, daily: 10am–4pm. *May to September*, daily: 10am–5pm. (Check for exact dates of opening and closing.) Closed January & February.

ADMISSION CHARGES: Free

🅿 ♿ ⚠ 📷

DIRECTIONS: On the seafront adjacent to the Wish Tower. See directions for the puppet museum.

EASTBOURNE
The Wish Tower Puppet Museum ✳
Martello Tower No. 73, King Edward Parade, Eastbourne, East Sussex BN21 4BU

TEL: 01323 417776 FAX: 01323 644440

E-MAIL: puppet.workshop@virgin.net

WEBSITE: www.puppets.co.uk

COLLECTION: Punch and Judy, Indonesian and Italian puppets, in fact puppets of all kinds of origins are displayed at the museum, from early shadow puppets through to puppets of the Victorian period and puppets from TV and film. There are also model theatres, special exhibitions and puppet performances. Guided tours of the exhibition by an experienced puppeteer are available by appointment.

BUILDING: A Martello tower built in 1802 as a defence against Napoleon, very small. Toilets and a café are adjacent to the building.

OPENING TIMES: *Good Friday to the end of October*, daily: 11am–4pm.

ADMISSION CHARGES: ①

🅿 ⚠ 📷 🚻

DIRECTIONS: Aim for the seafront and pier. From the pier turn westward and walk until you see the Martello tower.

HASTINGS
Hastings Fishermen's Museum ❄ ☀

Rock-a-Nore Road, Hastings, Sussex TN34

TEL: 01424 461446

COLLECTION: Outside are fishermen's boats and a fisherman's cottage made from an upturned boat. Inside the museum is the last of the Hastings sailing luggers and models of ships, and exhibits relating to Hastings fishing industry and general maritime history.

BUILDING: A small fishermen's church built in 1854 as a chapel of ease (two rooms). Toilets and café nearby.

OPENING TIMES: *April to October*: 10am–5pm, *November to March*: 11am–4pm every day except Christmas Day.

ADMISSION CHARGES: Free (donations welcome)

🅿 ♿ ⚠ 📷 🚻

DIRECTIONS: Museum stands on the beach at the far (eastern) end of Hastings Old Town.

NEWHAVEN
Newhaven Fort ☀

Fort Road, Newhaven, East Sussex N9 9DL

TEL: 01273 517622   FAX: 01273 512059

E-MAIL: ian.everest@newhavenfort.org.uk   WEBSITE: www.newhavenfort.org.uk

COLLECTION: Bread and water and solitary confinement were the lot of any prisoners in the cells at Newhaven Fort, a ten-acre Victorian clifftop fortress. The barracks, living quarters, an Anderson shelter, a blitzed home and a spooky tunnel leading down through the cliffs all help set the atmosphere and tell the history of the fort.

BUILDING: Built in the 1860s to deter invaders. The displays are housed within the original barrack rooms. Picnic tables are situated around the site. The fort is a scheduled ancient monument. Some areas may be difficult for wheelchairs, but most of the displays are accessible. There is a disabled toilet. The canteen is open most Sundays and during the high season.

OPENING TIMES: *Beginning of April to end of October*, daily: 10.30am–6pm. *March*: open at weekends.

ADMISSION CHARGES: ②

Ⓟ ♿ 🆆🅲 🚻 ✕ 🅰 📷 ⛺

DIRECTIONS: Newhaven is between Brighton and Eastbourne on the A259. It is well signposted from the A27. All roads into the town have signs for Newhaven Fort.

West Sussex

CHICHESTER
Royal Military Police Museum ❊ ❉

Roussilon Barrack, Broyle Road, Chichester, West Sussex PO19 4BN
TEL: 01243 534225 FAX: 01243 534288
E-MAIL: museum@rhqrmp.freeserve.co.uk
WEBSITE: www.rhqrmp.freeserve.co.uk
COLLECTION: Protecting very important people (VIPs) as part of a Close Protection Team., or combating crime in the army as part of the Special Investigation Branch, is the work of military policemen. They are both soldiers and policemen and became a permanent corps in Britain in 1885. From then they carried out traffic and straggler patrols during World War I and were deployed on all the fronts during World War II. Since then they have been active in Northern Ireland, the Falklands and the Gulf. The museum displays the history of the Royal Military Police, medals, uniforms and badges. Permission is needed for taking photographs.
BUILDING: The keep, built in 1803.
OPENING TIMES: *1 April to 30 September*, Tuesday to Friday: 10.30am–12.30pm & 1.30pm–4.30pm. Saturday & Sunday: 2pm–5pm. (Closed Monday.) *1 October to 31 March*, Tuesday to Friday: 10.30am–12.30pm & 1.30-pm–4.30pm. (Closed Monday, Saturday & Sunday.) Closed January.
ADMISSION CHARGES: Free

Ⓟ ♿ 🆆🅲 🅰 📷 ⛺

DIRECTIONS: Take the A286 out of Chichester, going north towards Midhurst, past Chichester Theatre. The Roussillon Barracks lies behind the A286, not far out of the city. Broyle Road runs parallel to the A286.

COULTERSHAW BRIDGE
Coultershaw Beam Pump ✳

Coultershaw Bridge, Station Road, Petworth, West Sussex GU28 0JE

TEL: 01798 865569 FAX: 01798 865672

COLLECTION: Built in 1782 to pump water from the River Roth to Petworth, the Coultershaw Beam Pump supplemented the water supply to Petworth House and the town. The present wheel was cast in the mid-19th century and the wheel and pump were running until 1960. Restored by the Sussex Industrial Society, the beam pump is now working again. Also on display are smaller water pumps, and the history of pumping and of the Rother Navigation to Midhurst.

BUILDING: The original stone pump-house now has a weather-boarded upper storey, with a clay-tiled roof from a wagon-shed on the Goodwood Estate.

OPENING TIMES: *April to September*, first and third Sundays in the month, plus Bank Holiday Mondays: 11am–4pm.

ADMISSION CHARGES: ①

Ⓟ 🖛 🏥

DIRECTIONS: The Beam Pump is on the River Rother, on the A285, Petworth to Chichester road.

PORTFIELD
Mechanical Music and Doll Collection ✳

Church Road, Portfield, Chichester, West Sussex PO19 4HN

TEL: 01243 372646

COLLECTION: Restored instruments play the music of a Victorian public house in 1890 or popular songs of the Victorian parlour. A guided demonstration tour allows the visitor to hear and see the range of mechanical music instruments, plus early horned gramophones and Edison phonographs. In addition there are over 100 dolls dating from 1830 to 1930, many in their original clothes.

BUILDING: A large hall inside a Victorian church.

OPENING TIMES: *June to September*, daily: 1pm–4pm. Group visitors are welcome throughout the year, day or evening. Telephone for details.

ADMISSION CHARGES: ①

Ⓟ ♿ Ⓢ 🖛 🏥

DIRECTIONS: Portfield is one mile east of Chichester City Centre and the museum is signposted from the A27.

3. South Central

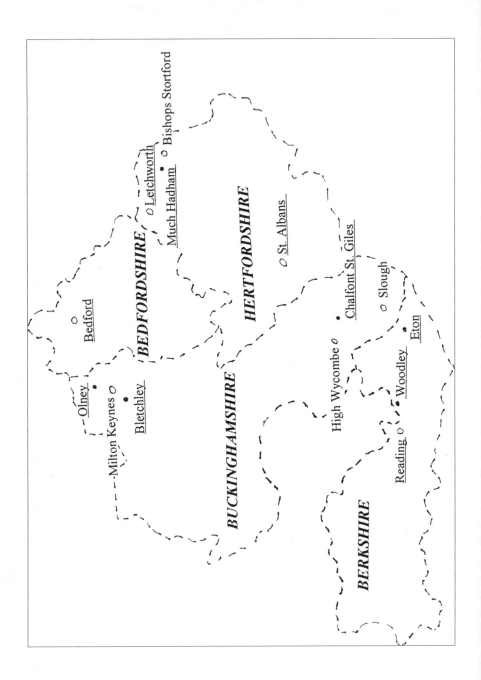

Bedfordshire

BEDFORD
John Bunyan Museum ✳

Bunyan Meeting Free Church, Mill Street, Bedford MK40 3EU

TEL: 01234 213722

COLLECTION: Author of *The Pilgrim's Progress*, John Bunyan was also a preacher and pastor. He lived from 1628 to 1688 and was born in Elstow, near Bedford, the son of a tinker. His religious convictions led to his imprisonment in Bedford jail, where he wrote two-thirds of his famous work. The museum shows some of the objects associated with his life and explains his life and times. There is a modern display illustrating scenes from *The Pilgrim's Progress*.

BUILDING: Purpose-built museum, opened in 1998. It has disabled access, ramps, a disabled toilet and a platform lift. The church occupies the site of the barn, which the congregation bought in 1672. The present church was built in 1849. It has magnificent bronze doors depicting scenes from *The Pilgrim's Progress* and 20th-century stained-glass windows. Coffee bar in church foyer.

OPENING TIMES: *First Tuesday in March to last Saturday in October*, Tuesday to Saturday: 11am–4pm (last entry 3.45pm). (Closed Sunday, Monday and Good Friday.)

ADMISSION CHARGES: Free

🄿 ⅋ 🆆 ⅃ ⚠ 👫

DIRECTIONS: The museum is off the High Street and north of the river. Turn down Mill Street, then right and right again into Castle Lane. There is a car-park off Castle Lane.

Berkshire

ETON, WINDSOR
Museum of Eton Life ✳ ✳

Eton College, Windsor, Berkshire SL4 6DW

TEL: 01753 671177 FAX: 01753 671265

E-MAIL: visits@etoncollege.org.uk

COLLECTION: Founded in 1440 by Henry VI, Eton College is one of the oldest schools in the country. The museum illustrates the history of Eton College and the life of the boys at the school. A guided tour of various parts of the college and the museum is offered.

BUILDING: Within the historic buildings of Eton College.

Prison scene, John
Bunyan Museum,
Bedford

OPENING TIMES: Term times (check for dates).

ADMISSION CHARGES: ② (includes the tour)

🅿 ♿ 🚾 ⚠

DIRECTIONS: From the M4 take junction 5 and follow signs for Eton. Pedestrian access to Eton from Windsor. Cross Windsor Bridge and walk up Eton High Street. There are car-parks in Windsor.

READING
Cole Museum of Zoology ❄ ✳

Whiteknights, Reading, Berkshire RG6 2AJ

TEL: 01734 318903

COLLECTION: One of the finest teaching collections of zoological specimens in the country. It was built up in the first part of the 20th century by the late Professor Cole. The original theme was to illustrate the relationship between form and function in the animal kingdom. A gorilla, other primates and an elephant are on view.

BUILDING: On the ground floor of the School of Animal and Microbial Science building in Whiteknights Park. Staff/student canteen close by. Access ramp for the disabled and a disabled toilet.

OPENING TIMES: *All year*, Monday to Friday: 9am–5pm. (Closed Saturday and Sunday.)

ADMISSION CHARGES: Free

Ⓟ ♿ WC 🎥 👫

DIRECTIONS: The university building is on the A327 out of Reading. It is off Shinefield Road.

Also on the same site is the *Museum of English Rural Life*, in which the collections cover most aspects of the economic and social life of the countryside. It is open to the public Tuesday to Friday: 10am–4.30pm and Saturday 10am–1pm & 2pm–4.30pm.

At the Faculty of Letters and Social Sciences in the ground floor wing nearest the Palmer Building is the *Ure Museum of Greek Archaelogy*. Built up since 1922, the museum contains a collection of pottery of Greek lands. Open Monday to Friday during term time: 9am–5pm.

WOODLEY
The Museum of Berkshire Aviation ❄ ✳

Mohawk Way (off Bader Way), Woodley, nr. Reading, Berkshire RC5 4UE

TEL: 0118 9340712 (museum answering service) 0118 9448089

WEBSITE: fly.to/museumofBerkshireAviation

COLLECTION: Woodley was once the centre of a thriving aircraft industry, with the Miles and Handley Page aircraft factory. The museum tells the story of Berkshire's dynamic contribution to aviation history. Aircraft such as Handley Page Herald and Miles Magister are on display, as well as the wind tunnel model for the first ever supersonic aircraft. Several aircraft restoration projects are in progress. There is a reference library.

BUILDING: At the site of Woodley Airfield in a Robins aircraft hangar, built in the mid-1930s.

OPENING TIMES: *Easter to end of October*, Wednesday, Saturday & Sunday and bank holidays: 10.30am–5pm. *November to March*, Wednesday & Sunday: 12 noon–4pm.

ADMISSION CHARGES: ①

Ⓟ ♿ WC ↻ ♿ 🎥 👫

DIRECTIONS: Leave the A329(M) Reading to Bracknell road at the junction marked Winnersh, Woodley & L. Earley. Go up Bader Way to the roundabout and turn right into Mohawk Way. The museum is off to the right. From the A4 Reading to Maidenhead road turn off at roundabout into Butts Hill Road. Turn left into Headly Road East, right at the roundabout, straight over the next roundabout and then left into Mohawk Way to the museum.

Buckinghamshire

BLETCHLEY
Bletchley Park ❊ ✷
Station X (home of the code-breakers of World War II)

Bletchley Park Trust, The Mansion, Bletchley, Milton Keynes, Buckinghamshire
MK3 6EB

TEL: 01908 640404

WEBSITE: www.bletchleypark.org.uk

COLLECTION: Code-breaking at Station X shortened World War II and saved millions of lives. The Cryptology Trail takes the visitor through the process of a coded message, from its interception to decoding and interpretation. Examples of coding machines such as the Enigma machine, which was the main coding device for the German armed forces, and the rebuilt Colossus computer are on show. Free guided tours are available. There are many other exhibits within the park, uniforms and World War II memorabilia and military vehicles. Within the mansion there is a period toy museum and a Winston Churchill collection.

BUILDING: Bletchley Park consists of 50 acres with the original mansion as the centrepiece. Station X is housed in the various wooden and brick buildings in the grounds.

OPENING TIMES: Open every other weekend: 10.30am–5pm. Contact Bletchley Park for details.

ADMISSION CHARGES: ②

ⓟ ♿ 🚾 ⬧ ✕ ⚠ 🎥 ⛪

DIRECTIONS: See map.

CHALFONT ST GILES
Milton's Cottage ✷

Chalfont St Giles, Buckinghamshire HP8 4JH

TEL: 01494 872313

E-MAIL: pbirger@clara.net WEBSITE: www.clara.net.pbirger

COLLECTION: It was at this cottage that John Milton completed *Paradise Lost* and started *Paradise Regained*. Milton's career is described, and on show are his portrait by Sir Godfrey Kneller and many specific items relating to Milton. There are first editions of his 17th-century poetry and prose works. Civil War items are also exhibited.

BUILDING: A Grade I listed building, built in 1580. There are three rooms upstairs and three down. Outside is an attractive cottage garden. There is a restaurant opposite the museum.

OPENING TIMES: *1 March to 31 October*, Tuesday to Sunday (closed Monday): 10am–1pm

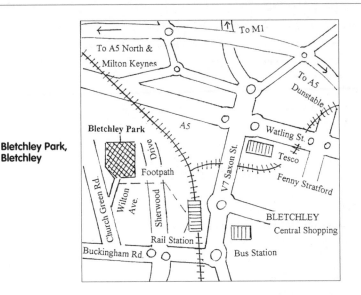

Bletchley Park, Bletchley

(map labels: To M1; To A5 North & Milton Keynes; To A5 Dunstable; Bletchley Park; A5; Watling St.; Tesco; Footpath; Fenny Stratford; V7 Saxon St.; Drive; Church Green Rd.; Wilton Ave.; Sherwood; BLETCHLEY Central Shopping; Rail Station; Buckingham Rd.; Bus Station)

& 2pm–6pm. Open spring and summer bank holidays.

ADMISSION CHARGES: ①

Ⓟ ♿ [WC] ⚠

DIRECTIONS: From the A413 Amersham to Denham road turn off into Chalfont St Giles. Milton's Cottage is on the left.

OLNEY

The Cowper and Newton Museum ❊ ✳

Orchard Side, Market Place, Olney, Buckinghamshire MK46 4AJ

TEL: 01234 711516

E-MAIL: museum@olney.co.uk

WEBSITE: www.oloi.demon.co.uk/cnmhome.html

COLLECTION: Home of William Cowper, the poet, for 18 years from 1768, the museum displays Cowper memorabilia. In his garden, the summer-house where he wrote several of his poems still stands. A room is devoted to John Newton, Cowper's friend. Newton came to Olney as a curate in 1764. As well as helping in the fight against slavery, he wrote many famous hymns, such as *Amazing Grace,* together with Cowper. There are additional exhibits and a lace collection, reflecting the importance of the industry to Olney and collections of local history items.

BUILDING: Grade II listed building. Only the ground floor and the garden are accessible by wheelchair. Research facilities are available by appointment.

There are a number of cafés and restaurants in Olney.

Buckinghamshire

OPENING TIMES: *1 March to 23 December*, Tuesday to Saturday: 10am–1pm & 2pm–5pm. (Closed Sunday & Monday.) Open on all Bank Holiday Mondays and Shrove Tuesday. *June, July & August*, open Sunday: 2pm–5pm. Closed Good Friday.

ADMISSION CHARGES: ①

P WC ⑤ 📷

DIRECTIONS: Leave the M1 at junction 14 on to the A509 for Olney. The museum is in a central position in Olney's marketplace.

Hertfordshire

LETCHWORTH
The First Garden City Heritage Museum ❄ ❋

296 Norton Way South, Letchworth Garden City, Hertfordshire SG6 1SU

TEL: 01462 482710 FAX: 01462 486056

E-MAIL: fgchm@letchworth.com

COLLECTION: One small book published in 1898, written by Ebeneezer Howard, changed the whole concept of town planning. Howard's idea of the garden city was a marriage of town and country. To put his ideas into operation the Garden City Association was formed and in 1903 it bought land at Letchworth to develop the first garden city. The museum celebrates this achievement with models and artefacts from Letchworth's history, plus posters, books, plans and diagrams. Photography requires the permission of the curator.

BUILDING: In the drawing office of the original town architects, Parker and Unwin. Two-thirds of the building are accessible by wheelchair but there are no other facilities for the disabled.

The First Garden
City Heritage
Museum,
Letchworth

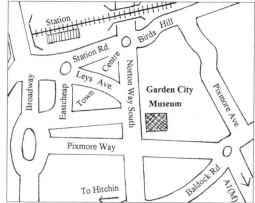

The Forge
Museum,
Much
Hadham

OPENING TIMES: *All year*, Monday to Saturday: 10am–5pm. (Closed Sunday.)
ADMISSION CHARGES: ①

🅿 ♿ WC Ⓢ 🎦 👪

DIRECTIONS: Letchworth is on the A505 and not far from the A1(M).
For directions to the museum see map.

MUCH HADHAM
The Forge Museum ❄ ✳

High Street, Much Hadham, Hertfordshire SG10 6BS
TEL/FAX: 01279 843301
COLLECTION: From 1811 to 1983 the Page family ran a smithy in Much Hadham. The
daughter of the last Page blacksmith gave the buildings to the Hertfordshire Building
Preservation trust in 1988. A blacksmith still works in the forge and the displays tell the
story of the craft of blacksmithing over the years. There are smaller exhibits about local
village life, a number of blacksmithing tools and tools from other trades.
BUILDING: The museum is set in Grade II listed buildings. The earlier building, once a
farmhouse, dates from the 15th century. The forge and bellows room are part of a 17th-
century barn conversion and in 1811 the shoeing room and blacksmith's shop were added
when the Page family moved in. Not all the site is accessible by wheelchair and there are
no facilities for the disabled. Snacks are sold and refreshments can be arranged with
advance warning.
OPENING TIMES: *All year*, Friday, Saturday, Sunday and bank holidays: 11am–5pm (dusk
in winter).

Hertfordshire

ADMISSION CHARGES: ①

🅿 ♿ 🚾 ⚠ 🎥 👫

DIRECTIONS: Much Hadham is south west of Cambridge on the B1004. The museum is in the High Street.

ST ALBANS
St Albans Organ Museum ❄ ❋

326 Camp Road, St Albans, Hertfordshire AL1 5PB

TEL/FAX: 01727 851557

COLLECTION: The sounds of these old organs ring out during opening times and a commentary adds to the understanding of the instruments. There are two theatre organs, the 'Mighty Wurlitzer' from the Granada Cinema in Edmonton, North London, and the Rutt Theatre Organ. In addition there is a 95-key Bursens Café Organ and a Mills Violano-Virtuoso, which produces its own unique sound of a four-string violin and 44-note piano. Musical boxes from the 1880s are also demonstrated, plus hand-turned Victorian table organettes.

BUILDING: One exhibition hall. The building is all on the level and there are ramps at the entrance, but wheelchairs cannot access the toilets.

OPENING TIMES: *All year*, every Sunday: 2pm–4.30pm. Organised groups are welcome at other times, by arrangement. Evenings preferred.

ADMISSION CHARGES: ②

Ⓟ ♿ 🚾 ⛟ ⚠ 🎥 👫

DIRECTIONS: See map.

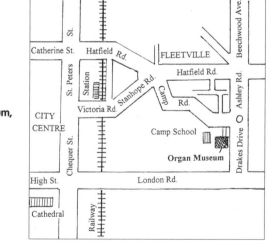

Organ Museum, St Albans

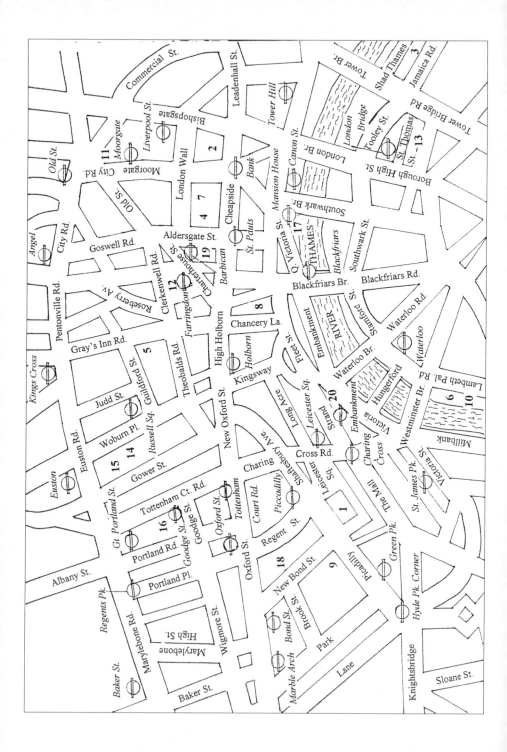

CENTRAL LONDON MUSEUMS

Key to Map

1. Alfred Dunhill Gallery
2. Bank of England Museum
3. Bramah Museum of Tea and Coffee
4. Chartered Insurance Institute Museum
5. The Dickens House Museum
6. Florence Nightingale Museum
7. Guildhall Clock Museum
8. Dr Johnson's House
9. The Michael Faraday Museum
10. Museum of Garden History

11. The Museum of Methodism
12. Museum of the Order of St John
13. The Old Operating Theatre Museum and Herb Garret
14. The Percival Foundation of Chinese Art
15. The Petrie Museum of Egyptian Archaeology
16. Pollock Toy Theatres
17. The Salvation Army International Heritage Centre
18. Smythson
19. St Bartholomew Hospital Museum
20. Twinings in the Strand.

Central London

Alfred Dunhill Gallery ❋ ❊

On corner of 48 German Street and 30 Duke Street St James, off Piccadilly,
London W1

TEL: (museum shop) 0207 290 8622 (head office) 0207 838 8000

COLLECTION: In 1893 Alfred Dunhill took over his father's business catering for the
horse-carriage trade. He began to realise the increasing importance of the motor-car
and switched his attention to motoring accessories, selling veils, waterproofs, straw
motor-caps, and jackets. The museum has large leather overcoats and luggage on display,
but the emphasis of the collection is on the cigarette-lighters. Housed in glass cases in a
curved, underground room, they tell the history of smoking fashion and the famous.
There is Harpo Marx's gold lighter and a silver-plated lighter given to Picasso by Dora
Maar, the Yugoslav photographer with whom he lived from 1936. Dora's portrait, engraved by Picasso, is on the lid. There are laquered lighters and a very rare eggshell laquer
of the 1920s, plus fountain-pens, cigarette-holders, old tinder lighters and pipes.

BUILDING: Below Dunhill's present shop, which sells shirts, multi-coloured luggage and
many other things.

OPENING TIMES: *All year*, Monday to Friday: 9.30am–6pm, Saturday: 10am–6pm (except
the usual shop holidays).

ADMISSION CHARGES: Free

🅿 ♿ 🚾 ⚠ 🎥

DIRECTIONS: Off the south side of Piccadilly between the Underground stations of
Piccadilly and Green Park.

Bank of England Museum ❋ ❊

Bank of England, Threadneedle Street, London EC2 8AH

TEL: 020 7601 5545 FAX: 020 7601 5808

WEBSITE: www.bankofEngland.co.uk

COLLECTION: Gold bars, coins and a unique collection of banknotes might catch the
eye, but the purpose of the museum is to trace the history of the Bank from its foundation
by Royal Charter in 1694 to its role today as the nation's central bank. There is a reconstruction of a late 18th-century banking hall based on John Soane's original drawings,
documents and pictures. Research facilities are available by appointment. Interactive computers allow visitors to examine the making of banknotes and such things as stock-
dealing.

BUILDING: Housed within the Bank of England, a seven-storey building, enclosed on a

Bank of England Museum

three-and-a-half-acre site by a curtain wall completed by John Soane in 1828. The museum entrance is in Bartholomew Lane.

OPENING TIMES: *All year,* Monday to Friday: 10am–5pm. Closed weekends and public and bank holidays. Open on the day of the Lord Mayor's Show and Open House Weekend.

ADMISSION CHARGES: Free

  ♿ WC ⚠ 🚻

DIRECTIONS: Underground: Bank. British Rail: Liverpool Street, Fenchurch Street.

Bramah Museum of Tea and Coffee ❄ ✳

Maguire Street, Butler's Wharf, London SE1 2NQ

TEL: 020 7378 0222 FAX: 020 7378 0219

E-MAIL: e.bramah@virgin.net WEBSITE: bramahmuseum.co.uk

COLLECTION: How to make a pot of leaf tea and learning about the history and quality of tea form part of a special tea seminar. This must be pre-booked. For those who do not wish to participate so actively, the museum offers teapots galore, machines for coffee-making, old prints and the history of the Dutch and English trading companies, and a range of displays to tell the history of tea and coffee from 1650 to 1950. Instant coffee and tea-bags bring the story up to date.

BUILDING: The Butler's Wharf site was chosen because the area was involved in the unloading of ships handling tea and coffee over 350 years ago. The museums are now

Reading
the tea
leaves,
Bramah
Museum of
Tea and
Coffee

separated, with the tea museum in Maguire Street and the coffee museum in Gainsford Street. The entrance fee is for both museums.

OPENING TIMES: *All year*, daily, except Christmas Day and Boxing Day: 10am–6pm.

ADMISSION CHARGES: ②

🅿 🆆🅲 ☕ ⚠

DIRECTIONS: South of the River Thames off Shad Thomas, by Tower Bridge. Nearest Underground: London Bridge, Tower Hill.

Chartered Insurance Institute Museum ❋ ✳

The Hall, 20 Aldermanbury, London EC2 V7HY

TEL: 020 7417 4426

COLLECTION: In the centre of this one-room museum is a 19th-century, horse-drawn fire-engine, a reminder that fire was one of the main hazards to the buildings of London and that it took the Great Fire of London to inspire fire insurance. Firemen's helmets and buckets, plus plaques that were placed on buildings to mark an insured property, are on display around the walls. Other insurances also feature, such as accident insurance and cover on steam-boilers, which were apt to explode. Marine insurance was introduced in 1601 by Francis Bacon, supported by Sir Walter Raleigh. Life assurance proves to be the oldest of all, and is supposed to have been introduced by the Greeks and Romans. In Britain it dates back to the Anglo-Saxon burial societies. The first policy, however, dates from 1583. Many of the displays feature the hand-written policies themselves.

BUILDING: Within the rather imposing Chartered Insurance building.

OPENING TIMES: *All year*, Monday to Thursday: 9am–5pm, Friday: 9am–4.45pm. The

room may be used for functions, so it is advisable to telephone in advance of a visit.
ADMISSION CHARGES: Free

P 📷

DIRECTIONS: Ask directions at the reception desk as the room is upstairs. Underground: Moorgate, Bank.

The Dickens House Museum ❄ ✳

48 Doughty Street, London WC1N 2LF
TEL: 020 7405 2127 FAX: 020 7831 5175
E-MAIL: Dmuseum@rmple.co.uk WEBSITE: www.dickensmuseum.com
COLLECTION: Dickens' manuscripts, writing desk, personal items and memorabilia, plus illustrations to his books, are on display. There are also various portraits of the man himself. A large number of Dickens' editions are housed in the basement, together with a video giving a short history of the writer. There is a photographic and research library, to be viewed by appointment only.
BUILDING: A Georgian terraced house built in 1801. In fact Dickens lived in the house only from 1837 to 1839, but it is his only London residence still standing.
OPENING TIMES: Monday to Saturday: 10am–5pm. (Closed Sunday.)
ADMISSION CHARGES: ②

P WC ♿ 📷

DIRECTIONS: Underground: Russell Square, Kings Cross, Chancery Lane.

Florence Nightingale Museum ❄ ✳

St Thomas' Hospital, 2 Lambeth Palace Road, London SE1 7EW
TEL: 020 7620 0347 FAX: 020 7928 1760
E-MAIL: curator@florence-nightingale.co.uk
WEBSITE: www.florence-nightingale.co.uk
COLLECTION: The full horror of the Crimean War is conveyed by paintings and a reconstruction of a ward at Scutari. It was here that Florence Nightingale earned the reputation of 'ministering angel' among the soldiers, as she carried out her nursing duties. Her influence on modern nursing is well known and the museum helps to explain her work, both during the Crimean War and later, for she spent years campaigning for health reform and setting up a training school for nurses. Her clothes, medicine chest, lantern and a signed copy of her notes on nursing all help in telling her story. There is a Resource Centre open to researchers by appointment.
BUILDING: In the basement of St Thomas' Hospital, displays are laid out in different bays. Canteen in St Thomas' Hospital.
OPENING TIMES: *All year*, Monday to Friday: 10am–5pm, Saturday, Sunday, bank holidays:

11.30am–4.30pm. (Last admission one hour before closure.) Closed Good Friday, Easter Sunday & 24 December–2 January.

ADMISSION CHARGES: ②

Ⓟ ♿ WC ⚠ ♟

DIRECTIONS: South of the River Thames and Westminster Bridge. Underground: Waterloo.

Guildhall Clock Museum ❊ ✺

Guildhall, Aldermanbury, London EC2P 2EJ

TEL: 020 7332 1868 or 1870

COLLECTION: This is the museum of the Worshipful Company of Clockmakers and clocks as early as 1600 are on display in numerous glass cases. A rather large travelling clock for railways and carriages, smaller watches in silver or enamel, and watches from France and Switzerland are on view. Long case clocks, including one of 1672 and another of 1728 by James Harrison, line two walls. Chronometers, measuring time at sea, form a major display, the centre of which is an example of the work of John Harrison, hero of the book *Longitude*.

BUILDING: Within the Guildhall Library. Be ready to be checked by a luggage x-ray machine. The museum is having a complete overhaul in 2001, so check opening hours for 2002.

OPENING TIMES: *All year*, Monday to Friday: 9.30am–4.45pm.

ADMISSION CHARGES: Free

Ⓟ ♿ WC ♟

DIRECTIONS: Go through the doors into the Guildhall Library off Aldermanbury and the museum is on your left. Underground: St Paul's, Moorgate, Bank, Mansion House.

Dr Johnson's House ❊ ✺

17 Gough Square, Fleet Street, London EC4A 3DE

TEL: 020 7353 3745

E-MAIL: curator@drjh.dircon.co.uk WEBSITE: www.drjh.dircon.co.uk

COLLECTION: 'Dictionary Johnson' is what Dr Johnson came to be called, for he compiled the first comprehensive English dictionary. He lived at the house from 1748 to 1759. Memorabilia, paintings, books and a video show help to bring Dr Johnson and his work to life. A library is available by appointment.

BUILDING: The house was rescued from demolition by the late Cecil Harmsworth in 1911 and opened to the public. It is one of the few residential houses of its age that survive in the City. It has been restored to the condition of the time of Dr Johnson's stay there.

OPENING TIMES: *May to September*, Monday to Saturday: 11am–5.30pm. *October to April*,

Monday to Saturday: 11am–5pm. (Closed Sunday and bank holidays.)
ADMISSION CHARGES: ②

🅿 WC ⅍ 📷

DIRECTIONS: Underground: Blackfriars, Chancery Lane. The house is well signposted from Fetter Lane, Shoe Lane and Fleet Street.

The Michael Faraday Museum ❄ ✳

The Royal Institution, 21 Albermarle Street, London W1S 4BS

TEL: 020 7409 2992

E-MAIL: ri@ri.ac.uk WEBSITE: www.ri.ac.uk/History/M.Faraday

COLLECTION: The restored laboratory and museum reveal the work of Michael Faraday. It was his discovery of electromagnetic induction that made a major advance towards developing the electrical industries of today. Among the items on display are his working apparatus and generator, plus early batteries.

BUILDING: Within an 18th-century building that has undergone much renovation.

OPENING TIMES: Monday to Friday: 10am–5.30pm. (Closed Saturday and Sunday.)

ADMISSION CHARGES: ①

🅿 ♿ WC ⅍ 📷 👫

DIRECTIONS: Underground: Green Park.

Museum of Garden History ❄ ✳

St Mary-at-Lambeth, Lambeth Palace Road, London SE1 7LB

TEL: 020 7401 8865 FAX: 020 7401 8869

E-MAIL: info@museumgardenhistory.org

WEBSITE: www.Museumgardenhistory.org

COLLECTION: Victorian lawnmowers and old garden tools are a reminder of the hard work gardening can involve. Displays about garden pioneers such as the Tradescants and famous garden designers such as Gertrude Jekyll are an inspiration. The exhibits tell the history of gardening. Outside is a 17th-century-style knot garden, full of plants traced back to that period. There are changing exhibits in the gallery.

BUILDING: The historic church of St Mary-at-Lambeth. The Tradescant family tomb can be seen in the garden. The church was saved from demolition in 1977 and was restored.

OPENING TIMES: *Early February to late December*, Sunday to Friday: 10.30am–5pm. (Closed Saturday.)

ADMISSION CHARGES: Free (donations appreciated)

🅿 ♿ WC ☕ ⅍ 📷 👫

DIRECTIONS: South of the river and Westminster Bridge. Underground: Waterloo, Westminster, Lambeth North.

Central

The Museum of Methodism ❄ ✳

Wesley's Chapel and House, 49 City Road, London EC1 1AU

TEL: 020 7253 2262 FAX: 020 7608 3852

COLLECTION: A pack of religious playing-cards and a ceramic Wesleyan chapel are surprises in one of the world's largest collections of Weslyan ceramics held by the museum, plus Methodist paintings. The museum tells the history of Methodism to the present day and the story of John Wesley (1703–91), the founder of Methodism. In Wesley's house are his belongings and his study chair. There is also Wesley's gruesome electric shock machine used to treat cases of depression.

BUILDING: John Wesley's house was built in 1779. He lived there for eleven years. (The house is not accessible by wheelchair.) Wesley built the chapel in 1778 as his London base. It was designed by the architect George Dance the Younger.

OPENING TIMES: *All year*, Monday to Saturday: 10am–4pm, Sunday: 12 noon–2pm. Closed every Thursday between 12.45 and 1.30pm and public and bank holidays.

ADMISSION CHARGES: ②

🅿 ♿ WC Ⓢ 📷

DIRECTIONS: Underground: Old Street and Moorgate.

Museum of the Order of St John ❄ ✳

St John's Gate, St John's Lane, Clerkenwell, London EC1M 4DA

TEL: 020 7253 6644 FAX: 020 7336 0587

WEBSITE: www.sja.org.uk/history

COLLECTION: Armour and a rare chain-mail outfit are reminders of the fighting side of the Order of St John. Maltese furniture, pharmacy jars, paintings, prints and drawings all contribute to tell the story of the Order from the time of the Crusades to the present. Included in the display is information on the foundation of St John Ambulance and St John Ophthalmic Hospital in Jerusalem. The guided tour includes access to parts of the gatehouse not normally seen and to the Grand Priory Church and Crypt. A photographic archive and the Order's history library and St John Ambulance library are available by appointment.

BUILDING: St John's Gate was built in 1504 and was the entrance to the English headquarters of the Order. Their Grand Priory in Clerkenwell existed from 1140 until the reign of Henry VIII.

OPENING TIMES: *All year*, Monday to Friday: 10am–5pm, Saturday: 10am–4pm. Closed Sunday, Saturdays of bank holidays and Monday.

ADMISSION CHARGES: Free (donations for tours are requested)

🅿 ♿ WC Ⓢ 📷 👪

DIRECTIONS: Underground: Farringdon.

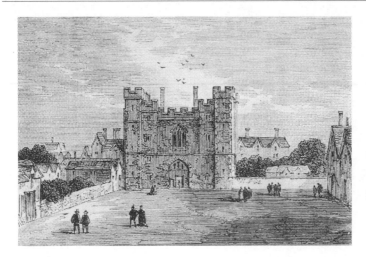

Engraving
by Hollar of
St John's
Gate,
Museum of
the Order of
St John

The Old Operating Theatre Museum and Herb Garret ✻ ✺

9a St Thomas' Street, Southwark, London SE1 9RY

TEL: 020 7955 4791 FAX: 020 7378 8383

E-MAIL: curator@thegarret.org.uk WEBSITE: www.thegarret.org.uk

COLLECTION: A gruesome but atmospheric reminder of the days when operations were performed without anaesthetics or antiseptics. Dating from 1822, it is the only 19th-century operating theatre surviving in Britain and the operating table and viewing benches are still there. So are medical instruments for amputation and other purposes, which are on show next door in the garret. This room was used by the apothecary of St Thomas' Hospital for the storage and curing of medicinal herbs.

BUILDING: In the garret of St Thomas' Church. Formally a 13th-century Augustinian monastery and nunnery, the church and hospital were largely rebuilt in the 17th century.

OPENING TIMES: *All year*, daily: 10.30am–5pm (last admission 4.45pm). Closed 15 December–5 January.

ADMISSION CHARGES: ②

🅿 ⓦⓒ ♿ 📷 👫

DIRECTIONS: South of the River Thames and London Bridge. Underground: London Bridge.

The Percival David Foundation of Chinese Art ✻ ✺

53 Gordon Square, London WC1 0PD

TEL: 020 7387 3909 FAX: 020 7383 5163

COLLECTION: Glass cases full of wonderful Chinese ceramics. This is the finest collection

The Old
Operating
Theatre
Museum

outside China. There are Ru, Guan and Jun wares, made especially for the court or given as a tribute. The late Sir Percival David presented this collection and a library of books relating to Chinese art and culture to the University of London in 1950. The familiar blue and white ceramics feature alongside pale green cracked glaze, creamware and much more, all dating from the 10th century to the 18th centuries. The library is meant for students or qualified researchers and permission to visit must be requested of the curator in advance. Photography is possible but without a flash. Children must be accompanied by an adult.

BUILDING: A separate building from the university on the south west corner of Gordon Square. There are three floors.

OPENING TIMES: *All year*, Monday to Friday: 10.30am–5pm. Closed on bank holidays and weekends. The library is open Monday to Friday: 10.30am–1pm & 2pm–4.45pm.

ADMISSION CHARGES: Free

🅿 📶 ♿ 📷

DIRECTIONS: Underground: Russell Square, Goodge Street, Euston Square.

Petrie Museum of Egyptian Archaeology ❋ ✳

University College London, Malet Place, London WC1E 6BT

TEL: 020 7679 2884 FAX: 020 7679 2886

E-MAIL: petrie.museum@ucl.ac.uk

COLLECTION: A warren of display-cases full of fascinating objects from Egypt, including the world's earliest surviving dress (around 2800 BC), painted funerary portraits, even a skeleton in a burial pot. Most of the items on display were excavated, or bought in Egypt by William Flinders Petrie (1853-1942). The displays illustrate life in the Nile Valley from prehistory through to Roman and Islamic times. There are many small personal items not seen in other museums and one of the largest collections of Roman mummy portraits. The museum is recognised as a teaching and research resource. Researchers must make arrangements with the museum well in advance. Photography is allowed but without a flash.

BUILDING: Part of University College London. The museum is upstairs.

OPENING TIMES: *All year*, Tuesday to Friday: 1pm–5pm, Saturday: 10am–1pm. Closed for one week at Christmas and Easter.

ADMISSION CHARGES: Free

P WC ⚠ 📷 ⛄

DIRECTIONS: See map. Underground: Euston, Euston Square, Warren Street, Russell Square, Goodge Street.

Pollock's Toy Theatres ❄ ❋

1 Scala Street, London W1P 1LT

TEL: 020 7636 3452

E-MAIL: toytheatres@hotmail.com WEBSITE: www.pollocks.cwc.net

COLLECTION: The Penny Plain and Twopence Coloured Victorian Toy Theatre sheets were the subject of hours of childrens' pleasure in the Pollock's Toy Theatres. Benjamin Pollock devoted his life to making toy theatres as his father-in-law, John Redington, had taught him. The museum also houses toys from all countries, puppets, wax dolls, teddy bears and a collection of toy theatres.

BUILDING: Two small houses joined together. The rooms are small and connected by narrow winding staircases.

OPENING TIMES: Monday to Saturday: 10am–5pm (Closed Sunday.)

ADMISSION CHARGES: ①

P WC ⚠ 📷 ⛄

DIRECTIONS: Underground: Goodge Street.

The Salvation Army International Heritage Centre ❄ ❋

101 Queen Victoria Street, London EC4 4EP

TEL: 020 7332 0101 ext 8704/8705 FAX: 020 7332 8099

E-MAIL: heritage@salvationarmy.org WEBSITE: www.salvationarmy.org

COLLECTION: At 15 years of age William Booth (1829-1912) decided to 'go in for God'. From this belief grew the Salvation Army and the museum tells its history. Memorabilia and the *Salvation Soldier's Song Book* fill display cases. Videos show historic moments in

Central

Salvation Army history. There are fun worksheets for children. Research facilities are available by appointment.

BUILDING: The Salvation Army's International Headquarters, built in 1963. The museum maybe relocated within the next two years. Phone before visiting.

OPENING TIMES: *All year*, Monday to Friday: 9.30am–3.30pm (Closed Sunday & public holidays.)

ADMISSION CHARGES: Free

🅿 ♿ 🚾 �🥤 ✕ ⚠ 📷

DIRECTIONS: On Queen Victoria Street, opposite the road to St Paul's Cathedral and by the road to the Millennium Bridge. Underground: Mansion House, Blackfriars.

Smythson ❄ ✳

40 New Bond Street, London W1S 2DE

TEL: 020 7629 8558

COLLECTION: The shop of Smythson opened in 1887. Displayed in glass cases in a small cave-like room at the back of the shop is the history of this supplier of stationery to the rich. A brief history of paper begins the display and then a collection of Smythson's wares, including 1932 diaries, engagement books, wax seals and stamps, tells the development of the firm's goods. There is an album of stationery supplied to the Maharaja of Cooch Behar, and lightweight travel notebooks hint at the lifestyles of those who came to the shop.

BUILDING: At the back of Smythson's shop.

OPENING TIMES: *All year*, Monday to Wednesday & Friday: 9.30am–6pm, Thursday & Saturday: 10am–6pm. Closed Sunday and usual shop holidays.

ADMISSION CHARGES: Free

🅿 ♿ ⚠ 📷

DIRECTIONS: Underground: Bond Street.

St Bartholomew's Hospital Museum ❄ ✳

St Bartholomew's Hospital, West Smithfield, London EC1A 7BE

TEL: 0207 601 8033/8152

COLLECTION: Founded in 1123, St Bartholomew's (Bart's) is one of the oldest hospitals in the world. The museum tells the story of nine centuries of caring for the sick and displays the surgical instruments and medical equipment used. The stories of the doctors and nurses of Bart's are also told. The hospital archives are open to researchers by appointment only. Food is available in the hospital canteen and there is a disabled toilet in the Out-Patients' Department.

BUILDING: In the historic North Wing of the hospital, under the arch leading to the West Smith Square.

Twinings
in the
Strand

OPENING TIMES: *All year*, Tuesday to Friday: 10am–4pm. (Closed Saturday to Monday.) Closed public holidays.

ADMISSION CHARGES: Free

🅿 ♿ 🚻 ⚠ 📷 👪

DIRECTIONS: Near Smithfield Market, a few minutes' walk from St Paul's Cathedral and the Museum of London. Underground: St Paul's, Farringdon and Barbican.

Twinings in the Strand ❄ ✳

216 Strand, WC2R 1AP

TEL: 020 7353 3511

COLLECTION: A narrow corridor, in which tea and coffee are sold, leads to a small room at the rear. The history of the firm from 1706, when Thomas Twining set up as a tea merchant, is told via photographs on the walls. Displayed around the room are many objects associated with the trade. There are former tea packagings, a tea urn and a T.I.P. box, which customers of the coffee-houses used to pay money into to ensure prompt service.

BUILDING: In Twinings shop, which seems to concentrate upon sending orders out, although it does have a very small shop.

OPENING TIMES: *All year*, Monday to Friday: 9.30am–4.55pm. Closed weekends and usual shop holidays.

ADMISSION CHARGES: Free

🅿 ♿ ⚠ 📷

DIRECTIONS: Underground: Temple.

Central

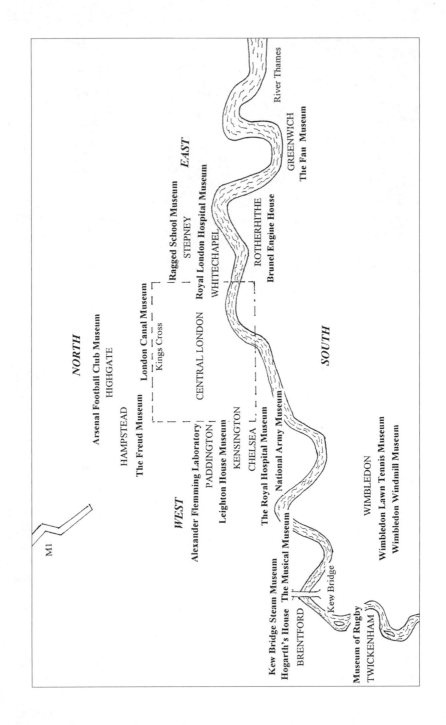

Outer London

EAST
Ragged School Museum ❊ ❊

46-50 Copperfield Road, London E3 4RR

TEL: 020 8980 6405 FAX: 020 8983 3481

E-MAIL: museum@raggedschool.freeserve.co.uk WEBSITE: www.raggedschoolmuseum

COLLECTION: A Victorian schoolroom is re-created to show what school was like over 100 years ago. Dr Thomas Barnardo leased these warehouses and in 1896 the ragged schools had 1,075 children registered for day schools, 178 young women for evening classes and 2,460 pupils for Sunday school. The museum relates the work of Dr Barnardo and education in London. It also shows the life of the East End in the 19th and early 20th centuries.

BUILDING: Built as warehouses in 1872, number 46 was leased by Dr Barnardo in 1876, number 48 in 1895. The Ragged School Museum Trust, founded by people from the local community, purchased numbers 46-50 in 1986. Numbers 46 and 48 have Grade II listed building status. Only the ground floor is accessible by wheelchair.

OPENING TIMES: *All year*, Wednesday & Thursday: 10am–5pm, first Sunday of each month: 2pm–5pm.

ADMISSION CHARGES: Free

DIRECTIONS: From Stepney Green Underground turn towards Regent's Canal and Mile End Park. Turn right down Harford Street and left into Ben Jonson Road. Then left up Copperfield Road. The museum is on the left. From Mile End Underground walk towards Mile End Park, turn left down Burdett Road and then right into St Paul's Way. Copperfield Road is on your right.

EAST
The Royal London Hospital Archives and Museum ❊ ❊

Royal London Hospital, Whitechapel High Street, London E1 1BB

TEL: 020 7377 7608

E-MAIL: r.j.evans@mds.qmw.ac.uk

COLLECTION: Information on Joseph Merrick, the 'Elephant Man', and George Washington's dentures form some of the more bizarre exhibits. The main exhibition tells the history of the Royal London Hospital, founded in 1740, and includes paintings, sculpture, uniforms, surgical instruments and x-ray and nursing equipment. The lives of individuals such as Edith Cavell and Eva Luckes are also told. Archive research facilities are available by prior appointment. Toilets and canteen are in the Out-Patients' Department.

BUILDING: In the crypt of the former hospital church, St Augustine with St Philip's, a Grade II listed building, dating from 1890.

OPENING TIMES: *All year*, weekdays: 10am–4.30pm. (Closed Saturday, Sunday and bank holidays and adjacent days and between Christmas and New Year.)

ADMISSION CHARGES: Free (donations welcome)

🅿 ⚠ 📷 ⅲ

DIRECTIONS: The hospital is opposite Whitechapel Underground.

NORTH
Arsenal Football Club Museum ❄ ✳

Arsenal Stadium, Avenell Road, Highbury, London N5 1BU

TEL: 020 7704 4101   FAX: 020 774 4101

COLLECTION: The club's first football was bought by a group of munitions workers collecting all their sixpences in 1886. The museum tells the story of the club from this small beginning to the present day. There are life-like waxworks of the club's stars, a shirt worn by Alex James in the 1936 FA Cup Final and, to outline the club's history, a short film.

BUILDING: On the second floor of the North Bank stand. The club shop is 200 metres from the museum.

OPENING TIMES: *All year*, Friday: 9.30 am–4pm. (Also open on other selected days. Check for dates.) (Arsenal Football Club may be relocating some time in the future. Check before visiting.)

ADMISSION CHARGES: ①

🅿 ♿ 🆆🅲 ⚠ 📷 ⅲ

DIRECTIONS: Underground: Arsenal. Railway stations: Drayton Park, Finsbury Park.

NORTH
The Freud Museum ❄ ✳

20 Maresfield Gardens, London NW3 5SX

TEL: 020 7435 2002   FAX: 020 7431 5452

E-MAIL: freud@gn.apc.org

WEBSITE: www.freud.org.uk

COLLECTION: Sigmund Freud's study and couch are the centrepiece of the museum but there are also many antiques to enjoy. Freud (1856-1939) was an avid collector and there are Oriental rugs, ceramic and glass to view. Anna Freud, the only one of his six children to become a psychoanalyst, lived in the house until her death in 1982. There is an archive available to accredited postgraduate researchers, by appointment.

BUILDING: The Freud family home. Freud and his family moved into this house in 1938,

Freud's
couch,
The Freud
Museum

after they had fled from Nazi persecution. Only the ground floor is suitable for wheel-chairs. No flash photography is allowed.

OPENING TIMES: *All year*, Wednesday to Sunday: 12 noon–5pm. (Closed Saturday to Tuesday.)

ADMISSION CHARGES: ②

Ⓟ ♿ ⓦⓒ ⚠ 📹

DIRECTIONS: From Swiss Cottage Underground walk north up College Crescent into Fitzjohn's Avenue. Turn left into Maresfield Gardens. From Hampstead Underground walk south down Fitzjohn's Avenue and turn right into Maresfield Gardens.

NORTH
London Canal Museum ❄ ✹

12–13 New Wharf Road, London N1 9RT

TEL: 020 7713 0836 WAP MOBILE SITE: www.canalmuseum.org.uk/wap/index-wm/
WEBSITE: www.canalmuseum.org.uk

COLLECTION: Discovering how a canal lock works and cramming into the small space of a canal barge are all part of what the museum has to offer. It tells the story of London's canals from the early days as trade routes to today's use for leisure. There is information on cargoes and canal crafts, the people who made a living on the canals and the horses that pulled the boats. There is a library for research use by appointment. The museum also tells the story of the ice and icecream trade.

BUILDING: Once an ice warehouse built in the 1860s for Carlo Gatti, the famous ice-cream maker. Ice from Norway was stored in two vast ice-wells beneath the building. One well can be viewed. Wheelchair access to the ground floor, first floor by appointment only.

OPENING TIMES: *All year*, Tuesday to Sunday (closed Monday) but open on Bank Holiday Mondays: 10am–4.30pm (last entry 3.45pm).

ADMISSION CHARGES: ①

🅿 ♿ WC ⚠ 🎥 ♦♦♦

DIRECTIONS: Rail: Kings Cross, St Pancras. From Kings Cross Station turn up York Way towards the Regent's Canal, then right down Wharfdale Road. Turn left up New Wharf Road. The museum is on the left.

SOUTH
Brunel Engine House ❄ ❀

Brunel Exhibition, Railway Avenue, Rotherhithe, London SE16 4LF

TEL: 020 7231 3840 INFO LINE: 020 8806 4325

WEBSITE: www.museumweb.freeserve.co.uk/brunel.htm

COLLECTION: The achievements of Sir Marc Isambard Brunel and his son are celebrated in this exhibition about the world's first major underwater tunnel (1825–43). It links Rotherhithe on the south bank of the River Thames to Wapping on the north bank and is still used by London Underground. Inside the museum is the only surviving compound horizontal V steam engine, built by J. & G. Rennie in 1885.

BUILDING: Now a listed building and a designated ancient monument, the Engine House was built by Brunel to contain boilers for his River Thames Tunnel. It is partially accessible by wheelchair. No café but tea, coffee and biscuits are served.

OPENING TIMES: *April to October*, Saturday & Sunday: 1pm–5pm. *November to March*, Sunday: 1pm –5pm (telephone about other times of opening).

ADMISSION CHARGES: ①

🅿 ♿ WC ⚠ 🎥

DIRECTIONS: From Rotherhithe Underground go up Railway Avenue. Brunel Engine House is near the top on the left.

SOUTH
The Fan Museum ❄ ❀

12 Crooms Hill, Greenwich, London SE10 8ER

TEL: 020 8305 1441 FAX: 020 8293 1889

E-MAIL: admin@fan-museum.org WEBSITE: www.fan-museum.org

COLLECTION: This is the only museum in the world devoted entirely to all aspects of the fan. The history of fans, the craft of making fans and the sources of fans are on display.

Over 2,000 items form part of the Hélène Alexander collection, which she gifted to the nation. Regular exhibitions offer specific themes such as 'Art Nouveau Fans' or 'The lure of the East, Chinoiserie Fans'. There are study and research facilities and a reference library, by appointment only.

BUILDING: Two listed and restored Georgian townhouses. The café is open only Tuesday and Sunday afternoons. There is a lift and a disabled toilet. The toilets won the 'Loo of the Year Award' for 1999.

OPENING TIMES: *All year*, Tuesday to Saturday: 11am–5pm, Sunday: 12noon–5pm. (Closed Monday.)

ADMISSION CHARGES: ②

🅿 ♿ 🚾 ⛱ ⚠ 🚻

DIRECTIONS: Rail: Greenwich Station. From Greenwich Rail Station turn left up the High Road and right down Wells Street into Crooms Hill. The museum is on the right.

SOUTH
Wimbledon Lawn Tennis Museum ❄ ✻

Centre Court, The All England Lawn Tennis and Croquet Club, Church Road, Wimbledon, London SW19 5AE

TEL: 020 8946 6131 FAX: 020 8944 6497

WEBSITE: www.wimbledon.org

COLLECTION: The Ladies' Singles Salver and the Men's Singles Cup feature among the exhibits, which include tennis fashion, the modern game and the history of lawn tennis.

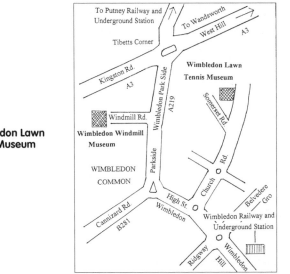

**Wimbledon Lawn
Tennis Museum**

From medieval royal tennis to the polite game on the lawns of Victorian England to today's game, tennis has come a long way. Memorabilia, equipment, a racquet-maker's workshop and paintings help to tell the story, and there is film and video footage of the great players in action. The Kenneth Ritchie Wimbledon Library is open to researchers by appointment only.

BUILDING: Established in 1977 and located within the Centre Court.

OPENING TIMES: *All year*, daily: 10.30am–5pm. During the championships the museum is open only to tournament visitors, and it is closed a few days before and after the championships. (Telephone for details.) Closed 24–26 December and 1 January.

ADMISSION CHARGES: ②

Ⓟ ♿ 🚾 ⬇ ⚠ �

DIRECTIONS: Entrance is through Gate 4. By car take the A3 Portsmouth Road and just before Tibbet's Corner turn left into the A219, towards Wimbledon, down Parkside and left into Church Road. Underground to Southfields on the District Line, then taxi or a 15-minute walk down Wimbledon Park Road. By rail from Waterloo to Wimbledon, then a 25-minute walk along Wimbledon Hill or take a taxi. (See map).

SOUTH
Wimbledon Windmill Museum ❋

Windmill Road, Wimbledon Common, London SW19 5NR

TEL: 020 8947 2825

WEBSITE: www.wimbledonwindmillmuseum.org.uk

COLLECTION: Working models and original machinery help to tell the history of the development of the windmill in the UK. There are 'hands-on' exhibits for children. Also displayed is a collection of woodworking tools. Displays upstairs show the Wimbledon windmill as it was in 1825 and the interior of the mill when it was working.

BUILDING: A hollow post windmill, built in 1817 and last worked in 1864. It is a Grade II listed building. Only the ground floor is accessible by wheelchair.

OPENING TIMES: *April to October* (inclusive), Saturday: 2pm–5pm, Sunday and public holidays: 11am–5pm. (Other times by appointment.)

ADMISSION CHARGES: ①

Ⓟ ♿ 🚾 ⬇ ✕ ⚠ 🚌 ♥

DIRECTIONS: See map.

WEST
Alexander Fleming Laboratory ❄ ❋

St Mary's Hospital, Praed Street, London W2 1NY

TEL: 020 7886 6528 FAX: 020 7886 6739

COLLECTION: A petri dish of mould made Alexander Fleming famous for the discovery

Wimbledon Windmill Museum

of penicillin. Fleming (1881-1955) was awarded the Nobel Prize in 1945, and his work began the search for new antibiotics to fight bacteria. The laboratory where this remarkable discovery took place has been reconstructed to show how it looked in 1928. An accompanying display and video presentation tell the story of Fleming and penicillin. The museum offers educational visits to schools and colleges. The archives of St Mary's Hospital are open to bona fide researchers by appointment only.

BUILDING: The Clarence Memorial Wing of St Mary's Hospital is a Grade II listed building (1891–1904). The museum is on four floors and has five rooms.

OPENING TIMES: *All year*, Monday to Thursday: 10am–1pm. (Closed Friday to Sunday.) Closed public holidays. Open at other times by appointment.

ADMISSION CHARGES: ①

WC

The Arab Hall, Leighton
House Museum

DIRECTIONS: Underground: Paddington. Rail: Paddington. Turn left along Praed Street. The hospital is on the left.

WEST
Leighton House Museum ❄ ✳

12 Holland Park Road, London, W14 8LZ

TEL: 020 7602 3316 FAX: 020 7371 2467

WEBSITE: www.aboutbritain.com/LeightonHouseArtGallery.htm

COLLECTION: President of the Royal Academy and classical painter, Lord Leighton lived from 1830 to 1896. The house is certainly a work of art, with the Arab Hall as its centrepiece. Leighton's studio has great north windows, a gilded dome and an apse. The house contains a fine collection of Victorian art and paintings by Leighton, Burne-Jones, Millais and other contemporaries are displayed throughout the house. Research facilities are

London

available on request. The museum also runs a programme of temporary exhibitions throughout the year.

BUILDING: Built between 1864 and 1879 to designs by George Aitchison.

OPENING TIMES: *All year*, Wednesday to Monday: 11am–5.30pm. (Closed Tuesday.) Open on Sundays and spring and summer bank holidays.

ADMISSION CHARGES: Free

P WC ♿

DIRECTIONS: Undergound: High Street Kensington. The museum is north of Kensington High Street, off Melbury Road.

WEST
National Army Museum ✽ ✻

Royal Hospital Road, Chelsea, London SW3 4HT

TEL: 020 7730 0717 FAX: 020 7823 6573

E-MAIL: pr@national-army-museum.ac.uk

WEBSITE: www.national-army-museum.ac.uk

COLLECTION: Campaigns and battles fought by the British Army from Tudor times to the present day are illustrated in the museum. A cavalryman and his horse from the Civil War and a recruiting sergeant of 1806 are just some of the life-size models that help to tell the story of the soldier. A Tudor canon, English Civil War pistols and a 17th-century sword bring the battles to life. Paintings, photographs, uniforms and equipment, plus reconstructions such as a World War I trench, help to complete the picture. There is an archive for researchers available by appointment.

BUILDING: Purpose-built with nine rooms, a lecture theatre and a reading room for researchers.

OPENING TIMES: *All year*, daily: 10am–5.30pm. Closed 24–26 December, 1 January, Good Friday and early May bank holiday.

ADMISSION CHARGES: Free

P ♿ WC ⛉ ♿ 👪

DIRECTIONS: See map. Underground: Sloane Square.

Outskirts of London

Hogarth's House ✽ ✻

Hogarth Lane, Great West Road, London W4 2QN

TEL: 020 8994 6757

WEBSITE: www.cip.org.uk/heritage/hogarth.htm

COLLECTION: The paintings 'The Rake's Progress' and 'The Harlot's Progress' are on

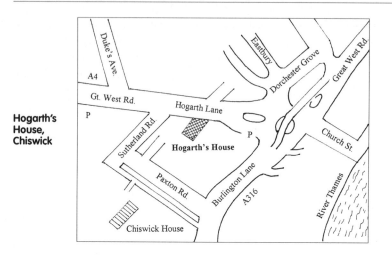

Hogarth's House, Chiswick

display in what was once Hogarth's country home. Many other of his famous moral commentaries on society, such as 'Gin Lane' and 'Beer Street' are also here, alongside engravings and a special exhibition on aspects of Hogarth's life and work.

BUILDING: An early 18th-century house, fully restored in 1997. Only the ground floor is suitable for wheelchairs.

OPENING TIMES: *April to September*, Tuesday to Friday: 1pm–5pm and Saturday & Sunday: 1pm–6pm. *November to December* and *February to March*, Tuesday to Friday: 1pm–4pm. Saturday & Sunday: 1pm–5pm. Closed Monday (except bank holidays) and closed Good Friday, Christmas and Boxing Day and the month of January.

ADMISSION CHARGES: Free

Ⓟ ♿ WC ⚠ ☎

DIRECTIONS: Parking: at Axis Centre next to house, named spaces and Chiswick House grounds car-park. For directions see map.

Kew Bridge Steam Museum ❄ ✳

Green Dragon Lane, Brentford, Middlesex TW8 0EN

TEL: 020 8658 4757

WEBSITE: www.kbsm.org

COLLECTION: Walking through a piece of Thames Water Ring Main is just one of the features of this museum. Information on fighting cholera and how the toshers made a living by scavenging in the sewers are also part of the Water for Life Gallery. There is a collection of water-pumping machinery and many of the engines are in steam every weekend, including the Grand Junction 90, the massive Cornish beam engine that pumped water to West London for over a century. It is the largest working beam engine

London

in the world. Two small steam locomotives are run occasionally. The museum's collections database is accessible during opening hours. Other research by appointment.

BUILDING: A 19th-century pumping station. Grade I listed buildings. The site includes other buildings such as a forge and workshops. There is partial wheelchair access. The café is open at weekends only.

OPENING TIMES: *All year*, daily: 11am–5pm. The engines operate at weekends and Bank Holiday Mondays and there is a higher admission charge.

ADMISSION CHARGES: ① (engines static), ② (in steam)

Ⓟ ♿ WC �–½ â–³ ≢ ∯

DIRECTIONS: Underground: Gunnersbury then 237 or 267 bus, or Kew Gardens then 391 bus. Main line rail: Kew Bridge or Gunnersbury. The museum is located about 100 yards from the North side of Kew Bridge, next to the tall Victorian tower.

Museum of Rugby ❋ ✳

Twickenham Stadium, Rugby Road, Twickenham, Middlesex TW1 1DZ

TEL: 020 8892 8877 FAX: 020 8892 2817

E-MAIL: museum@RFU.com WEBSITE: www.RFU.com

COLLECTION: Testing your strength on the scrum machine is one way of getting to grips with the game of rugby. Other ways include looking at the Twickenham players' baths, made in 1930, and viewing the oldest rugby jersey in existence. The history of rugby is told and a collection of rugby memorabilia creates the atmosphere. There are interactive touch-screen computers, video footage and an audio-visual theatre to view past games. There is a library for research purposes. A tour of the stadium is available and

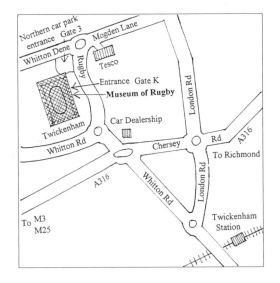

Museum of Rugby, Twickenham

ticket prices are therefore higher to include the tour. It is advisable to pre-book the tour. The café is within the stadium.

BUILDING: In the east stand of the Twickenham stadium. The museum was opened in 1996.

OPENING TIMES: *All year,* Tuesday to Saturday: 10am–5pm, Sunday: 2pm–5pm, bank holidays: 10am–5pm. The last admission is 4.30pm on all days. Closed Mondays, Good Friday, 24, 25 & 26 December.

ADMISSION CHARGES: ①

Ⓟ ♿ 🚾 ⛛ ✕ ⚠ 🏃

DIRECTIONS: By road from the M25/M3 follow the A316 towards Twickenham. See map for position of museum. Entrance is by Gate K.

The Musical Museum ✳

368 High Street, Brentford, Middlesex TW8 0BD

TEL: 020 8560 8108

COLLECTION: Automatic musical instruments are put through a continuous demonstration in which the instruments are explained and played. The tour lasts about 90 minutes. One of the stars is the Wurlitzer cinema organ, while other fascinating instruments are the Mills Violano-Virtuoso, which plays a violin and a piano, and the Steinway Duo-Art grand piano, which reproduces the performance of pianists such as Gershwin or Myra Hess. The original collection was made by Frank W. Holland. There is a large library of rolls for different instruments. This is available on written request. A programme of concerts is held through the summer. There is a café at the nearby Watermans Arts Centre.

BUILDING: A church building. There is no disabled toilet. If using a wheelchair, advance warning for the museum is helpful.

OPENING TIMES: *April to October* (inclusive), Saturdays & Sundays: 2pm–5pm, *July and August,* in addition to weekends, Wednesdays: 2pm–4pm.

ADMISSION CHARGES: ②

Ⓟ ♿ 🚾 ⚠ 📷 🏃

DIRECTIONS: Underground: Gunnesbury (District Line) then 237 or 267 bus. South Ealing (Piccadilly Line) then 65 bus. Parking in North Road or Pottery Road. The museum is past the Kew Bridge Steam Museum (see above). Turn right out of Kew Bridge Station and walk along Kew Bridge Road, past the Steam Museum. The Musical Museum is on your right, just before North Road. Further along on your left is Watermans Art Centre.

5. Eastern Region

Cambridgeshire

CAMBRIDGE
Cambridge Museum of Technology ❄ ✳
(preserved Victorian pumping station and working museum)

The Old Pumping Station, Cheddars Lane, Cambridgeshire CB5 8LD

TEL: 01223 368650

COLLECTION: Untreated sewage used to flow into the River Cam through a network of collapsing and over-used sewers. The steam pumping station was built to pump the drainage to the sewage farm at Milton and it continued working for 74 years from 1895 to 1968. Rescued by enthusiasts from demolition in 1968, both the building and the machines inside tell the history of the pumping station from steam power through to the addition of electrical power to help cope with storm surges. Among the various machinery are a Hathorn Davey steam engine and Babcock and Wilcox boilers, the oldest water-tube boilers in existence. Some of the steam engines run on particular days.

BUILDING: The Cambridge Sewage pumping station built in 1894, designated a National Monument (No. 65). A unique feature is the destructors, which burned domestic rubbish to produce the steam to fire the boilers. Not all the collection is accessible by wheelchair.

OPENING TIMES: Not in steam: *Easter to November*, every Sunday: 2pm–5pm. *November to Easter*, first Sunday in the month: 2pm–5pm. Open when the engines are in steam at certain times during the school holidays: 11am–5pm. (Telephone for details.) The admission price is higher for the steaming days.

ADMISSION CHARGES: ①

🄿 ♿ 🆆🅲 ▽ Ⓢ 📷 🚻

DIRECTIONS: See map.

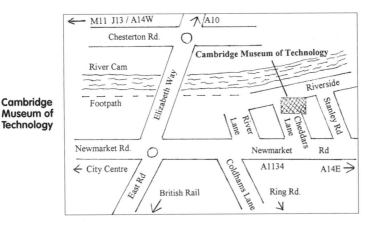

CAMBRIDGE
Cavendish Laboratory Museum ❄ ✳

Madingley Road, Cambridgeshire CB3 0HE

TEL: 01223 337419 FAX: 01223 766360

E-MAIL: r.hag@phy.cam.ac.uk WEBSITE: www.phy.cam.ac.uk/cavendish/geography/

COLLECTION: Here is the apparatus used at the Cavendish laboratory since its foundation in 1874. A cathode-ray tube used by J. J. Thomson to discover the electron is on display. In Rutherford's chamber the first nuclear disintegration was observed, which resulted in the coining of the term proton as a constituent of a nucleus. Chadwick's chamber, in which the neutron was discovered, is also on display.

BUILDING: The new Cavendish Laboratory opened in 1974 (100 years after the Old Cavendish). The building houses the University of Cambridge Department of Physics. There is a canteen for the laboratory, which could be made available by appointment. Coaches may park at the museum by appointment.

OPENING TIMES: *All year*, Monday to Friday: 9am–5pm. (Closed Saturday & Sunday.) Closed on public holidays.

ADMISSION CHARGES: Free

🅿 ♿ WC 📷

DIRECTIONS: The Cavendish Laboratory is on the West Cambridgeshire site of the University of Cambridge. If travelling by car up the M11, exit at junction 13 and turn towards Cambridge on the A1303. The site is signed to the right off this road. There is a long traffic island and a break in the island for the entrance to the laboratory. You pass several buildings but the laboratory is just after the Veterinary School and is signed 'University West Cambridge site'.

CAMBRIDGE
Scott Polar Research Institute ❄ ✳

University of Cambridge, Lensfield Road, Cambridgeshire CB2 1ER

TEL: 01223 336540 FAX: 01223 336549

WEBSITE: www.spri.cam.ac.uk/

COLLECTION: The institute was founded in 1920 in memory of the late Captain R. F. Scott, who died on an expedition to the South Pole. Among the information on Scott and other Arctic and Antarctic explorers is a display on the expedition led by Franklin Scott Shackleton. Maps, journals, clothing, equipment and artefacts are on show as well as paintings and photographs. There is at least one special exhibition annually. A series of Saturday night lectures is run during the first two terms of the academic year. Research facilities are available by appointment. Flash photography is prohibited.

BUILDING: The building dates from 1934 with modern additions. Most of the museum is accessible by wheelchair.

Eastern Region

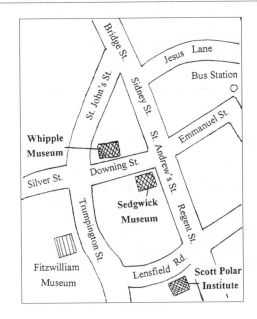

Scott Polar Institute, Sedgwick and Whipple Museums, Cambridge

OPENING TIMES: *All year,* Monday to Friday: 2.30pm –4pm. (Closed Saturday & Sunday.) Check for closing times during public holidays.

ADMISSION CHARGES: Free

DIRECTIONS: See map.

CAMBRIDGE
The Sedgwick Museum (Museum of Fossils) ❊ ❋

Department of Earth Sciences, Downing Street, Cambridge CB2 3EQ

TEL: 01233 333456 FAX: 01223 333450

WEBSITE: www.esc.cam.ac.uk/SedgwickMuseum

COLLECTION: A hippopotamus, 125,000 years old, from nearby Barrington gravel-pit features in the collection. Over 9,000 rare and curious specimens of fossils, minerals, rocks, shells, plant material and a few human artefacts form the oldest intact geological collection. Gathered by Dr John Woodward (1665–1728), some of the collection is displayed in the original early 18th-century walnut cabinets. In addition the museum holds a range of fossils and even the bones of a giant deer and wolves and bears from the local Fenland deposits. The Whewell Gallery is devoted to displaying minerals and gemstones.

BUILDING: Adam Sedgwick (1785–1873) built up a major geological school at Cambridge and one of the finest geological research museums in the world. After his death,

Cambridgeshire

The Grand Orrery,
Whipple Museum
of the History of
Science,
Cambridge

friends and colleagues opened a public subscription to build the present Sedgwick Museum as a memorial. It was opened in 1904 by King Edward VII. Although the museum itself is accessible by wheelchair, the initial entry is difficult. Telephone if special assistance is needed.

OPENING TIMES: *All year*, Monday to Friday: 9am–1pm, 2pm–5pm, Saturday: 10am–1pm. (Closed Sunday.) Closed Christmas & Easter.

ADMISSION CHARGES: Free

DIRECTIONS: See map.

CAMBRIDGE
Whipple Museum of the History of Science ❆ ❋

Free School Lane, Cambridge CB2 3RH

TEL: 01223 334500

WEBSITE: www.hps.cam.ac.uk

COLLECTION: Sextants and astrolabes, telescopes, sundials and laboratory equipment form part of this collection of scientific instruments and models, dating from the Middle Ages. To bring the instruments up to date there are even pocket electronic calculators on display. A boost to the collection came in 1974 with a gift of apparatus manufactured by the Cambridge Instrument Company. Whipple, having joined the company in 1898, became managing director and chairman.

Eastern Region

BUILDING: The main gallery of the museum is in a large hall with Elizabethan hammer-beam roof-trusses. It was built in 1618 as the first Cambridge Free School, the Old Perse School. Two other galleries have recently been redesigned. If using a wheelchair, telephone first. There are no disabled toilets.

OPENING TIMES: *All year*, Monday to Friday: 1.30pm–4.30pm. The museum is not always open during the university vacations, so check beforehand. (Closed Saturday & Sunday.)

ADMISSION CHARGES: Free

🅿 ♿ 🆆🅲 Ⓢ 🎥 👫

DIRECTIONS: See map.

ELY
The Stained Glass Museum ❊ ✳

The South Triforium, Ely Cathedral, Ely CB7 4DL

TEL: 01353 660347 FAX: 01353 665025

E-MAIL: stainedgm@lineone.net

COLLECTION: For at least 1,300 years, stained glass has been made in Britain and the first gallery shows how a stained-glass window is made. In the main gallery there are 100 panels on display dating from 1240 to 2000, mostly rescued from redundant churches. The museum has a fine Victorian collection and recently acquired two high-quality panels from the early 16th century. Established in 1972, this is the only museum in Britain devoted exclusively to stained glass.

BUILDING: Within Ely cathedral, which is well worth a visit on its own account. The museum is up some narrow stairs. It has recently been refurbished. There is one small gallery for temporary exhibitions. The café and toilets are in a separate part of the cathedral.

OPENING TIMES: *Easter to October*, Monday to Friday: 10.30am–5pm, Saturday: 10.30am–5.30pm, Sunday: 12 noon–6pm. *November to Easter*, Monday to Friday: 10.30am–4.30pm, Saturday: 10.30am–5pm, Sunday: 12 noon–4.30pm. (Last admissions half an hour before closing.)

ADMISSION CHARGES: ②

🅿 🆆🅲 ♿ Ⓐ 👫

DIRECTIONS: Ely is north east of Cambridge on the A10. The cathedral dominates the town. It is at the top of the town, parallel to the High Street.

GRANCHESTER
Rupert Brooke Museum ❊ ✳

The Orchard Tea Rooms, Mill Way, Granchester, Cambridgeshire CB3 9ND

TEL: (Tea Rooms) 01223 845788 FAX: (Tea Rooms) 01223 845862

COLLECTION: Photos, editions of Rupert Brooke's poems and copies of his verse are

Cambridgeshire

ranged around this small hut.The poet (1887–1915) was an undergraduate at Cambridge and in 1909 took lodgings at Orchard House. In 1868, Cambridge students asked Mrs Stevenson of Orchard House if she would serve them tea beneath the fruit trees instead of on the front lawn.The Orchard Tea Rooms were created and are still there today. Friends of Rupert Brook from Cambridge would visit him at his lodgings and therefore the Tea Rooms are closely associated with his time as an undergraduate and his poem 'The Old Vicarage, Granchester'.

BUILDING: A wooden hut near the car park at the Tea Rooms. There is a step up into the hut.

OPENING TIMES: Thursdays and Sundays. Check if you are travelling any distance as the museum is not always open. However, if you arrive and the museum is closed, enjoy the delightful Orchard Tea Rooms.There is an inside café too.

ADMISSION CHARGES: Free

Ⓟ ♿ 🚻 ↻ ✕ 🎥

DIRECTIONS: Granchester is south west of Cambridge but only a few miles from the city. In the village of Granchester, a large sign for the Orchard Tea Rooms is at the entrance to the car park.

HUNTINGDON
Cromwell Museum ❄ ✳

Grammar School Walk, Huntingdon PE18 6LF

TEL: 01480 375830

E-MAIL: CromwellMuseum@cambridge.gov.uk

WEBSITE: www.cromwell.argonet.co.uk EDWEB: camenty.gov.uk/cromwell

COLLECTION: Opinions vary about the career of Oliver Cromwell (1599-1658), but some idea of the man, who defeated the Royalists and ruled England as Lord Protector, can be gained from this museum. It is the only public collection relating specifically to Cromwell. Portaits of him and his family and leading figures of the day hang on the walls. Coins and medals and objects which belonged to Cromwell are on display, amongst them a Florentine cabinet, a gift from the Grand Duke of Tuscany.

BUILDING:The building was once Cromwell's school.A small stone building, originally part of an extensive medieval hospital founded in the late 12th century, it later became the town grammar school and remained in use from the 16th century until fairly recently.

OPENING TIMES: *April to October,*Tuesday to Friday: 11am–1pm, 2pm –5pm, Saturday & Sunday: 11am–1pm, 2pm –4pm. (Closed Monday.) *November to March,* Tuesday to Friday: 1pm –4pm, Saturday: 11am–1pm, 2pm–4pm. Sunday 2pm–4pm. (Closed Monday.) Closed bank holidays except Good Friday.

ADMISSION CHARGES: Free

🅿 ♿ Ⓢ 🎥 🚻

DIRECTIONS: Huntingdon is north west of Cambridge off the A14. Follow the signs for the town centre car-parks and then follow the pedestrian signing for the museum.

PETERBOROUGH
Railworld ❄ ✳

Oundle Road, Peterborough PE2 9NR

TEL/FAX: 01733 344340

WEBSITE: www.railworld.net

COLLECTION: Three hundred trains a day pass through Peterborough and it stands at the intersection of three railway routes. It also has the Nene Valley Railway, a restored line from Wansford to Peterborough running steam trains and home of the famed tank engine named Thomas. So it seems the right place for a museum such as Railworld, which looks both backwards, telling the history of rail both national and local, and forwards to look to 'global rail travel'. On view is Britain's unique hovertrain with some sample track and the only compound system loco in the UK. A library is available to view by prior arrangement.

BUILDING: The museum and exhibition centre are housed in second-hand timber buildings. The visitor centre opened in 1993. The site is a twelve-acre brownfield area still being developed.

OPENING TIMES: *March to October*, daily: 11am–4pm. *November to February*, Monday to Friday only: 11am–4pm. Visits at Christmas and New Year by arrangement.

ADMISSION CHARGES: ①

Ⓟ ♿ WC 🖭 👫

DIRECTIONS: See map.

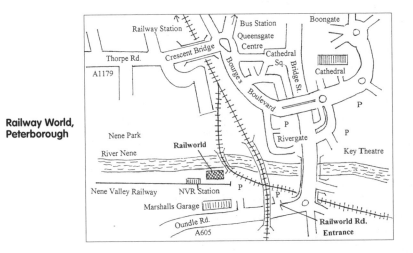

Railway World, Peterborough

Steam pumping
engine, Prickwillow
Drainage Engine
Museum,
Prickwillow

PRICKWILLOW
Prickwillow Drainage Engine Museum ✳

Main Street, Prickwillow, Ely, Cambridgeshire CB7 4UN

TEL: 01353 688360 After 7pm: 01353 720419

COLLECTION: Ever since man tried to drain the low-lying, waterlogged Fens, the peat has been shrinking and the land sinking. Water has had to be lifted up into the rivers and drainage channels, first by the use of windmills, later by steam, then by diesel and now by electricity. The museum contains many of the formidable drainage engines such as the 1924 Mirrlees, five-cylinder diesel engine. An exhibition of photographs shows Fen life and there is also an exhibition of old tools and implements associated with the drainage of the Fens.

BUILDING: The old engine house built in 1880 to house a beam engine. The building was extended and improved in 1995 to provide more facilities.

OPENING TIMES: *May to September*, daily: 11am–5pm. *March, April, October, November*, Saturday, Sunday and bank holidays only: 11am–4pm. (Closed Monday to Friday.) Closed December to February.

Eastern Region

ADMISSION CHARGES: ①

ⓟ ♿ 🚾 ⊍ ⚠ 🍴 ⑆

DIRECTIONS: In Prickwillow, which is four miles east of Ely on the B1382.

STRETHAM
The Stretham Old Engine ✳

Geenend Road, Stretham, Cambridgeshire

TEL: 01353 649210

WEBSITE: www.ely.org.uk/soe/index.html

COLLECTION: To drain the Fens the steam-powered double-acting rotative beam engine was installed in 1831. It is the last surviving complete example of its kind in the Fens. Working successfully until 1925, it was replaced by a diesel engine, which is also on display. Although the old steam engine cannot be run on steam, an electrical drive has been installed to show the former operation of the engine and is run on certain weekends. An old cottage, the home of the engine stoker, is also on view. There is a bookstall but not a shop.

BUILDING: Now an ancient monument, the engine house was built in 1831 to house the steam engine.

OPENING TIMES: *Good Friday to the last Sunday in September*, Sundays and bank holidays only: 11.30am–5pm. (Closed Monday to Saturday.) (Check opening times before visiting.)

ADMISSION CHARGES: ①

The
Stretham
Old Engine
Pumping
Station,
Stretham

Cambridgeshire

P WC 🎥 ⛟

DIRECTIONS: The access road to Stretham Old Engine is off the A1123 Haddenham to Soham and Wicken Fen Road. Coming from Haddenham, just after crossing the A10, look for a small road to the right just as the road bends round to the left into the village of Stretham.

Essex

BRAINTREE
The Working Silk Museum ❋ ❋

New Mills, Braintree, Essex CM7 3GB

TEL: 01376 553393 FAX: 01376 330642

COLLECTION: Exiled French Huguenots first brought silk-weaving to this country and the trade arrived in Braintree in the early 19th century from Spitalfields, London. Daniel Walters set up his silk-weaving factory over 150 years ago. Hand-looms were installed and these worked until 1971, when the firm finally closed. Ten of his original hand-looms are now restored and back in daily use. In the exhibition area there are fine silks on display, plus treasures from the company's industrial archive. When the firm closed Richard Humphries, the last textile designer to be trained on the old looms, managed to rescue some of the machinery and started the present silk mill. This is a working museum and visitors can watch the process of producing the many coloured silks.

BUILDING: The New Mills building was built by Daniel Walters over 150 years ago and

The Working Silk Museum, Braintree

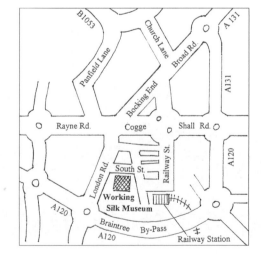

is now restored. There are cafés and local restaurants near the Silk Museum. There is a disabled toilet. There is a certain amount of noise from the machinery (below 92 decibels).

OPENING TIMES: *All year*, Monday to Friday: 10am–12.30pm & 1.20pm–5pm. Last entry to factory 12 noon & 4pm. Closed Saturday (except for booked parties), Sundays and bank holidays.

ADMISSION CHARGES: ②

ⓟ ♿ 🚾 ⚠ 🚻

DIRECTIONS: Braintree is north east of London. For directions to the museum see map.

BURNHAM-ON-CROUCH
Mangapps Railway Museum ❄ ✳

Southminster Road, Burnham-on-Crouch, Essex CM0 8QQ

TEL: 01621 784898

WEBSITE: www.mangapps.co.uk

COLLECTION: From tickets to trains and buttons to buildings, Mangapps has one of the largest collections of historic railway items on public display in Britain. It has a ¾-mill standard gauge passenger carrying line, with restored stations, signal boxes and equipment removed from various sites throughout East Anglia. To operate the line the museum has steam and diesel locomotives and a number of historic carriages. Most of the exhibits are under cover.

BUILDING: Various buildings on the site. On Old Heath Station the main building came from Laxfield Mid-Suffolk Light Railway. The café is housed in a railway carriage.

OPENING TIMES: *All year*, every weekend: 1pm–5pm. Closed January. Open bank holidays (except Christmas). *August & Easter fortnight*, open every day. Steam-hauled passenger trains on first Sunday of each month, every Sunday in August and Bank Holiday Sunday & Monday. (Diesel hauled at other times.)

ADMISSION CHARGES: Museum & steam rides: ②

ⓟ 🚾 ⛴ ⚠ 🎥 🚻

DIRECTIONS: Follow signs to Burnham-on-Crouch, then look out for the brown tourist sign. Mangapps is one mile north of Burnham-on-Crouch main line station.

CANVEY ISLAND
Castle Point Transport Museum ✳

105 Point Road, Canvey Island, Essex SS8 7TP

TEL: 01268 684272

COLLECTION: Some of these old and rare buses have made appearances on television, and the Bristol open-top double-decker is one of the buses depicted on the Royal Mail Special Issue of British Buses. The collection ranges from 1944 to 1972 and includes a

Bristol open-top
double-decker,
Castle Point
Transport
Museum,
Canvey Island

very rare GPO Telephones Maudslay box-van. There are buses from Glasgow, Blackpool and Stoke and other items include a military fully equipped, three-axle Scammell recovery unit. Visitors can see the full range of restoration work under way on the vehicles.
BUILDING: The former Canvey and District Bus Depot built in 1935 and vacated by Easter National in 1978. The museum is accessible by wheelchair but there are no other facilities for the disabled.
OPENING TIMES: *April to mid-October*, every Sunday: 10am–5pm. On the second Sunday in October an end of season Transport Show is held.
ADMISSION CHARGES: Free, except for the Transport Show
Ⓟ ♿ [WC] 📷 👪
DIRECTIONS: Canvey Island is south east of Basildon. Brown signs direct visitors to the museum as they come to Canvey Island.

COLCHESTER
Tymperleys Clock Museum ✳

Trinity Street, Colchester, Essex
TEL: (Museum Resource Centre) 01206 282931/2
COLLECTION: A lantern clock inscribed Thomas Thorp, Colchester, was bought by Bernard Mason in 1927. This clock stimulated Mason's interest and he began to search for clocks by Colchester makers. His collection totals 216 clocks and twelve watches. The earliest clocks are by William Bacon and John Groome, who worked during the

second half of the 1600s. Nathaniel Hedge (1710–95), plus generations of the Hedge family, were clockmakers. The collection contains many more 18th- and 19th-century makers. Long-case clocks line the walls of two rooms and smaller clocks fill a display case.

BUILDING: Mason bought and restored a medieval timber-framed house to house his collection. Built just before 1500, it was extended in 1580. It is called 'Tymperleys' after the house that once stood facing the street and was the home of William Gilberd, the Elizabethan scientist.

OPENING TIMES: *1 April to 31 October*, Monday to Saturday: 10am–5pm, Sunday: 11am–5pm.

ADMISSION CHARGES: Free

P & 🎥

DIRECTIONS: Trinity Street is one of the small lanes between the High Street and St John's Street. It connects to St John's Street, almost opposite the shopping centre entrance. The museum is in a courtyard off the street to the left as you walk up from St John's Street.

KELVEDON HATCH
Kelvedon Hatch Secret Nuclear Bunker ❄ ✳

Kelvedon Hall Lane, Kelvedon Hatch, Brentwood, Essex CM14 5TL
TEL: 01277 364883 FAX: 01277 372562
E-MAIL: bunker@japar.demon.co.uk WEBSITE: www.japar.demon.co.uk
COLLECTION: A bungalow built into a hillside hides an extraordinary secret. Built in 1952, this is where central government and military commanders would have run the region had the UK been attacked and nuclear war broken out. A military operations command centre, a room for members of the government, a scientists' centre and a BBC studio are all in place, plus a dormitory, a sick-bay, a and canteen and a massive power and filtration plant. The bunker is built from 40,000 tons of concrete, 80 feet below the Essex countryside. Photography is allowed with a licence. The bunker houses the National Library for the Emergency Planners.

BUILDING: The bunker is set in woodland open to the public and there is a picnic area. There are no lifts. Wide, shallow stairs connect the three stories. Flat shoes are recommended. There are facilities for the disabled.

OPENING TIMES: *1 March to 31 October*, Monday to Friday: 10am–4pm (last entry), Saturday, Sunday and bank holidays: 10am–5pm (last entry). *1 November to 28 February*, Thursday to Sunday: 10am–4pm (last entry). (Closed Monday to Wednesday.)

ADMISSION CHARGES: ②

P WC 🚻 ⚠ 🎥 👫

DIRECTIONS: From the M11 take the A414 (Chelmsford) to Ongar and then the A128 to Ongar. From the M25 exit at junction 28, the A12 interchange, take the A1023 to Brentwood, and then the A128 to Ongar. The bunker is off the A128 Ongar to Brentwood road at Kelvedon Hatch.

ST OSYTH
East Essex Aviation Society Museum ❄ ✳

Martello Tower, Orchards Holiday Camp, Point Clear, St Osyth, Clacton, Essex

TEL: 01255 428028 or 01225 860966

COLLECTION: Pride of place is given to the remains of a crashed American P51 Mustang of the US 479th Fighter Group. Its recovery from the sea in 1985 was the stimulus for the formation of the East Essex Aviation Society. Alongside this are many other items from local aircraft crash sites, all treated and preserved in the workshop within the building. On the first floor there is a wide range of memorabilia such as uniforms and equipment. There is also memorabilia from World War I. On cold nights a roaring log fire burns in the grate. The roof is also open to visitors and there are more displays up there of parts of aircraft. The views stretch for miles on a clear day.

BUILDING: One of the first Napoleonic forts built in 1805 to repel invasion from France. It is one of the only Martello towers still open to the public along the Essex coast. The tower is near a pub, which has a restaurant.

OPENING TIMES: *All year*, Monday: 7pm–10pm. *February to October*, plus Sunday: 10am – 2pm. *June to September*, plus Wednesday: 10am–2pm.

ADMISSION CHARGES: Free

Ⓟ 🎥 👪

DIRECTIONS: Point Clear is three miles outside St Osyth. The Martello tower is at the end of the Orchards Caravan Park, next to the Ferry Boat Inn.

TIPTREE
Tiptree Museum ❄ ✳

Wilkin & Sons Limited, Tiptree, Colchester, Essex CO5 0RF

TEL: 01621 815407 FAX: 01621 814555

E-MAIL: tiptree@tiptree.com WEBSITE: www.tiptree.com

COLLECTION: Over 50 years ago, John Wilkin began collecting the paraphernalia of preserve-making and Essex village life. He stored these away in corners of the factory. Now on display in the museum are pictures, documents and redundant machines, all helping to tell the story of what life was like 50 years ago and how jam-making has changed over the years.

BUILDING: A renovated farm building at Tiptree. The museum is in one room, and there is a jam shop and tea-room.

OPENING TIMES: *All year*, Monday to Saturday: 10am–5pm. (Closed Sunday.) *June, July*

& August, open on Sunday: 12noon–5pm. For group bookings telephone 01621 814524.
ADMISSION CHARGES: Free

ⓟ ♿ 🚻 ⛲ ⚠ 📷 ⴲ

DIRECTIONS: Tiptree is on the crossroads of the B 1023 Kelvedon to Tollesbury road and the B 1022 Malden to Colchester road. Travelling towards Tollesbury, the Tiptree Museum is just outside Tiptree village on the right-hand side.

Lincolnshire

LINCOLN
The Incredibly Fantastic Old Toy Show ✳

26 Westgate, Lincoln LN1 3BD

TEL: 01522 520534

COLLECTION: Thousands of toys bring to life two centuries of childhood. Toy soldiers, dolls, trains, cars, boats, dolls' houses and aeroplanes are just some of the exhibits. There is also the fun of distorting mirrors, 'what the butler saw' machines and working models. On the walls are old photographs of children with their toys, and some of these toys are displayed nearby.

BUILDING: An old Methodist chapel. The museum is accessible by wheelchair but there are no other facilities for the disabled.

OPENING TIMES: *Easter Saturday to the end of September*, Tuesday to Saturday: 11am–5pm, Sunday & Bank Holiday Mondays: 12 noon–4pm. Closed on other Mondays. *October to December*, Saturday: 11am–5pm, Sunday: 12 noon–4pm. Closed Monday to Friday, except during school holidays. Then open Tuesday to Friday: 11am–5pm. Closed Christmas until Easter Saturday.

ADMISSION CHARGES: ①

🅿 ♿ ⚠ ⴲ

DIRECTIONS: The museum is opposite the car-cark behind the castle.

PINCHBECK
Pinchbeck Pumping Engine and Land Drainage Museum ✳

Pinchbeck Marsh, Spalding, Lincolnshire PE11

TEL: 01775 725468 FAX: 01775 762715

COLLECTION: The nature of the area, its problems and man's attempt at drainage are explained in the Land Drainage Museum. To lift the water up from the shrinking land into rivers and drainage channels, windmills and then steam-powered pumps were introduced. The Pinchbeck Engine, a restored working beam engine driven by steam, was built in 1833 and each year lifted an average of 3,000,000 tons of water.

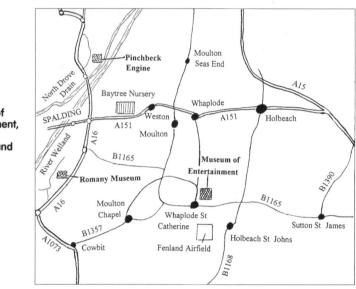

Museum of
Entertainment,
Romany
Museum and
Pinchbeck
Engine,
Spalding

BUILDING: The steam pumping house.

OPENING TIMES: *April to October*, daily: 10am–4pm (other times by arrangement).

ADMISSION CHARGES: Free

Ⓟ 🄵🄲 ♿ 🚻

DIRECTIONS: The museum is off the A16 and signposted by a brown sign. See map.

SANDTOFT
Sandtoft Transport Museum ❄ ☀

Belton Road, Sandtoft, North Lincolnshire DN8 5SX

TEL: (information line) 01724 711391

E-MAIL: enquries@sandtoft.org.uk   WEBSITE: www.sandtoft.org.uk

COLLECTION: Travel on a trolley-bus or even drive one on a simulator. Wander amongst vehicles dating from 1927 to 1985, including six-wheeled doubled-decker trolley-buses and a one-and-a-half-decker from Aachen in Germany. The museum has a wealth of vehicles to view. There is a steam and electric-hauled miniature railway and a place to watch clips from films about trolley-buses.

BUILDING: Site contains 51 buses and trolley-buses.

OPENING TIMES: Selected days during the year. Mostly weekends and usually twice a month, especially Easter, May Day and Spring Bank Holiday. Telephone or go to the website for details of the year's open days.

ADMISSION CHARGES: ②

ⓟ ♿ 🆆🅒 🛏 🍴 ⚠ 🎥 🚻

DIRECTIONS: Two minutes south from junction 2 of the M180 motorway.

SPALDING
Gordon Boswell Romany Museum ✳

Clay Lake, Spalding, Lincolnshire PE12 6BL

TEL: 01775 710599

COLLECTION: Brightly painted gypsy caravans, known as Vardos, line the walls. The interior of each looks as if its occupant has just left. The luxury end of the Romany life is a silver caravan. Carts and harnesses, a fortune-telling tent and photographs help to tell the story of Romany life. There is also video of travelling to Appleby Horse Fair. Groups can book a talk on Romany life.

BUILDING: A large barn.

OPENING TIMES: *March to October*, Wednesday to Sunday: 10.30am–5pm. (Closed Monday & Tuesday.) Open Bank Holiday Mondays.

ADMISSION CHARGES: ①

ⓟ ♿ ⚠ 🎥 🚻

DIRECTIONS: See map.

SPALDING
Museum of Entertainment ✳

Whaplode Sreet, Catherine, nr. Spalding, Lincolnshire PE12 6SF

TEL: 01406 540379

COLLECTION: Nearly every music machine can be encouraged to play some tune, and guided tours bring the history of the late Ray Tunicliffe's collection alive. A collector and restorer of fairground organs, Ray increased the range of his collection and it now includes music boxes, early gramophones, harmoniums and the first mobile disco. It even has a church organ. Tiller's Royal Marionettes are of historical interest and date from 1790.

BUILDING: An old threshing barn. Four rooms in all. There is a small caravan site behind the museum.

OPENING TIMES: Good Friday to Easter Monday: 1pm–5pm. *Easter to end of June*, Sundays only: 1pm–5pm. *July, August, September*, Sunday to Thursday: 1pm–5pm. (Closed Friday & Saturday.) Other times by appointment for group tours. Closed October to Easter.

ADMISSION CHARGES: ①

ⓟ ♿ 🆆🅒 🛏 ⚠ 🎥 🚻

DIRECTIONS: Follow the brown signs from Spalding. Also see map.

SOUTH WITHAM
Geeson Bros. Motorcycle Museum and Workshop ✳

South Witham, Grantham, Lincolnshire NG33 5PH

TEL: 01572 767280/768195

COLLECTION: The Geeson brothers, Len and George, once shared a 1924 250cc Round Tank BSA. They have returned to that first enthusiasm to restore a whole range of motorcycles, veteran, vintage and classic. The core of the collections consists of British machines of the 1920s and 1930s. Three bikes at a time can be restored in their workshop. Len died in 1994 but George carries on the restoration and collection of motorcycles.

BUILDING: A former Congregational chapel, built in 1843. There are no disabled toilets.

OPENING TIMES: *March to December*, open days held about once a month: 10.30am–5pm. Telephone for details. The museum and workshop are open for club and group visits by special arrangement.

ADMISSION CHARGES: ①

🅿 ♿ 🚾 ☕ 🎥

DIRECTIONS: South Witham is half-way between Grantham and Stamford, three-quarters of a mile from the A1 on the west side.

Norfolk

BURSTON
Burston Strike School ❄ ✳

Burston, Diss, Norfolk

TEL: (the curator's home) 01379 741565

COLLECTION: The school is the scene of the longest school strike in history, from 1914 to 1939. Two new teachers, Annie and Tom Higden, arrived at the school and made an impression on pupils and parents alike for their good teaching methods. For those who controlled the school it was a different story. The teachers supported farm-workers against farmers, and Tom Higdon tried to get the workers to join a trade union. After three years the teachers were dismissed and the pupils and parents were furious. Annie and Tom began to teach the pupils on the Green, and then inside a carpenter's shop when the winter came. The parents were fined for not letting their children attend the old school. Support for the parents came from all over the country and there was enough money to pay Tom and Annie and build a new school, the School of the Green, where the two teachers continued work until 1939, when Tom died. Story-boards, life-size figures and children's toys set the scene.

BUILDING: The original school, built in 1917. There is a portable ramp but no special toilet for the disabled. There is no shop but some goods are on sale.

OPENING TIMES: *All year*, except polling days for national and local elections. Open in daylight hours. The key is available.

ADMISSION CHARGES: Free

Ⓟ ♿ WC 📷 ⅋

DIRECTIONS: Burston is off the A140 Norwich to Needham Market road. It is north east of Diss. In the village, heading towards Diss, the turning is just after the crossroads and the church.

CROMER
Henry Blogg Lifeboat Museum ✳

No. 2 Boathouse, The Promenade, Cromer, Norfolk NR27 9HE

TEL: 01263 511294

COLLECTION: Henry Blogg's boat is on show, along with a World War II lifeboat, *H.F. Bailey*, plus photographs and models of Cromer lifeboats and crews.

BUILDING: 1900 lifeboat house. Toilets and cafés nearby. Wheelchair access.

OPENING TIMES: *Easter to end of October*, daily: 10am–4pm.

ADMISSION CHARGES: Free

Ⓟ ♿ ⚠ 📷 ⅋

DIRECTIONS: On the promenade, 200 yards east of the pier.

DEREHAM (or EAST DEREHAM)
Hobbies Museum of Fretwork ✳

34–36 Swaffham Road, Dereham, Norfolk NR19 2AZ

TEL: 01362 692985

COLLECTION: Over 3,000 years ago the Chinese first established fretwork, which is the carving of wood in decorative patterns. This collection begins a little later and displays a number of treadle fretsaws first made in the late 19th century. To make these machines the firm Hobbies was formed in 1897 and became the largest firm of manufacturers and suppliers of fretwork tools in the world. Surviving World War I and a major fire, the firm improved its machinery and also sold plans and materials for fathers to make dolls' houses and forts. After the closure of the firm in 1969, the sales manager, Mr Stroulger, established a new firm to sell fretwork kits, which still flourishes. The museum was created in the 1990s and now houses the fretwork machines, including treadles and examples of fretwork such as firescreens and bookcases.

BUILDING: The museum buildings were converted from an almost derelict merchant's house and stables in 1992. Only the ground floor is accessible by wheelchair and there are no other facilities for the disabled. The toilets are in attached premises.

OPENING TIMES: *April to August*, Monday to Friday only: 10am–12noon, 2pm–4pm. (Closed Saturday & Sunday.)

Gas Light Fittings, Fakenham Museum of Gas and Local History

ADMISSION CHARGES: Free

Ⓟ ♿ WC Ⓢ 🎥

DIRECTIONS: Dereham is off the main A47 between Swaffham and Norwich. The museum and craft centre are five-minutes' walk from Dereham Town Centre on the Swaffham road, at the junction of the Swaffham road and Sandy Lane

FAKENHAM

Fakenham Museum of Gas and Local History ❄ ✹

Hempton Road, Fakenham, Norfolk

TEL: 01328 851696 or 855237 or 863150

COLLECTION: First opened in 1846, the Fakenham gas works are now the only remaining complete gas works in England and Wales and now have ancient monument status. They produced gas by the carbonisation of coal. They were closed in 1965, the Norfolk

Industrial Archeaological Society stepped in and they are now a museum, with the various working buildings preserved, a gas-holder and within several rooms a collection of gas appliances, gas heaters, gaslight mantels and globes, gauges, meters and tools. In two upstairs rooms there is information on the history of Fakenham.

BUILDING: The gas works site. Wheelchair access possible but not upstairs in the cottage.

OPENING TIMES: *End of May to the beginning of September*, Thursday: 10.30am–3pm. *September to May*, Thursday: 10.30am–1pm. (Closed Friday to Wednesday.)

ADMISSION CHARGES: Free

P & WC 📷 ♦♦♦

DIRECTIONS: South of the River Wensum and north of the racecourse, the museum is on the left-hand side on Hempton Road as you walk south from the town and not long after the bridge. The racecourse is off Hempton Road.

GLANDFORD
The Shell Museum ✳

Glandford, Holt, Norfolk NR25 7JR

TEL: 01263 740081

COLLECTION: Shells from all over the world, from a humble limpet to a giant tortoise shell, were collected over 60 years by Sir Alfred Jodrell and finally arranged, by him and his sister, in their cases in the museum, which opened in 1915. There are carved and painted shells, shells of every colour and rarity and objects made out of shells, such as a bag made out of cowrie shells. The collection of shells has been added to over the years. Also on display are jewels, fragments of pottery and a tapestry.

BUILDING: A small building with Dutch gables, purpose-built in 1915 by the late Sir Alfred Jodrell. It is the oldest purpose-built museum in Norfolk. The museum is accessible by wheelchair but there are no other facilities for the disabled.

OPENING TIMES: *March to October*, Tuesday to Saturday: 10am–12.30pm & 2pm–4.30pm. (Closed Sunday & Monday.) Open bank holidays. During the winter opening can be organised by prior arrangement.

ADMISSION CHARGES: ①

P & △ 📷 ♦♦♦

DIRECTIONS: From the A149 north Norfolk coast road, take the B1156 at Blakeney to Glandford. The Shell Museum is well signposted in the village.

NORWICH
Colman's Mustard Shop and Museum � ✳

15 Royal Arcade, Norwich, Norfolk NR2 1NQ

TEL: 01603 627889 FAX: 01603 762142

COLLECTION: Mustard has been grown in England since Roman times. The museum,

The Museum
of the Broads,
Stalham

within Colman's shop, tells the story of Jeremiah Colman when he started his mustard empire in the early 19th century through the development of the industry. Colman's began contract farming of mustard in 1878. The museum shows the harvesting and making of various kinds of mustard together with a display of photographs.

BUILDING: Within a Victorian shopping arcade, 101 years old in art deco style.

OPENING TIMES: Monday to Saturday: 9.30am–5pm. Sunday and bank holidays: 11am–4pm.

ADMISSION CHARGES: Free

DIRECTIONS: The Royal Arcade is just behind the marketplace. It connects Gentleman's Walk and Castle Street.

STALHAM
The Museum of the Broads ✳

The Staithe, Stalham, Norwich, Norfolk NR12 9DA

TEL: 01692 581681

WEBSITE: www.whitesswan.u-net.com

COLLECTION: Originally medieval peat diggings, the broads became shallow lakes joined by cuts and dykes to the rivers of the area. Now they give pleasure to thousands of holiday-makers, but they are also important for their wildlife. The museum explains how the mystery of the origins of the Broads was solved and displays the tools of the traditional Broads industries such as thatching, eel-catching and reed-cutting. Gun punts with their big gun for wildfowl and even a concrete dinghy are also to be seen, as well as videos and side-shows.

BUILDING: In an old wherry shed on the side of the Staithe, in Marshmans building, an old storage barn and a boat-shed.

OPENING TIMES: *Easter to the end of September,* Monday to Friday (and weekends during school holidays): 11am–5pm.

ADMISSION CHARGES: ①

🅿 ♿ 🆆🅲 ⓢ 📷 ⛄

DIRECTIONS: Stalham is off the A149 Great Yarmouth road between Wayford Bridge and Potter Heighham. Park at Richardson's boatyard. By water the museum is at the end of Stalham Dyke, leading off the River Ant. Moorings are available at Richardson's boatyard.

THURSFORD
The Thursford Collection (fairground equipment and organs and steam engines) ❄ ✳

Thursford Green, Thursford, nr. Fakenham, Norfolk NR21 0AS

TEL: 01328 878477

COLLECTION: George Cushing first saw steam engines at a fair in 1920. He became obsessed by them, eventually driving a steam traction engine, then buying it. His collection had begun. Over the years it increased. Ancient rusting machines were discovered and then lovingly restored. Now they stand gleaming inside a huge barn for all to enjoy. There are steam engines for all purposes: pulling, threshing, ploughing and static engines. Engines of all makes are featured – an Aveling Light, a Savage, a Ruston Proctor, a Burrell. Magnificent fairground organs are ranged the other side of the barn with the centrepiece a 19th-century roundabout. These machines are demonstrated after the daily live musical shows featuring the Wurlitzer organ concert and resident organist.

BUILDING: Converted farm buildings, with many facilities, shops and outside seating area.

OPENING TIMES: *Good Friday to near the end of October* (check the exact date of closure), daily: 12 noon–5pm.

ADMISSION CHARGES: ②

Ⓟ ♿ 🆆🅲 🍴 ⓢ 📷 ⛄

DIRECTIONS: Thursford is on the A148 Kings Lynn to Cromer road, near Fakenham. The Thursford collection is signposted along the road.

Suffolk

COTTON
Mechanical Music Museum and Bygones ✳

    Cotton, nr. Stowmarket, Suffolk IP14 4QN

TEL: 01449 613876

COLLECTION: A musical Christmas tree, a musical chair and even a musical chamber-pot form part of this collection. The stars, however, are the organs: a Wurlitzer theatre pipe organ, fairground organs, reed organ, barrel organs, player organs and a gigantic café organ. Sreet pianos and pianolas, horn gramophones and old gramophone records make up the collection. It was started by Robert Finbow in the 1960s with a Gavioli barrel organ, housed in a van, which he took to steam engine rallies and fêtes. The collection slowly grew and now everyone can enjoy the looks and the sounds of the various mechanical music machines.

BUILDING: Purpose-built and consisting of one large hall and a small room. No disabled toilets as yet but they are planned. The building is accessible by wheelchair.

OPENING TIMES: *June, July, August & September*, Sunday: 2.30pm–5.30pm.

ADMISSION CHARGES: ①

    Ⓟ ♿ 🚾 ⬆ 📷 👪

DIRECTIONS: Turn off the A140 Norwich to Ipswich road at Stoke Ash, to Cotton and Finningham. The White Horse Inn is on the corner. Cross over the railway line and at the crossroads with another White Horse Inn on the corner, turn left. Go under the railway and then turn left into Blacksmiths Road. The museum is on the left.

DUNWICH
Dunwich Museum ✳

    St James Street, Dunwich, Suffolk

TEL: 01728 648796

COLLECTION: In 1919, standing on the edge of the cliff at Dunwich was the ruin of the tower of All Saints Church. The constant cliff erosion has slowly reduced Dunwich from a prosperous port in the 11th century to the small village it is today. Most of the town, including all of the old church, is under the sea. The museum tells the story of Dunwich from Roman fort through to the height of its prosperity and consequent decline. It also looks at the importance of the wild life of the area.

BUILDING: One of the terraced houses built by Frederick Barne in the 1860s to replace the earlier hovels. Parking, toilets and café on the seafront. The Ship Inn serves food.

OPENING TIMES: *March*, weekends only: 2pm–4pm. *Good Friday to end of September*, daily: 11.30am–4.30pm. *October*, daily: 12 noon–4pm.

Eastern Region

Ninety-two
key Mortier
Café Organ,
Mechanical
Music Museum
and Bygones,
Cotton

ADMISSION CHARGES: Free

🅿 ♿ 🍴 👫

DIRECTIONS: Dunwich is between Walberswick and Sizewell on the east coast. Park at the seafront and walk into the village. The museum is only a few minutes away from the sea.

FLIXTON
Norfolk and Suffolk Aviation Museum ✳

East Anglia's Aviation Heritage Centre, Buckeroo Way, The Street, Flixton,
nr. Bungay, Suffolk NR35 1NZ

TEL: 01986 896644

E-MAIL: nsam.flixton@virgin.net WEBSITE: www.aviationmuseum.net

COLLECTION: World War II wreckage is on display, as well as 30 complete historic aircraft. There are also aviation artefacts to view and special displays on World War II decoy sites, plus exhibitions on Boulton and Paul of Norwich, the Civil Defence Corps and aircraft cameras.

BUILDING: A World War II hangar and other buildings. There is a raised boardwalk to the River Waveney. There are picnic tables on the site.

OPENING TIMES: *April to October*, Sunday to Thursday: 10am–5pm. (Closed Friday & Saturday.)

ADMISSION CHARGES: Free

🅿 ♿ 🚻 🍴 👫

DIRECTIONS: On the B1062, off the A143, two miles south west of Bungay.

Suffolk

IPSWICH
Ipswich Transport Museum ✳

Old Trolley-Bus Depot, Cobham Road, Ipswich, Suffolk IP3 9JD

TEL: 01473 715666

WEBSITE: www.ipswichtransportmuseum.co.uk

COLLECTION: All the vehicles in the museum were either built or operated in and around Ipswich. This makes the museum unique among collections of transport vehicles. A tram, trolley-buses and coaches stand near fire-engines, tractors, military vehicles, cranes and even milk-floats. There are many more vehicles to see, plus uniforms, ticket-machines and pictures. An archive is available Friday mornings. (Telephone for exact dates and times.)

BUILDING: The former operational depot of the Ipswich trolley-bus fleet. It was built in 1937. The museum is accessible by wheelchair and there is a disabled toilet.

OPENING TIMES: *April to November*, Sunday and Bank Holiday Mondays: 11am–4.30pm. School holidays, May half-term, October half-term, Monday to Friday: 1pm–4pm. (At least an hour is needed to look round the museum.)

ADMISSION CHARGES: ①

ⓅⓀ🚾↪⚠🍴👫

DIRECTIONS: Leave the A14 at the slip-road signed Nacton and Ransomes Europark. Follow signs for town centre and Cliff Quay. Straight over the roundabout by the Thrasher public house, into Nacton Road. After approximately half a mile turn right into Lindburgh Road and continue along into Cobham Road. The museum is visible on the left.

IPSWICH
Museum of Knots and Sailor's Ropework ✣ ✳

501 Wherstead Road, Ispwich, Suffolk IP2 8LL

TEL: 01473 690090

COLLECTION: There is much more to see than a few knots: the museum has a good selection of sailors' sea chest handles, blackjacks, knives with ropework handles, walking-sticks and a shaving brush, all from the 19th century. Also in the collection are 50-year-old sennit rope mats and many examples of rope fenders, plus modern examples of knotwork from several countries. Tools for working with rope and canvas are also on display, from a whalebone fid (a conical pin used for splicing rope) to the most modern tools for splicing hi-tech yacht ropes. Research is possible in the reserve collection and in Des Pawson's library on all aspects of knots and ropework.

BUILDING: Opened in 1996, one room.

OPENING TIMES: By appointment only.

ADMISSION CHARGES: Free

P WC & 📹

DIRECTIONS: Wherstead Road is on the A137 to Brantham, leaving Ipswich town centre. The museum is just inside the town boundary.

KESSINGLAND
The Cock Robin Collection ✳
Kessingland, Lowestoft, Suffolk

TEL: (home of the curator, Arthur Brown, cousin to Mr Brown) 01502 730063
COLLECTION: 'Cock Robin' was really Stanley James Brown (1907–97) whose nickname stuck after he shot a robin mistaking it for a sparrow when he was a boy. He was the son of a fisherman and a part-time fisherman himself. He was also a great hoarder of all kinds of things, many of which are to do with the fishing industry in Kessingland before it died out. On display are records of fish caught and sold, notebooks of size and placing of nets, photographs of fishing-boats, nets, books and many other items.
BUILDING: Originally a wooden storage shed for fishermen's nets. Toilets and a pub are nearby. The building is small but on one level.
OPENING TIMES: *April to end of September*, Sunday: 10am–1pm.
ADMISSION CHARGES: ①

P & 📹

DIRECTIONS: Opposite the Caravan Club site and near the beach.

LOWESTOFT
East Anglian Transport Museum ✳
Chapel Road, Carlton Colville, Lowestoft, Suffolk NR33 8BL

TEL: 01502 518459
COLLECTION: An old Lowestoft tramcar, No. 14, was the first in a whole line of vehicles that needed extensive renovation, eventually to become exhibits at this museum. Tramcar No. 14 was rescued by four enthusiasts and the idea of the museum grew. In 1965 the museum became a reality, but it has taken years to develop and is still doing so. To see and ride on are trams and trolley-buses. The museum specialises in these, but there are also cars, a steam-roller, a forklift truck and the East Suffolk Light Railway.
BUILDING: Once a disused meadow, it now has various buildings, tramways and roads.
OPENING TIMES: *Easter & May*, Easter weekend, then every Sunday, plus daily during May half-term holiday: 11am–5.30pm. *June*, Wednesday & Saturday: 2pm–5pm. *Mid-July to the end of August*, daily: 2pm–5pm. *September*, Wednesday & Saturday: 2pm–5pm. Sunday: 11am–5.30pm. Bank holidays: 11am–5.30pm. (As times and days may change, telephone for details.)
ADMISSION CHARGES: ②

P & WC ☕ & 📹 ⛲

DIRECTIONS: Three miles south west of Lowestoft on the B1384, just off the A146 Norwich to Lowestoft road. Brown signs from the A12, A117 and A146.

LOWESTOFT
Maritime Heritage Museum ✳

Sparrows Nest, Whapload Road, Lowestoft, Suffolk NR32 1XG

TEL: 01502 561963

COLLECTION: The crew quarters in the aft cabin of a steam-drifter are just one of the exhibits at the museum, which specialises in the history of the Lowestoft fishing fleet. From early sail to steam through to modern diesel vessels, the museum explains the history of fishing vessels, methods of fishing and the evolution of lifeboats. Also on display are shipwrights' and coopers' tools and a picture gallery. Photography is allowed with permission.

BUILDING: A small four-room flint and brick house, rebuilt in 1878. An extension was added in 1980. Toilets and cafés are nearby.

OPENING TIMES: *May to October (inclusive)*, daily: 10am–5pm (last admissions 4.30pm).

ADMISSION CHARGES: ①

🅿 ⅖ ⚠ 📷 👫

DIRECTIONS: Take the A12 into Lowestoft. Whapload Road is parallel to the High Street and on the seaward side. The museum is on the left as you go north. There is a free car-park to the right at the top of Whapload Road.

NEWMARKET
The National Horseracing Museum ✳

99 High Street, Newmarket, Suffolk CB8 8JL

TEL: 01638 667333 FAX: 01638 665600

COLLECTION: Visitors can ride a race-horse simulator in the museum. Telling the story of the sport's origins in England in Tudor times, the museum displays a wealth of material such as a reconstructed 19th-century weighing-room, a horse skeleton and jockey colours. The jockeys, the involvement of kings, the personalities of the racecourse and the bloodlines of the horses are all explained. The museum undertakes research and has an extensive archive. Telephone for details. Photography is allowed only in the Practical Gallery.

BUILDING: Opened as a museum in 1983. There is a new extension to house temporary exhibitions.

OPENING TIMES: *April to October (inclusive)*, Tuesday to Sunday: 10am–5pm. (Closed Monday.) Open on bank holidays and on Monday during July and August. Open other times by prior appointment.

ADMISSION CHARGES: ②

🅿 ⅖ 🆆🅲 🚻 ⚠ 👫

Maritime
Heritage
Museum,
Lowestoft

DIRECTIONS: In Newmarket High Street near Tattersals, where parking is possible.

SOUTHWOLD
The Amber Museum ❄ ✳

Amber Shop, 15 Market Place, Southwold, Suffolk IP18 6EA

TEL: 01502 723394 FAX: 01728 454411

WEBSITE: www.Ambershop.co.uk

COLLECTION: Creatures trapped in amber 30 to 50 million years ago are just one of the delights of this small room, lined with glass cases. Amber artefacts of all shades and all ages fill the shelves. There is a Burmese red amber dragonfly by a Polish artist, a Russian-made amber musical box and a crown of sterling silver and amber, commissioned by an old German family and made around 1920. This is the only purpose-built museum dedicated to the story and history of amber.

BUILDING: At the back of the Amber Shop in one small room.

OPENING TIMES: All year Monday to Saturday: 10am–5pm. (Closed Sunday.)

ADMISSION CHARGES: Free

🅿 ♿ ⚠ 🖼 👪

DIRECTIONS: The shop is opposite the Swan Hotel in the marketplace, in the centre of Southwold.

WETHERINGSETT
Mid-Suffolk Light Railway Museum ✳

Brockford Station, Wetheringsett, Stowmarket, Suffolk IP14 5PW

TEL: 01473 286907

COLLECTION: Original station buildings that have been returned to the site provide the setting for a collection of photographs and railway relics associated with the line. Vintage rolling-stock is on display.

BUILDING: The site is partly under cover and partly outdoor. At the station there are three buildings of the original railway company. Refreshments and a shop are housed in old railway carriage bodies. There are disabled toilets.

OPENING TIMES: *Easter Sunday to the last Sunday in September,* Sunday and Bank Holiday Mondays.

ADMISSION CHARGES: ①

Ⓟ ♿ WC ⛨ ⚠ ☕ ♨

DIRECTIONS: Wetheringsett is off the A140 Ipswich to Norwich road. The museum is outside the village. Travelling north turn right off the A140 at the Mendlesham Mast, then left at the T-junction into Station Road, then right into Hall Lane.

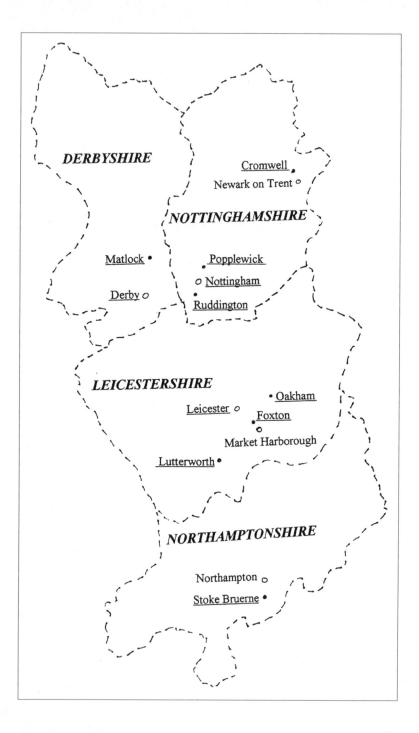

DERBYSHIRE

Cromwell •
Newark on Trent ○

NOTTINGHAMSHIRE

Matlock •

Popplewick •
○ Nottingham
Derby ○
Ruddington •

LEICESTERSHIRE

• Oakham
Leicester ○
• Foxton
○
Market Harborough

Lutterworth •

NORTHAMPTONSHIRE

Northampton ○
Stoke Bruerne •

Derbyshire

DERBY
Royal Crown Derby Visitor Centre ❋ ❋

194 Osmaston Road, Derby DE24 8JZ

TEL: 01332 712841 FAX: 01332 712863

WEBSITE: www.royal-doulton.com

COLLECTION: Collected by aristocracy and royalty, Royal Crown Derby can trace its history back to 1748. The museum displays a wealth of pieces, such as the moustache cup, designed with a lip to allow gentlemen to keep their moustaches dry, and a plate from the dinner service for the *Titanic*. The Ronald William Rauen room houses a magnificent collection from 1748 to the 1920s. There is also a collection of paperweights from 1981 to the present day. A ticket for the museum includes the demonstration studio. Factory tours are available twice daily on weekdays.

BUILDING: Victorian building. Approach to the museum is via a short staircase.

OPENING TIMES: *All year,* Monday to Saturday: 9.30am–5pm, Sunday: 10am–5pm.

ADMISSION CHARGES: Visitor Centre (studio and museum): ① Factory Tour: ②

Ⓟ 👤 🚻 🦖 ✕ ⚠ 🚻

DIRECTIONS: The Visitor Centre is on the A514 Derby to Ashby road, south east out of Derby, two minutes by car out of the city centre and opposite the Derby Royal Infirmary.

MATLOCK
Peak District Mining Museum ❋ ❋

The Pavilion, Matlock Bath, Derbyshire DE4 3NR

TEL/FAX: 01629 583834

COLLECTION: The centrepiece of the museum is a water-pressure engine and pump, which was cast at Colebrookdale and operated 360 feet below ground at Wills Founder Mine between Elton and Winster in Derbyshire. Display boards tell the history of Derbyshire mineral-mining for the past 2,000 years, and mining tools and working models are exhibited. In addition the eminent geologist Professor Howie's collection of minerals, about 1,700 items, is on show. It is possible to visit Temple Mine for a tour.

BUILDING: In the Pavilion at Matlock Bath, built about 80 years ago. The museum is next to a pump-room, where there was a pump that tapped the thermal springs from the hills. Public toilets are nearby.

OPENING TIMES: *All year, 1 November to 31 March,* daily: 11am–3pm, *1 April to 31 October,* daily: 10am–5pm, later at weekends.

ADMISSION CHARGES: Museum: ① Mine: ① Joint ticket: ②

Ⓟ 👤 🦖 ⚠ 🚃 🚻

DIRECTIONS: The Pavilion is a large cream building, easily recognisable by its dome tower. It is in Matlock Bath, which is south of Matlock on the A6. The Pavilion is between the A6 and the River Derwent.

Leicestershire and Rutland

FOXTON
Foxton Canal Museum ❄ ✳

Middle Lock, Gumley Road, Foxton, Leicestershire LE16 7RA

TEL: 0116 2792657

COLLECTION: On the Grand Junction Canal at Foxton there are ten locks. Raising a boat by about 75 feet and using 25,000 gallons (113,650 litres) of water per passage, they took 45 minutes to negotiate. To speed up this process the Canal Company decided to build an inclined plane boat lift to compete against the railways for traffic. It was completed in 1900 but closed in 1911 to save money. Now it forms one of the central features of the Canal Museum, plus the ten locks. Inside the museum are displays covering the social history of canals, interactive computer displays, costumes and working models. Photography is not allowed inside the museum but is permitted outside.

BUILDING: The Lift Boilerhouse, which has been reconstructed. It is situated half-way down the 1814 lock site. There is an education room in a stable built in 1810. Pub, tea-room and shop are at the bottom lock. Toilets at the country car-park. Wheelchair-users may need assistance for the steep path to the museum.

OPENING TIMES: *Easter to October*, daily: 10am–5pm. *October to Easter*, Saturday & Sunday, some weekdays. (Telephone for details.)

ADMISSION CHARGES: ①

🅿 ♿ 🆆🅲 ⛴ ✗ ⚠ ♨

DIRECTIONS: Follow the brown signs from the A6–B6047 roundabout near Market Harborough. Or from junction 20 of the M1, follow the A4304 to Lubenham and turn left at brown sign to Foxton. Parking is at the LCC Country Park, Gumley Road, near the top lock. There are ample moorings and water points at the top and bottom locks.

LEICESTER
Abbey Pumping Station ❄ ✳

Corporation Road, Leicester LE4 5PX

TEL: 0116 2995111 FAX: 0116 2995125

WEBSITE: : www.leicestermuseums.ac.uk

COLLECTION: There are four massive steam beam pumping engines in this museum, relics of the building's former function. In addition there are industrial artefacts relating

East Central

The Thomas' Boat Lift, Foxton Canal Museum

to Leicester, such as the road transport system, narrow-gauge railway, steam engines, textile machines, engineering and typewriters. There are hands-on science interactives and two museum galleries with public health displays. An archive is available as well as a railway worked by volunteers, which carries passengers.

BUILDING: A Victorian sewage-pumping station. Only the museum gallery is suitable for wheelchairs but there is a disabled toilet.

OPENING TIMES: *All year*, Monday–Friday: 1pm–5pm, Saturday: 10.30am–5pm, Sunday: 2pm–5pm.

ADMISSION CHARGES: Free (except on Steam Day): ①

Ⓟ ♿ 🚾 ♿ ⛟ 🚻

DIRECTIONS: One and a half miles north from Leicester city centre off the A6 Loughborough road.

LEICESTER
GN Sikh Museum of Sikh History and Culture ❀ ❋

9 Holybones, Leicester LE1 4LJ

TEL: 0116 2628606 FAX: 0116 2624264

E-MAIL: gnpleicester@virgin.net

COLLECTION: It all began with a model of Harimander Sahib, or the Golden Temple, in 1992. Artefacts and paintings have been added to illustrate the origins and development of Sikh history and culture. There are five models of 'Takhats' (the seats of authority of the Sikh nation). A collection of photographs illustrates the roles of Sikh soldiers in World

Leicestershire and Rutland

War I and World War II and a collection of artefacts and rare coins is being established. Photography of individual items is not allowed.

BUILDING: Within the Guru Nanak Gurdwara complex. There is a lift but no disabled toilet.

OPENING TIMES: Thursdays only: 1pm–4pm. (Other times for group visits by appointment.)

ADMISSION CHARGES: Free (donations are welcome)

Ⓟ ♿ 🚾 ⛁ 🎥 ♞

DIRECTIONS: With Shires Shopping Centre on your right walk down the High Street to St Nicholas Circle. Turn up any side-street on the north side of the circle and this will connect with Holybones, which runs parallel to the north side of the circle.

LEICESTER
Leicester Royal Infirmary Museum ❄ ❅

Knighton Street Nurses' Home, Leicester Royal Infirmary NHS Trust, Aylestone Road, Leicester LE1 5WW

TEL: 01858 565532

COLLECTION: The Royal Infirmary opened in 1771 and its story is told in the museum by means of pictures, prints and memorabilia. Medical equipment and artefacts illustrate the history of medicine during the last 200 years. The collection is more suited to older children.

BUILDING: Former nurses' home, built around 1910. The museum is housed in the recreation room. The hospital canteen is open to visitors and there are disabled toilets in the hospital.

OPENING TIMES: *All year*, Tuesday & Wednesday: 12 noon–2pm. (Closed bank holidays and the Tuesday following.)

ADMISSION CHARGES: Free

🅿 ♿ 🚾 🎥 ♞

DIRECTIONS: Leicester Royal Infirmary is on Aylestone Road, which is the A426 from Rugby. The road leads into Leicester from the south, into Oxford Street and up to St Nicholas Circle, which is off the west end of the High Street.

LUTTERWORTH
Stanford Hall Motorcycle Museum ❅

Lutterworth, Leicestershire LE17 6DH

TEL: 01788 860250 FAX: 01788 860870

COLLECTION: Enthusiasts C. E. 'Titch' Allen and the late John P. Griffith assembled an outstanding collection of vintage motorcycles. With help from the late Lord Braye, a pioneer motorcyclist and owner of Stanford Hall, the museum was set up in the Hall's stable block. Here there are some unique machines, a Norton–Villiers–BSA experimental model, plus famous names such as Norton, BSA, Triumph and Douglas Ariel. There are about 65 motorcycles on display, plus 2 cycle-cars and 15 bicycles including a 1980 Hera Plastic Cycle.

BUILDING: The stable block of Stanford Hall. Stanford Hall was built in the 1690s. There is a disabled toilet.

OPENING TIMES: *Easter Sunday to end of September*, Saturdays, Sunday, Bank Holiday Mondays and Tuesdays following: 2.30pm–5pm. (last admission 5pm.) On bank holidays & event days open 12 noon (house 2.30pm).

ADMISSION CHARGES: House and grounds ② Extra charge for motorcycle museum: ①

Ⓟ ♿ WC ☝ ✕ ⚠

DIRECTIONS: Stanford Hall is off the minor road that connects Stanford on Avon to Swinford. The road is north and parallel to the A14, which connects to the M1 and the M6 just to the west of Swinford.

OAKHAM
Oakham Castle Horse Shoe Collection ❅ ✳

Oakham Castle, Oakham

TEL: (Rutland County Museum) 01572 758440

WEBSITE: www.rutnet.co.uk

COLLECTION: Horeshoes, from the enormous to the dainty, cover the walls of the Great Hall. There are over 200 of them and they are there because of a unique custom: every peer of the realm visiting Oakham for the first time had to forfeit a horseshoe to the Lord of the Manor, a custom that is at least 500 years old.

BUILDING: Oakham Castle is one of the finest examples of 12th-century domestic architecture in England. The Great Hall was built by Walkelin de Ferrers in about 1180. Full facilities are available at Rutland County Museum, Catmose Street.

OPENING TIMES: *Late March to late October*, Monday to Saturday: 10am–1pm & 1.30pm–5pm, Sunday: 1pm–5pm. *Late October to late March*: All closing times: 4pm. Closed on Good Friday, on court Mondays (normally once a month) and at Christmas.

ADMISSION CHARGES: Free

Ⓟ ♿ ⚠ 🚻 ⛹

DIRECTIONS: Oakham is between Leicester and Stamford. The castle is just off the marketplace in Oakham.

Northamptonshire and Nottinghamshire

STOKE BRUERNE
The Canal Museum ❄ ✳

Stoke Bruerne, Towcester, Northamptonshire NN12 7SE

TEL: 01604 862229 FAX: 01604 864199

E-MAIL: british.waterways@sosb.globalnet.co.uk

COLLECTION: Every aspect of the waterways from the amazing feats of engineering to the colourful decoration of the canal boats and canal ware is on display at the museum. There are working models, videos and pictorial and three-dimensional displays covering 200 years of inland waterways, with the emphasis on the narrowboat canals of the south and midlands. Outside is the canal itself, with its flight of locks, boats and Blisworth Tunnel. Photography allowed by arrangement. There is a library.

BUILDING: An 1840 corn mill, alongside the Grand Union Canal.

OPENING TIMES: *Easter to October*, daily: 10am–5pm, including bank holidays. *November to just before Easter*, Tuesday to Sunday: 10am–4pm. Closed on Mondays and Christmas Day and Boxing Day.

ADMISSION CHARGES: ①

℗ ⴴ 🆆🅲 ⚠ 🎥 ♂♀

DIRECTIONS: Travelling south on the A508 (Northampton to Old Stratford road) from junction 15 of the M1, or Northampton, turn right to Stoke Bruerne just before the canal. There are two turnings to the village. The museum is in the village.

CROMWELL
Vina Cooke Museum of Dolls and Bygone Childhood ❄ ✳

The Old Rectory, Cromwell, nr. Newark, Nottinghamshire NG23 6JE

TEL: 01636 821364

COLLECTION: Vina Cooke's handmade portrait dolls from Robin Hood to royalty are featured, plus a large collection of dolls from the 18th century to the present day. In addition there are toys, prams, dolls' houses, books, games, railway models, christening robes and children's and adults' costumes. Photography is allowed by arrangement.

BUILDING: Late 17th-century dower house and former rectory, with original staircase. A picnic area is available in the garden. There is a tea-room but it is booked for parties only. Only the ground floor is accessible by wheelchair. There are no other facilities for the disabled.

OPENING TIMES: *All year*, Saturday to Thursday: 10.30am–12 noon & 2pm–5pm. (Closed Friday.) Easter Monday there is an Extravaganza (Morris dancers, crafts, etc.).

ADMISSION CHARGES: ①

Vina
Cooke
Museum,
Cromwell

Ⓟ ♿ 🚾 ♿ 🎥 👫

DIRECTIONS: Signposted off the A1 (brown signs), four miles north of Newark and next to the church in the village of Cromwell.

NOTTINGHAM
Galleries of Justice ❄ ✳

Shire Hall, High Pavement, Lace Market, Nottingham NG1 1HN

TEL: (information line) 0115 9520558 and (group bookings and enquiries) 0115 9520555

WEBSITE: www.galleriesofjustice.org.uk

COLLECTION: A trial takes place in the Victorian courtroom. In an original 18th-century prison, hard labour can be experienced under the eye of the costumed gaoler, warder and fellow prisoner. The walls of the exercise yard are covered in graffiti and there is a view of the gallows. In addition there are displays of police memorabilia and material on some of the most famous trials in English history. The great train robber Buster Edwards's trial was held in Shire Hall and the museum displays some of his posessions. There are many more experiences to enjoy – an original bath-house and laundry and even a medieval cave system. This is the only museum of law in the country, and it brings the world of the law alive. There is a Children's Activity Centre. A library is available by appointment. Photography is allowed but without a flash.

BUILDING: Original Court buildings in use from the 1700s until the mid-1980s. The building is 80 per cent accessible by wheelchair. There are disabled toilets and a lift.

'On trial', Galleries of
Justice, Nottingham

OPENING TIMES: *All year*, Tuesday to Sunday & bank holidays: 10am–5pm. (Closed Mondays & 24–26 December & 1 January.)

ADMISSION CHARGES: ③ (savings on family tickets booked in advance)

🅿 ♿ 🆆🅲 ☕ ♨ 👫

DIRECTIONS: From the top north east corner of Broad Marsh Shopping Centre take High Pavement east towards St Mary's church. The Galleries of Justice are on the right almost opposite the church.

PAPPLEWICK
Papplewick Pumping Station ❄ ✳

Off Longdale Lane, Ravenshead, Nottinghamshire NG15 9AJ

TEL: 0115 9632938

WEBSITE: www.papplewickpumpingstation.co.uk

COLLECTION: Originally used to lift 1,500,000 gallons of water a day, the beam pumping engines then forced the water up to the storage reservoir on the hill behind the station. From there the water supplied the city of Nottingham. As well as housing the engines, the building has a stained-glass window and cast-iron stairs. The hand-operated winches,

East Central

used with block and tackle to raise machinery for maintenance, are still there. In the boilerhouse three boilers, out of the six, supplied steam for power. Across the courtyard there is a forge and a Visitor Centre, which contains other exhibits.

BUILDING: The original engine house, built in the early 1830s by Thomas Hawksley.

OPENING TIMES: *Easter to the end of October* (not in steam), Sunday: 2pm–5pm. Telephone for midweek opening times. *November to Easter*, Sunday: 2pm–4pm. Dates for 'steaming days' are about once a month from April to October and then over New Year. Telephone for dates. Times: Saturday: 2pm–5pm, Sunday/Monday: 11am–5pm.

ADMISSION CHARGES: ①

ⓟ 🆆🅒 🗋 ⚠ 📧 👫

DIRECTIONS: The Pumping Station is on a minor road that connects across from the A60 to the A614. There is also a minor road from Ravenshead south east to the Pumping Station.

RUDDINGTON
Ruddington Framework Knitters' Museum ✳

Chapel Street, Ruddington, Nottingham NG11 6HE

TEL: 0115 9846914

COLLECTION: Knitting part of a sock, on a circular sock machine, is just one of the experiences in this museum. Built during the transition from cottage industry to factory production, this knitters' yard has living and working quarters on one site. Across the yard there is another frameshop with two frames and a workshop where repairs to the machinery are carried out. Upstairs is a large frameshop full of frames set close together. There are four cottages, which would have housed 29 people. Two of the cottages are restored, one to 1850 and one to 1900. Research facilities are available by appointment.

BUILDING: A purpose-built knitters' yard dating from 1829. It ceased work in 1929 and was bought by the Ruddington Framework Knitters' Shops Preservation Trust in 1971. They finally acquired the Primitive Methodist chapel in 1990. Only the ground floor is accessible by wheelchair. There is a village museum nearby.

OPENING TIMES: *Easter to December*, Wednesday to Saturday & Bank Holiday Mondays: 11am–4.30pm (last ticket sale: 4pm). *Easter to September*, Sunday: 1.30pm–4.30pm.

ADMISSION CHARGES: ①

🅿 ♿ 🆆🅒 🗋 ⚠ 📧 👫

DIRECTIONS: Ruddington is south of Nottingham on the A60. Leaving Nottingham and going south, turn right into the village at the traffic lights and go down Kirk Lane. Go straight over the crossroads to the T-junction of Asher Lane and turn left, then second right into Chapel Street. The street is just north of the village green.

Northamptonshire and Nottinghamshire

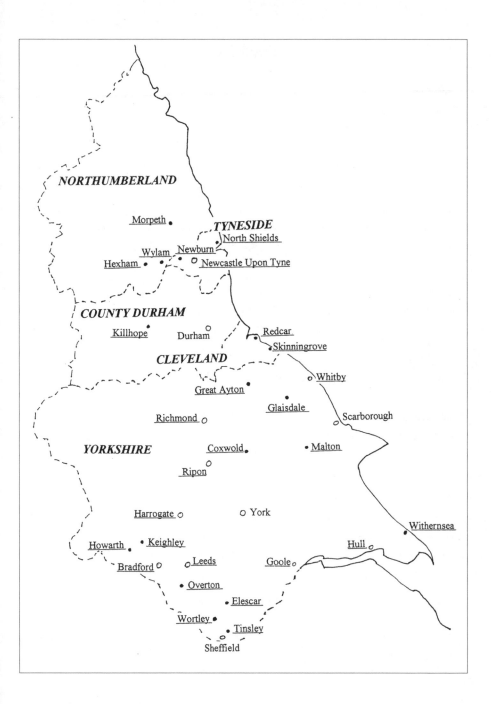

NORTHUMBERLAND

Morpeth •

TYNESIDE
• North Shields
Wylam Newburn
Hexham • • • ○ Newcastle Upon Tyne

COUNTY DURHAM
Killhope • Durham ○ • Redcar
• Skinningrove
CLEVELAND
○ Whitby
Great Ayton •
Glaisdale •
Richmond ○ Scarborough ○

YORKSHIRE Coxwold •
Ripon ○ • Malton

Harrogate ○ ○ York
Withernsea •
Howarth • • Keighley
Hull ○
Bradford ○ ○ Leeds Goole ○
• Overton
• Elescar
Wortley •
• Tinsley
○
Sheffield

Cleveland

REDCAR
The Zetland Museum ✳
The Esplanade, Redcar, Cleveland TS10 3AH
TEL: 01642 485370
COLLECTION: The *Zetland* is the oldest lifeboat in the world, built in 1802. The fishermen of Redcar raised £200 to bring the lifeboat to the village. Only one of the crew was ever lost and the boat made a memorable rescue in 1854 when the *Jane Erskine* ran aground. Local fishermen put to sea, but when the weather deteriorated the lifeboat was launched and picked up both the crew of the *Jane Erskine* and 26 fishermen. When the *Zetland* was damaged in a storm in 1864, the people of Redcar saved the boat from being broken up and raised money to repair it and house it in a shed on the seafront. It was replaced by a new lifeboat. There are marine photographs and the local history of fishing at the museum.
BUILDING: A listed building built in 1877 as a lifeboat house.
OPENING TIMES: *May to September*, daily: 11am–4pm.
ADMISSION CHARGES: Free
🅿 ♿ ⚠ 📷 ⛟
DIRECTIONS: On the Esplanade in Redcar.

SKINNINGROVE
Tom Leonard Mining Museum ✳
Deepdale, Skinningrove, Saltburn, Cleveland TS13 4AA
TEL: 01287 642877 FAX: 01287 642970
E-MAIL: visits@ironstonemuseum.co.uk
COLLECTION: Loftus Mine at Skinningrove produced ironstone to feed the ironworks of the North East, from 1848 until its closure in 1958. The museum is now the only ironstone museum in the UK. Visitors can enter the mine, explore the working space of the miners and see how the stone was drilled ready for explosives. There is a collection of mining tools and equipment, plus documents and archive photographs of the ironstone-mining era of Cleveland.
BUILDING: Housed in the mine buildings of Loftus Mine. The North Drift and ventilation areas are open to visitors.
OPENING TIMES: *1 April to 31 October*, daily: 1pm–5pm (last admission 3.45pm). Other times by arrangement for pre-booked parties.
ADMISSION CHARGES: ①

ⓟ ♿ 🅆🄲 Ⓢ 🎥 ♛

DIRECTIONS: On the coast in Skinningrove village, just off the A174, four miles south of Saltburn and 14 miles north of Whitby.

Durham and Humberside

KILLHOPE
Killhope Lead Mining Museum ✹
Killhope, Durham
TEL: 01388 537535

COLLECTION: Wearing helmets and cap-lamps and taken along about 50 metres of existing stone-arched tunnel and into a mine, the visitor can begin to experience the working conditions of the Victorian lead-miners. By taking a journey through the various buildings on the mine site, all aspects of lead-mining are revealed. The mineshop is where miners lived through the week. The washing rake, where lead ore was separated from other materials, and the park level mill, powered by a huge waterwheel, also cleaned the ore. The majority of the site, but not the mine, is accessible by wheelchair. Disabled toilets.

BUILDING: A 19th-century lead-mining separation site and mine, which has been restored (partly original, partly replica). The mine was one of Britain's richest and was worked from 1853 to 1910. There is a modern Visitors Centre.

OPENING TIMES: *April to October (inclusive)*, daily: 10.30am–5pm. *November*, Sunday: 10.30am–4pm. Other times by arrangement.

ADMISSION CHARGES: ②

ⓟ ♿ 🅆🄲 🛗 Ⓢ 🎥 ♛

DIRECTIONS: The Killhope museum is off the A689 Wolsingham to Alston road. It is between Cowshill and Nenthead.

HULL
Maritime Museum ❄ ✹
Queen Victoria Square, Hull HU1 3DX
TEL: 01482 613902 FAX: 01482 613710
WEBSITE: www.hullcc.gov.uk/museums

COLLECTION: Dominating the Whaling Gallery is the huge skeleton of a Greenland Right whale. Themed displays cover such subjects as whales and whaling, ships and shipping, fishing and the River Humber itself. Equipment, models, decorative figureheads and paintings form part of the displays. The nautical art includes an important collection of scrimshaw (whalebone decorated by sailors at sea). Research facilities are available by appointment. Two boats are within walking distance of the museum: the *Spurn Lightship*

(1927) in Hull Marina and the trawler *Arctic Corsair* (1960) on the River Hull, accessible via the Wilberforce House Museum.

BUILDING: Formerly the Town Docks offices, built in 1871.

OPENING TIMES: *All year*, Monday to Saturday: 10am–5pm, Sunday: 1.30pm–4.30pm. Closed Good Friday and Christmas holidays.

ADMISSION CHARGES: Free

🅿 ♿ 🆆🅲 ⚠ 📹 👪

DIRECTIONS: city centre, near the Queens Gardens.

HULL
Streetlife Transport Museum ❄ ✳

High Street, Hull HU1 1PS

TEL: 01482 613902 FAX: 01482 613710

WEBSITE: www.hullcc.gov.uk/museums

COLLECTION: The story of transport is told through various hands-on exhibits. The very latest in computer technology offers visitors a unique mail-coach ride. The golden age of steam is represented, and even the bicycle. There is a car gallery and a major extension of the carriage gallery, plus a street scene with shops.

BUILDING: Purpose-built museum.

OPENING TIMES: *All year*, Monday to Saturday: 10am–5pm, Sunday 1.30pm–4.30pm. Closed during the Christmas period.

ADMISSION CHARGES: Free

🅿 ♿ 🆆🅲 ⚠ 📹 👪

DIRECTIONS: In the High Street, which runs parallel to the River Hull. The museum is on the right as you walk up the High Street and near a fork in the road and Drypool Bridge.

Northumberland

HEXHAM
The Old Gaol, The Border History Museum ❄ ✳

The Old Gaol, Hallgate, Hexham, Northumberland NE46 3NH

TEL: 01434 652349 FAX: 01434 652425

COLLECTION: Forming a buffer zone between England and Scotland, the Border Marches were a breeding ground for a fiercely independent breed of warriors, known as Reivers. The museum is the first of its kind dedicated to telling their story. Blood and family ties were often more important than nationality and national borders to the

Reivers. Blending contemporary records and illustrations with modern interpretations, the museum creates the flavour of life and death in the 16th century.

BUILDING: The Old Gaol was completed in 1332-33. It is the earliest purpose-built prison in England and remained in use as a gaol until 1824. There are four rooms and a view of the dungeon. The museum is not accessible by wheelchair but it does offer induction loops, Braille and large-print guides.

OPENING TIMES: *April to October*, daily: 10am–4.30pm. *February, March & November*, Saturday, Monday & Tuesday: 10am–4.30pm (last admission 4pm). (Closed Sunday, Wednesday, Thursday, Friday.) Closed December and January.

ADMISSION CHARGES: ①

🅿 ⑤ 👫

DIRECTIONS: The Old Gaol is situated in Hexham town centre, a short walk from the main town car-park and just behind the marketplace. Hexham is south of the A69, which links the A1 in the east with the M6 to the west.

MORPETH
Bagpipe Museum ❄ ✳

Morpeth Chantry, Bridge Street, Morpeth, Northumberland NE61 1PD

TEL: 01670 519466

COLLECTION: The Northumbrian small pipes and their music are the speciality of this museum. Different pipes are displayed, and the visitor can listen to the sound of the pipes through headphones and also learn the difference between a rant and a reel. The information on these pipes is set in the context of bagpipes around the world. Research facilities are available by appointment.

BUILDING: A 13th-century chantry (a medieval ecclesiastical building), restored in the 1980s and now containing a Craft Centre, a Tourist Office and the museum. There is an induction loop.

OPENING TIMES: *All year*, Monday to Saturday: 10am–5pm, Sunday: 11am–5pm. Closed Sunday during December. Bank holidays: 11am–5pm.

ADMISSION CHARGES: ①

🅿 ⅦⅭ ⑤ 👫

DIRECTIONS: Bridge Street leads off the marketplace towards St George's church.

WYLAM
Wylam Railway Museum ❄ ✳

Falcon Centre, Falcon Terrace, Wylam, Northumberland

TEL: 01661 853520 or 852174

COLLECTION: Home to four of the world's most famous railway pioneers, Wylam is proud of its connections with the railway. George Stephenson, known as 'the Father of

Railways' was born in the village in 1781. William Hedley, colliery manager at Wylam, designed the historic locomotives 'Puffing Billy' and 'Wylam Dilly'. Timothy Hackworth was blacksmith at the colliery and first engineer of the Stockton and Darlington Railway. Stephenson's lifelong friend Nicholas Wood, a prominent Tyneside mining engineer, was born in Wylam. The museum celebrates the achievements of these men and displays railway relics from the area. Permission is required for photography.

BUILDING: The Falcon Centre was built as a school in 1910 but is on the site of the 19th-century ironworks where locomotives were built. A tea-shop, pubs and public toilets are nearby. Accessible by wheelchair.

OPENING TIMES: *All year*, Tuesday & Thursday: 2pm–5pm & 5.30pm–7.30pm, Saturday: 9am–12 noon. (Closed Monday, Wednesday, Friday & Sunday.)

ADMISSION CHARGES: Free

Ⓟ ♿ 🔺 📷 ♨

DIRECTIONS: Wylam is east of Newcastle and south of the A69 to Corbridge. The village is on the River Tyne. The museum is in the Falcon Centre. Turn off the main road through the village, alongside the Fox and Hounds inn into Falcon Terrace.

Tyne and Wear

NEWBURN
Newburn Hall Motor Museum ❄ ✳

35 Townfield Gardens, Newburn, Newcastle Upon Tyne NE15 8PY

TEL: 0191 2642977

COLLECTION: Visit one day and an exhibit of veteran motors (pre-1920) might be on display. Try another time and it could be cars featured on television or Grand Prix cars. The motors are often changed and exhibits are themed. There is a workshop and stores and a library.

BUILDING: Built in 1924 for the Territorial Army, the building was used by the TA until 1977. It was bought in 1979 to be rebuilt as a motor museum. The drill hall of 4,000 feet has been restored to form the main exhibition hall. The museum is accessible by wheelchair and there are disabled toilets.

OPENING TIMES: *All year*, daily: 9pm–6pm.

ADMISSION CHARGES: ①

Ⓟ ♿ 🚻 ✗ 📷 ♨

DIRECTIONS: Newburn is on the A6085 between Scotswood Bridge and Throckley. In Newburn turn down the road by the police station. Townfield Gardens and the museum are behind the police station.

NEWCASTLE UPON TYNE
Military Vehicle Museum ❄ ☀

Exhibition Park, Newcastle Upon Tyne NE2 4PZ

TEL: 0191 281722

COLLECTION: Jeeps, staff cars, trucks and heavy haulage lorries, plus fighting machines such as the 25-pounder field gun and the Mobat anti-tank gun, are all on display. These military vehicles and many others have been restored by enthusiasts. A mock-up World War I trench has been used for the television programme 'Voices of War' and cabinets around the museum house a large collection of small military and civilian items such as uniforms, medals, respirators and posters. Research facilities are available.

BUILDING: The last surviving structure of the 1929 North East Coast Exhibition. Originally used as the Pavilion of Fine Art, it is a steel-framed building designed to stand for six months but still standing 60 years later. It is now a listed building. There is a café in the park.

OPENING TIMES: *March to November*, daily: 10am–4pm. *November to March*, Saturday & Sunday only: 10am–4pm. (Closed weekdays in winter and Christmas and New Year.)

ADMISSION CHARGES: ①

🅿 [WC] ♿ 📷 🚻

DIRECTIONS: Exhibition Park and the Military Vehicle Museum are on the north side of Newcastle Upon Tyne, north of the university. No cars are allowed into the park. The car-park is off the roundabout that connects Queen Victoria Road and Claremont Road. (The Royal Victoria Infirmary is in Queen Victoria Road.) From the car-park walk north under the road and past the lake. The museum is north of the lake.

NORTH SHIELDS
Stephenson Railway Museum ☀

Middle Engine Lane, North Shields, Tyne and Wear

TEL: (enquiries): 0191 2007146

COLLECTION: 'Billy', the forerunner of Stephenson's world-famous 'Rocket' is on show alongside many other engines from the age of steam. The museum explains the impact of the coal industry on the region's railways and shows how electricity revolutionised transport on Tyneside in the early 1900s. There is a 'hands-on' exhibit demonstrating how trains work. A 1909 electric locomotive has recently been restored. The museum holds special events through the summer. Steam-train rides on the North Tyneside Railway are also on offer.

BUILDING: Former Tyne and Wear metro test track depot, built in the early 1970s. It stands on the site of the engine house of Brunton & Shields Railway. The museum is accessible by wheelchair and there is a disabled toilet.

OPENING TIMES: *1 May to the last Sunday in September*, daily, weekdays: 11am–3pm,

Tyne and Wear

Saturday, Sunday and bank holidays: 11am–4pm.

ADMISSION CHARGES: ①

ⓅⓀ🆆🅟▷⚠☞ⅲ

DIRECTIONS: The museum is well signposted from the A19/A1058 junction and is opposite the Siemens factory, adjacent to the Blythe and Tyne cycle route.

East Yorkshire

GOOLE
The Waterways Museum ❄ ❋

Dutch River Side, Goole, East Yorkshire DN14 5TB

TEL: 01405 768730 FAX: 01405 769868

E-MAIL: waterwaysmuseum@btinternet.com

WEBSITE: www.thewaterwaysmuseumadventurecentre.co.uk

COLLECTION: For over 120 years coal was carried from the coalfields down the Aire & Calder Navigation canal for shipment at the port of Goole. By 1900 Goole was the third largest port in the UK that dealt with the movement and shipment of coal. The museum celebrates this by telling the story of Goole port and the last 200 years of the waterways system. There are photographs dating from 1905 to the present day, model boats, news-cuttings and objects such as a splendid carved ship's figurehead that had lain in a work-shop for around 50 years. On display are the 'Tom Puddings', container boats capable of carrying up to 40 tons of coal. They were coupled together in trains and towed by special tugs. The museum is part of the 'Sobriety Project', a charity that takes its name from the first boat it was given more that 20 years ago. It runs workshops and educational trips on boats, and has a library for research.

BUILDING: A modern building, with a new extension now open. There is a nature trail and picnic area.

OPENING TIMES: *All year*, Monday to Friday: 10am–4.30pm. *Easter to mid-September*, plus Sunday: 10am–5pm. (Closed Saturday.)

ADMISSION CHARGES: ①

ⓅⓀ🆆▷⚠☞ⅲ

DIRECTIONS: The museum is just south of Goole, in Old Goole. Following the A161 north from Crowle into Old Goole, the road turns sharp left and then right and crosses the River Don (known as the Dutch River at this point). Turn left after the river. The museum is along this road between the River Don and the Aire & Calder Navigation canal.

WITHERNSEA
Withernsea Lighthouse Museum ✳

The Lighthouse, Hull Road, Withernsea, East Yorkshire HU19 2DY

TEL: 01964 614834

COLLECTION: In the late 19th century, when the captain of the fishing smack *Genesta* froze to death in the rigging while trying to work out his position at sea, the coroner commented that the tragedy would have been avoided if there had been a lighthouse at Withernsea. Shortly afterwards, in 1892, the lighthouse was under construction. Its light shone continuously, except for World Wars I and II, until 1976. The museum tells the story of the sea through exhibits such as 'H. M. Coastguard', 'Ships' Bells', models and old photographs. It also looks at the history of Withernsea and holds memorabilia of the 1950s star of stage and screen Kay Kendall, who was born in the town. Her grandfather worked on the construction of the lighthouse.

BUILDING: The lighthouse is 120 feet high and has a tapering tower. This tower is architecturally unusual in Britain. The lamp-room can be reached by climbing 144 steps and the views are worth the effort, with a certificate as a reward on descent. The base of the lighthouse and Lighthouse Keeps cottages have been used for the museum. Photography is allowed only from the top of the building. Only the ground floor is accessible by wheelchair, but there is a disabled toilet.

OPENING TIMES: *March to October*, Saturday, Sunday and bank holidays: 1pm–5pm. *Mid-June to mid-September*, Monday to Friday: 11am–5pm.

ADMISSION CHARGES: ①

🅿 ♿ 🆆🅲 ⛱ ⚠ 📷 🚻

DIRECTIONS: Withernsea is east of Hull on the A1033. The lighthouse stands behind the promenade. Turn down Seaside Road, right into Queen Street and then left into Hill Road.

North Yorkshire

COXWOLD
Shandy Hall and Gardens (home of writer Laurence Sterne) ✳

Coxwold, York, North Yorkshire YO61 4AD

TEL: 01347 868465

WEBSITE: www.shandy-hall.org.uk

COLLECTION: Laurence Sterne (1713–68) was curate of Coxwold. He is better known, however, for his two novels *Tristram Shandy* and *A Sentimental Journey*, written between 1760 and 1767. *Tristram Shandy* breaks all the laws of writing and is full of dashes, blank pages and eccentric punctuation. The museum contains the world's foremost collection

Museum of
Victorian
Science,
Glaisdale

of editions of Sterne's novels and contemporary prints and paintings illustrating his work. Photography is allowed only in the garden.

BUILDING: An early 15th-century house, added to by Sterne and surrounded by two-acres of garden, including a walled garden full of old-fashioned roses and unusual plants. The premises are accessible by wheelchair only with assistance. Food available in the village close by.

OPENING TIMES: *May to September*, Gardens open daily (except Saturday): 11am–4.30pm. House open: Wednesday: 2pm–4.30pm, Sunday: 2.30pm–4.30pm. (House closed Monday, Tuesday & Thursday to Saturday.)

ADMISSION CHARGES: House and garden: ②

Ⓟ WC ♿ ☞

DIRECTIONS: Coxwold is off the A19 York to Teeside road. The Hall is just north of the village.

GLAISDALE
Museum of Victorian Science ✳ ✺

Woodberry, Glaisdale, Whitby, North Yorkshire YO21 2QL

TEL: 01947 897440

COLLECTION: Over the last 30 years Tony Swift has painstakingly made Victorian machines that demonstrate such things as the 'Historical Development of Electro-statics', 'Electro-magnetism' and Marconi's early work in 'Wireless Telegraphy'. The room is full of miniaturised versions of huge machinery that made static electricity; one of the earliest reproduced pieces of machinery is from 1642. There are many other machines in this unique collection to delight the visitor. Nearly all the machines work, and they are demonstrated to visitors by Tony Swift.

BUILDING: In an annex to the main house and is a reproduction of a Victorian laboratory with gaslights. Public toilet nearby. Shop in development.

OPENING TIMES: By appointment only and only for three to six persons.

ADMISSION CHARGES: ①

ⓟ 🎥 🏛

DIRECTIONS: Glaisdale is south west of Whitby and off the A171 Whitby to Guisborough Road. Glaisdale is between the villages of Leaholm to the west and Egton to the east. The museum is between the railway station and the garage in the village of Glaisdale.

GREAT AYTON
The Captain Cook Schoolroom Museum ✳

101 High Street, Great Ayton, North Yorkshire TS9 6NB

TEL: 01642 724296

COLLECTION: The famous explorer and navigator of the seas Captain James Cook surveyed the coasts of St Lawrence and Newfoundland and made numerous discoveries in the Pacific. He was killed in Owhyhee (Hawaii) in 1779. His father worked for the lord of the manor, Thomas Skottowe, who paid James's school fees. James Cook went to school in Great Ayton from 1736 to 1740. The museum has a replica of an 18th-century school for the poor and a display where the visitor can stand next to Captain Cook on board ship and learn how to use a ship's sextant. There are also exhibits of his voyages.

BUILDING: The museum is housed within a building once used as a charity school and founded in 1704. Public toilets are next to the museum. There is wheelchair access and a wheelchair lift.

OPENING TIMES: *April to October*, daily: 1pm–4pm. *July & August*, daily: 11am–4pm.

ADMISSION CHARGES: ①

🅿 ♿ ⚠ 🎥 🏛

DIRECTIONS: Turn off the A173 through Great Ayton on to the High Street. The museum is on the right just past High Green.

HARROGATE
Royal Horticultural Society, Harlow Carr Museum of Gardening ❄ ✳

Crag Lane, Harrogate, North Yorkshire HG3 1QB

TEL: 01423 565418

COLLECTION: A potting shed of around 1920, complete with life-sized gardener, forms one of the exhibits. Tools used in gardening, ditching, hedging, pruning and felling, children's garden tools and chairs to sit on in the garden are on display. With many

Royal
Horticultural
Society
Garden
Harlow
Carr,
Harrogate

artefacts being in store, the exhibition is changed regularly. The museum holds a sub-stantial collection of gardening books, magazines and periodicals and seed catalogues. Research facilities are available by arrangement.

BUILDING: Within the gardens. One small room with open displays and cabinet displays. Toilets and café are nearby. Facilities for the disabled are available within the gardens.

OPENING TIMES: *All year*, daily: 10am–4pm. Closed Christmas Day.

ADMISSION CHARGES: ③ (admission charge to the gardens includes the museum)

Ⓟ ♿ WC 🚻 ✕ ♿ 📷

DIRECTIONS: West of Harrogate on the B6162 Otley Road. The gardens are on the right, travelling west, shortly before the road joins the B6161 at Beckwithshaw. The car-park is adjacent to the gardens.

MALTON
Eden Camp (The People's War 1939-45) ❄ ✳

Eden Camp, Malton, North Yorkshire YO17 6RT

TEL: 01653 697777 FAX: 01653 698243

E-MAIL: admin@edencamp.co.uk

WEBSITE: www.edencamp.co.uk

COLLECTION: When two Italian ex-prisoners of war visited the prisoner of war (POW) camp at Malton, they declared it had been Eden for them because they had food, shelter and kindness when they were there. From that sprang the idea of a museum. The camp had housed German prisoners of war as well as Italians who worked on local farms. In 1986 Stan Johnson bought the still intact POW camp. There are 29 huts, all housing different exhibits, mostly about World War II. History is brought to life in these huts: the

Blitz, with all its terrifying sounds, is in Hut 5, the Home Guard in Hut 2, women at war in Hut 8 and prisoners of war in Hut 10. Waxworks and tableaux, moving figures, authentic sound effects and smells, plus detailed re-creations of rooms and places make the war experience very real. This is a unique museum and it has won many awards. Among the huts are a cafeteria and a place to eat packed lunches. During term time there are school visits to the museum.

BUILDING: The POW camp, started in 1942 by the army and completed by Italian prisoners. The camp closed in 1948 and was about to be bulldozed when it was bought.

OPENING TIMES: *Second Monday in January to 23 December (inclusive)*, daily: 10am–5pm. (Allow at least three to four hours to see the museum properly.)

ADMISSION CHARGES: ②

Ⓟ & [WC] ⊓ ✕ Ⓐ 🍴 ♦♦♦

DIRECTIONS: Malton is on the A169 Malton to Pickering Road, which is off the A64, York to Scarborough road.

RICHMOND
The Georgian Theatre Royal and Theatre Museum ✳

Victoria Road, Richmond, North Yorkshire DL10 4DW

TEL: 01748 823710

COLLECTION: Famous actors Edmund Kean and William Charles Macready once trod the boards of this lovely 18th-century theatre, built in 1788 by actor-manager Samuel Butler and run by him until his death in 1812. The theatre finally closed in 1842 and was rescued from service as a corn chandler's, a furniture store and an auction room in the 1940s. The theatre museum tells the story of the theatre, shows a replica of the Georgian

Eden Camp,
Malton

North Yorkshire

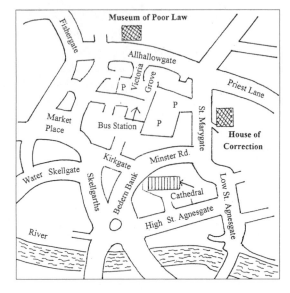

The Museum of Poor Law and House of Correction, Ripon

theatre stage and explains what happened to the building after it was closed and the stages of restoration. There are also model theatres showing different kinds of theatres from Ancient Greece to 20th-century Britain. Guided tours of the theatre help visitors to understand how it worked and the kinds of audience it attracted.

BUILDING: One of the most important theatres in Britain, as it is the most authentic public 18th-century theatre in existence.

OPENING TIMES: *Easter Saturday to near the end of May*, Monday to Saturday: 1.30pm–3.30pm (last tour). *End of May to September*, Monday to Saturday: 10.30am–3.30pm. *October*, Monday to Saturday: 1.30pm–3.30pm. (Closed Sunday except for party tours by prior arrangement.)

ADMISSION CHARGES: ①

🅿 ♿ 🆆🅲 ☕ ⚠ ♟

DIRECTIONS: The theatre is near the town square in Richmond.

RIPON
House of Correction Museum of Police and Prisons ✳

St Marygate, Ripon, North Yorkshire

TEL: 01765 690799 (Ripon Museum Trust)

COLLECTION: Hard labour in a prison meant the treadmill, the crank and picking oakum. The museum illustrates the life of a prisoner during the 19th century in photographs. Outside in the courtyard are medieval stocks, a pillory, a whipping-post and some 20th-century police call-boxes. Two hundred years of policing are demonstrated by a display

North East

of police uniforms, staves and handcuffs. Photography is allowed with permission. The museum publishes its own research booklets and these accompany the education packs for schools. A new museum about the Georgian Sessions Court is to be opened soon.

BUILDING: A prison building, known as the House of Correction, built in 1816. Not accessible by wheelchair.

OPENING TIMES: *Good Friday to near the end of October* (telephone for exact dates), daily: 10.30am–4pm. *March, April & November*, Saturday: 10.30am–3pm, Sunday: 12 noon–3pm. (Closed Monday to Friday.) For all dates: last admission 30 minutes before closing.

ADMISSION CHARGES: ①

P WC ⚠ 🎥 👫

DIRECTIONS: See map.

RIPON
The Workhouse Museum of Poor Law ✳

Allhallowgate, Ripon, North Yorkshire

TEL: (The Ripon Museum Trust) 01765 690799

COLLECTION: A hundred years ago vagrants could not expect kind treatment. Together with the desperately poor, they were put in workhouses. The harsh conditions of the Poor Law (amended in 1834) are illustrated in the 'Hard Times Gallery'. In the 14 night cells, where tramps were often locked up for the night, displays show the conditions of the poor in the 19th century. The functioning of the workhouse is made clear by viewing the ablution room, the day room and the work yard. Photography is allowed with permission. Research booklets are available, as are education packs for schools.

BUILDING: The museum is in the men's casual wards of the former Ripon Union Workhouse built in 1854. It has been refurbished to show the treatment of vagrants 100 years ago. Accessible by wheelchair.

OPENING TIMES: *Good Friday to near end of October* (telephone for exact dates), 10.30am–4pm. *March, April & November*, Saturday: 10. 30am–3pm, Sunday: 12 noon–3pm. (Closed Monday to Friday.) For all dates: last admission 30 minutes before closing.

ADMISSION CHARGES: ①

P ♿ WC ⚠ 🎥 👫

DIRECTIONS: See map.

WHITBY
Captain Cook Memorial Museum ✳

Grape Lane, Whitby, North Yorkshire YO22 4BA

TEL/FAX: 01947 601900

E-MAIL: captaincookmuseumwhitby@ukgateway.net

WEBSITE: www.cookmuseumwhitby.co.uk

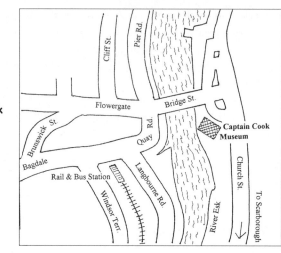

Captain Cook Memorial Museum, Whitby

COLLECTION: Seventeen apprentices were lodged in the attic of the ship-owner John Walker to learn their trade as seamen. Among them was the famous navigator James Cook, who was destined to put the Pacific Ocean, Eastern Australia, New Zealand and many South Sea islands on the map. The downstairs rooms have been furnished as Cook would have known them. In other rooms letters, pictures and models form exhibits relevant to his career, showing his nine years in Whitby, his voyages, artefacts from the voyages and the attic where he slept.

BUILDING: Built in 1688 but the building had its heyday in the mid-18th century, when Whitby was a shipbuilding centre and thriving seaport.

OPENING TIMES: *April to near the end of October* (telephone for exact dates), daily: 9.45 am–5pm (last admission 4.30pm). *March*, Saturday & Sunday: 11am–3pm. (Closed Monday to Friday.)

ADMISSION CHARGES: ①

🅿 ♿ ♔

DIRECTIONS: See map.

South Yorkshire

ELESCAR
Coddswallop Bottle Museum ❄ ❋

Building 11, Elescar Heritage Centre, Wath Road, Elescar, Barnsley, South Yorkshire S74 8HJ

TEL: (Secretary of the Codswallop Trust) 01226 288637

COLLECTION: A revolutionary invention in the 1870s meant that the fizzy drink known as 'pop' would no longer go flat. It was a glass marble stopper on wire. Invented by Hiram Codd, it was used to top the cheap beer of the day known as 'wallop'. The museum houses all manner of bottles, mainly concentrating upon Victorian bottles, such as pop, medicine and whisky bottles. There are pottery ginger beer and beer containers and a 1650 Bellarmin bottle. Since its beginnings in 1991, the museum has expanded its collection to include old adverts and shop and pub memorabilia.

BUILDING: In the Heritage centre, once the mid-19th-century Elescar ironworks workshops, which were bought by Barnsley Metropolitan Borough Council in 1988.

OPENING TIMES: *All year*, Monday to Friday: 9am–5pm, Saturday & Sunday: 11am–4pm.

ADMISSION CHARGES: ①

DIRECTIONS: Leave the M1 at junction 36. Follow the brown 'Elescar Heritage' signs (A6135) for approximately two miles. Left into Broad Carr Road for three-quarters of a mile. Right into Armroyd Lane, right at T-junction and again right after 100 yeards, left into main car park opposite Elescar Park. Enter the site by the side of the Market Hotel.

ELESCAR
Hot Metal Press ❆ ✳

Elescar Workshops, Wath Road, Elescar, Barnsley, South Yorkshire S74 8HJ

TEL: 01226 740498 FAX: 01226 350201

COLLECTION: This is a working museum, which uses many of its machines to produce printed material. A unique collection of typesetting equipment, together with a collection of letterpress printing machines and ancillary equipment, form the collection. There are over 100 cases of hand-set type and some wood-lettering for poster printing.

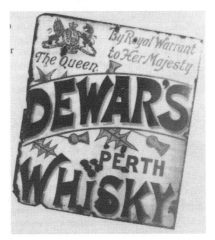

Coddswallop Bottle
Museum, Elescar

South Yorkshire

Amongst the printing presses are a Columbian 'Eagle' Double Royal Hand Press, circa 1830, and an Arab Hand Fed Platen, circa 1920.

BUILDING: In the Heritage Centre (as for Coddswallop Bottle Museum).

OPENING TIMES: *All year,* Wednesday & Saturday: 10am–5pm, occasional Sunday afternoons: 2pm–5pm. (Closed Monday, Tuesday, Thursday & Friday.)

ADMISSION CHARGES: Free

Ⓟ &. wc ⛱ ⚠ 📷 🚻

DIRECTIONS: As for Coddswallop Bottle Museum.

TINSLEY
Sheffield Bus Museum ✳

Tinsley Tram Sheds, Sheffield Road, Tinsley, Sheffield S9 2FY

TEL: 0114 2553010

WEBSITE: www.sheffieldbusmuseum.com

COLLECTION: Amongst the buses and artefacts are vehicles being restored by members of the Museum Trust. This collection of buses and coaches includes all kinds of makes and ages. There is also a tramcar from Sheffield Corporation Tramways. The miscellaneous collection even has a TET 135 Daimler from Rotherham Corporation, which was, in fact, a gritwagon. In addition there are destination blinds, tram stops, old road signs, timetables, tickets and models.

BUILDING: The former Tinsley Tram Depot was the first one built in Sheffield for the Sheffield Tramways Company in 1874. It was first built for horse-trams. The Sheffield Bus Museum Trust moved into part of Tinsley in 1987. Light refreshments available on open days. The museum is accessible by wheelchair but there are no other disabled facilities.

Sheffield Bus Museum

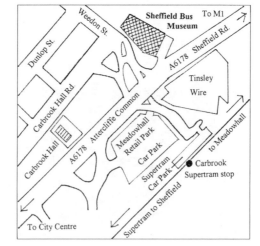

OPENING TIMES: Usually open every Saturday and Sunday afternoon for members to work on restoration of vehicles. From *April to December* it is open for special Sunday open days about once a month: 12 noon, last admission 4pm. Telephone for details and to check opening at weekends.

ADMISSION CHARGES: ①

🅿 ♿ 🆆🅲 ⚠ 📷 ⅲⅲ

DIRECTIONS: Leave the M1 at junction 34. There is unrestricted parking in Colebrook Hall Road on a Sunday. See map.

WORTLEY
Top Forge ❊ ✳

Wortley, South Yorkshire.

TEL: 0114 2817991

COLLECTION: Around 1700 the forge formed part of the Spencer Syndicate of Iron-masters. From 1850 until it closed in 1908 the forge, using only water power, made wrought-iron axles for railway wagons. The water-wheels still turn. The building houses part of South Yorkshire Industrial History Society's collection of historic steam engines and machine tools and a small collection illustrating the uses of iron.

BUILDING: Bought for preservation in the 1950s, the forge was by then derelict but the wheels and hammers were repairable. Volunteers have done most of the work to restore the buildings and machinery. Ninety per cent of the building is accessible by wheelchair but there are no other facilities for the disabled.

OPENING TIMES: *February to November*, Sunday only: 11am–5pm.

ADMISSION CHARGES: ①

Ⓟ ♿ 🆆🅲 ⚠ 📷 ⅲⅲ

DIRECTIONS: The forge is between Wortley, Thurgoland and Deepcar, just north of Wortley Bridge over the River Don. It is within three miles of junctions 35A and 36 on the M1.

West Yorkshire

BRADFORD
The Colour Museum ❊ ✳

1 Providence Street, Bradford, West Yorkshire BD1 2PW

TEL: 01274 390955 FAX: 01274 392888

COLLECTION: It is hard to imagine a world without colour. In the World of Colour gallery the importance of colour in everyday life is explored as well as the spectrum, primary colours, colour 'blindness' and many more aspects of the subject. Temporary

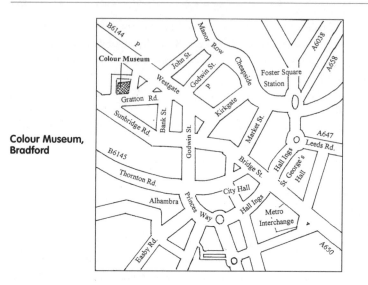

Colour Museum, Bradford

exhibitions on the theme of colour are held here. In the Colour and Textiles gallery, the exhibitions present the use of colour in textiles looking at natural dyes, synthetic fibre, textile printing and much more. This gallery gives an indication of the reason for such a museum, for it is run as an educational activity of the Society of Dyers and Colourists. The Society was founded in Bradford over a century ago. There is a small charge for photography within the building.

BUILDING: The museum is in part of the Society's headquarters building, which is a former wool warehouse, 19th or early 20th century. Ramp access and lift and disabled toilet.

OPENING TIMES: *All year*, Tuesday to Saturday: 10am–4pm. (Closed Sunday, Monday & bank holidays.) Open to pre-booked parties on Tuesday to Friday mornings. Telephone for bookings.

ADMISSION CHARGES: ①

🅿 ♿ 🚾 △ 📷 🚻

DIRECTIONS: See map.

HAWORTH
The Brontë Parsonage Museum ❀ ❋

Haworth, Keighley, West Yorkshire BD22 8DR

TEL: 01535 642323 FAX: 01535 647131

E-MAIL: bronte@bronte.prestel.co.uk WEBSITE: www.bronte.org.uk

COLLECTION: As each room is furnished with the Brontës' own furniture and possessions, it is possible to imagine that Charlotte, Branwell, Emily and Anne have not long left the house. The three sisters produced some famous novels, including *Wuthering Heights* by Emily, 1847, *Jane Eyre* by Charlotte, 1847 and *The Tenant of Wildfell Hall* by Anne, 1848. Individual items are changed but the main display of Charlotte's costume items, writing desks belonging to the sisters and manuscripts are always to be seen. Each year there is a temporary exhibition on aspects of the Brontës' life and work. Only the ground floor rooms are accessible by wheelchair. There is a Braille guide to borrow and free room-guides in many languages. A comprehensive library is open for research by prior appointment.

BUILDING: A Georgian house built in 1778 of local stone. Areas such as the kitchen have been reconstructed to appear as they would have been in the Brontës' time. There are local authority toilets in the nearby car-park and a number of cafés and pubs in the village.

OPENING TIMES: *April to September*, daily: 10am–5.30pm. *October to March*, daily: 11am–5pm. Closed over Christmas and from mid-January to the beginning of February. Telephone for exact dates.

ADMISSION CHARGES: ②

🅿 ♿ ⚠ 👥

DIRECTIONS: Haworth is off the A6033 Oxenhope to Keighley road. Once in Haworth go north over the river and at the fork turn left into the main street. The right fork is Rawden road. The museum is to the left of the main street.

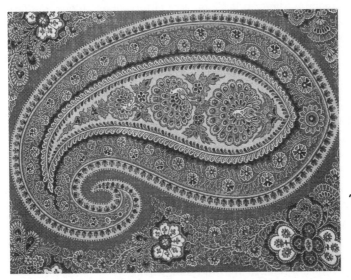

Turkey red 'Paisley' print, The Colour Museum, Bradford

West Yorkshire

The Vintage
Carriage
Museum,
Keighley

KEIGHLEY
The Vintage Carriage Museum ✳ ✸

The Railway Station, Haworth, Keighley, West Yorkshire BD22 8NJ

TEL: 01535 680425 or 01535 646472

WEBSITE: www.neotek.demon.co.uk/vct/

COLLECTION: Appearing in over 30 films and television programmes, these carriages are not only famous but historic. Pride of place in this collection goes to the 1876 Manchester, Sheffield & Lincolnshire railway carriage. There is also a Midland Railway six-wheeled composite coach built in 1886 and many others, including a very elderly steam locomotive. The visitor can walk into the carriages and feel what rail travel used to be like. Sound and video presentations, a collection of posters and other memorabilia from the age of steam help create the atmosphere. There is restoration work in progress too. A library is available for members of the Vintage Carriages Trust.

BUILDING: Built in 1990 and extended twice since then. There is no café but there are picnic tables outside, and confectionery, etc., for sale. Wheelchairs can access the guard's brake van areas but the carriage doors are too narrow. There is a disabled toilet and neck loop system.

OPENING TIMES: *All year*, daily: 11am–4.30pm. (Closed 25 & 26 December.)

ADMISSION CHARGES: ①

Ⓟ ♿ 🚾 ⚠ 🍴 ♟

DIRECTIONS: At Ingrow station, one mile from the centre of Keighley on the A629 Halifax road. Look out for the brown sign. By rail to Keighley main line station and then on the Worth Valley Railway to Ingrow West Station.

KEIGHLEY
Ingrow Loco Museum and Workshop ❄ ✳

The Railway Station, Haworth, Keighley, West Yorkshire BD22 8NJ

TEL: (Railway Station and Vintage Carriages Museum contact numbers) 01535 680425
or 01535 646472, (contact number for Bahamas Locomotive Society Ltd) 0161 432 7595
COLLECTION: To buy, preserve and maintain the former LMS Railway 'Jubilee' class
steam locomotive 45596 *Bahamas*, the Bahamas Locomotive Society was formed in 1967.
Having relocated from Derbyshire in 1990, the Society is continuing to develop the
Ingrow Railway Centre, where visitors can experience the bygone age of the steam train.
The museum portrays the evolution, construction and operation of steam railways using
drawings, photographs, tools, models and locomotives.
BUILDING: A stone- and wood-clad building next to Ingrow West Station. The building
is divided into the workshop, which overhauls steam locomotives, and the museum.
OPENING TIMES: As this museum plans to open in about May 2002 details of opening
and charges are not settled. Do telephone if travelling any distance.
ADMISSION CHARGES: Possibly free at first. Then charges will be decided

Ⓟ ♿ WC ⟨S⟩ 🎥 ♁

DIRECTIONS: For directions to Ingrow station see above (the Vintage Carriage Museum).
Ingrow Museum is adjacent to Ingrow station, Keighley and Worth Valley Railway.

LEEDS
Museum of the History of Education ❄ ✳

Parkinson Court, The University, Leeds LS2 9JT

TEL: (enquiries) 0113 2334545 or (direct line) 0113 2334665

FAX: 0113 2334541

COLLECTION: Established by W. E. Tate in the 1950s, the museum aims to document the
history of education and to promote research and publication. Desks, slates, pens, ink
and chalk, plus more sinister items such as a cane and a punishment book, suggest the
classroom atmosphere. There are also samples of work produced by trainee teachers and
detailed records of their progress. Also on display are books, scientific equipment and
needlework. A modern library on the history of education, records of educational
societies and archival material concerning education in the former West Riding county
are all open to researchers by appointment.
BUILDING: One room within the university.
OPENING TIMES: *All year*, Monday, Wednesday, Thursday and Friday: 2pm–4.30pm.
(Closed Tuesday, Saturday & Sunday.)
ADMISSION CHARGES: Free

🅿 ♿ WC ⟨P⟩ 🎥 ♁

DIRECTIONS: Leave Leeds city centre on the A660 to Ilkley. This is also the road to

Headingley Cricket Ground. Just north of the A58M and before Headingley, the university is on the left, in the area of Woodhouse. The museum is just off Woodhouse Lane.

LEEDS
Thackray Museum (medical) ❄ ✳

Beckett Street, Leeds, West Yorkshire LS9 7LN
TEL: (info hotline) 0113 2457084 or 0113 2444343 FAX: 0113 2470219
E-MAIL: info@thackraymuseum.org
WEBSITE: www.thackraymuseum.org
COLLECTION: An experience of the life and illness of Leeds, with a walk back in time through the slums of the city in 1840. The horrors of surgery without anaesthetics are explained, and there is a chance to enter the human gut. Among all these experiences there are displays about changing methods of surgery, from crude to high-tech. methods of today. A research library is available by appointment.
BUILDING: The former Leeds Union Workhouse, built in 1861.
OPENING TIMES: *All year*, Tuesday to Sunday: 10am–5pm. (Closed Monday.) Open Bank Holiday Mondays: 10am–5pm. Last admission 3pm. Closed for Christmas period and New Year.
ADMISSION CHARGES: ②

Ⓟ ♿ 🚻 🅿 ⚠ 🎥 👫

DIRECTIONS: From the M621 follow the signs for York (A64), then follow the museum's brown signs. From the north, take the A58 towards the city centre, then follow the brown signs. The museum is two miles to the north east of the city centre next to St James's Hospital.

OVERTON
The National Coalmining Museum For England ❄ ✳

Caphouse Colliery, New Road, Overton, Wakefield, West Yorkshire WF4 4RH
TEL: 01924 848806 FAX: 01924 840694
E-MAIL: info@ncm.org.uk WEBSITE: www.ncm.org.uk
COLLECTION: Riding the cage 450 feet underground, having collected a helmet and lamp from the lamp-room, brings the reality of working down the mine to life for the visitor. A one-hour tour underground with a local miner as guide enhances the experience. A shorter tour accessible by wheelchair and those not wanting to walk too far is also available. In addition to this experience the museum offers indoor exhibitions about mining and videos, outdoor machines, pit ponies and a working steam winder. There is a small train, a play area, a nature trail and a picnic area. Undergound filming equipment has to be checked by engineers to ensure it is safe. Usually smoking equipment and battery-operated equipment such as cameras and watches are not permitted under-

The National
Coalmining
Museum for
England,
Overton

ground. They can be deposited safely in the lamp-room. No children under five are allowed underground. A library is available. Telephone for details.

BUILDING: There was a shaft at the Caphouse site from 1789 to 1795. When the coal was finally exhausted in 1987 the colliery closed and the conversion to a museum began. It is a 17-acre site with some of the original buildings still standing. A modern visitor centre has been built.

OPENING TIMES: Daily: 10am–5pm. (Closed 24, 25, 26 December & 1 January.) Evening bookings may be made for parties of 19 or more.

ADMISSION CHARGES: ② (no charge for 16 years and younger or 60 years and over)
Ⓟ &. WC 🛈 ✕ ⚠ 🎥 👫

DIRECTIONS: The museum is on the A642 half-way between Wakefield and Huddersfield with easy signposted access from both the M1 and M62.

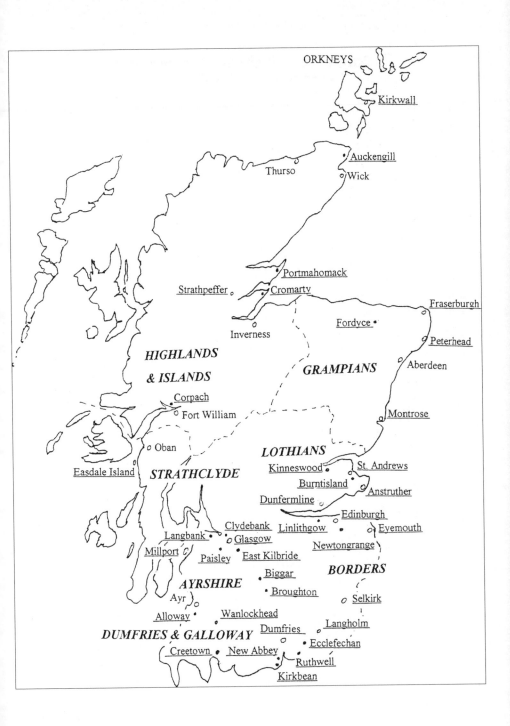

South West (includes Ayrshire and Dumfries and Galloway)

ALLOWAY
Burns Cottage and Museum ❄ ✳
Burns National Heritage Park, Murdoch's Lone, Alloway, Ayr KA7 4PQ
TEL: 01292 443700 FAX: 01292 441750
COLLECTION: Although he died when he was 37, Robert Burns produced poems and ballads in the Scottish dialect that made him famous and turned him into a Scottish icon. Built by Burns's father, the cottage now houses tableaux of the family, livestock and the famous bed where Robert Burns is said to have been born. The museum contains memorabilia such as an ink-bottle and leather case and quills, plus a pair of pistols. The collection of Burns's manuscripts is one of the most important in the world. Oil paintings illustrate Burns's life and times. Photography is allowed, except of the manuscript cases. Research facilities are available by prior arrangement.
BUILDING: The cottage, built in the 1750s, has whitewashed clay walls. It was an alehouse from before 1800 to 1880, but was bought by the Burns Monument Trustees. The museum was built in 1920. The tea-room is open June to September.
OPENING TIMES: *April to October*, daily: 9am–6pm. *November to March*, Monday to Saturday: 10am–4pm, Sunday: 12 noon–4pm.
ADMISSION CHARGES: ①

Ⓟ ♿ WC ⛱ ⚠ 🍴 ⚥

DIRECTIONS: Alloway is south of Ayr on the B7024 Maybole to Ayr road, which runs parallel to the A77. Coming into Alloway from Maybole, cross over the river into Monument Road. The museum is on your left after Greenfield Avenue.

BROUGHTON
The John Buchan Centre ✳
Broughton, Biggar ML12 6DT
TEL: 01899 830223 or (Biggar Museum Trust) 01899 221050
COLLECTION: Probably best known for his thriller *The Thirty-Nine Steps*, John Buchan did many other things with his life. He was a lawyer, politician, soldier, historian, biographer and finally governor-general of Canada. The museum explains his life and works and there is an extensive display of photographs illustrating his life from his schooldays in Glasgow to his last years. Over 100 of his books can be seen, plus his kilt and his uniforms. His sister Anna is also commemorated. As O. Douglas she wrote popular light novels.
BUILDING: The former church building, built around 1840, where Buchan's relatives

regularly worshipped and where he attended services when visiting Broughton. There is a ramp at the door but no disabled toilet.

OPENING TIMES: *Easter weekend*, Friday to Monday inclusive: 2pm–5pm. (Closed Tuesday to Thursday.) *May to mid- October*, daily: 2pm–5pm.

ADMISSION CHARGES: ①

Ⓟ ♿ 🆆🅲 ⚠ 🚻

DIRECTIONS: Broughton is on the A701, 29 miles from Edinburgh and 23 miles from Moffat. It is five miles from Biggar. The John Buchan Centre is at the south end of Broughton village.

CREETOWN
Gemrock Museum ❄ ✳

Chain Road, Creetown DG8 7HG

TEL: 01671 820357 or 820554

WEBSITE: www.gemrock.net

COLLECTION: Meteorites from space, a worldwide collection of natural, cut and polished crystals and gemstones, native gold from Scotland, malachite from Africa and jade from China fill this museum. Even fossil fish from Wyoming, USA, and a dinosaur egg and dung are on display. Owned and run by the Stephenson family, the museum houses one of the finest privately owned collections of gemstones, crystals and minerals. A new crystal cave has been developed.

BUILDING: Museum includes a themed tea-room, a Victorian prospector's drawing room with comfortable sofas and drawers full of gems and minerals. There is an Internet café.

OPENING TIMES: *Good Friday to 30 September*, daily: 9.30am–5.30pm. *1 October to 30 November*, daily: 10am–4pm. *1 December to 28 February*, weekends only: 10am–4pm (by appointment during the week). Closed 23 December to 31 January. *1 March to Good Friday*, daily: 10am–4pm. Last admittance half an hour before closing time.

ADMISSION CHARGES: ①

Ⓟ ♿ 🆆🅲 ▽ ⚠ 🎥 🚻

DIRECTIONS: Creetown is seven miles from Newton Stewart, eleven miles from Gatehouse-of-Fleet, just off the A75 Carlisle to Stranraer trunk road. Once in the village follow the signs to the Gemrock Museum.

DUMFRIES
Chrichton Museum (mental health care) ❄ ✳

Easterbrook Hall, Bankend Road, Dumfries DG1 4TG

TEL: 01387 244228

COLLECTION: Pioneering mental health care in S.W. Scotland for over 200 years, Chrichton Royal Mental Hospital had an amazing range of facilities for its patients. It was the result of Dr Easterbrook's grand scheme. He went to the USA and Canada on a study tour in 1913 to research ideas for the building. World War I prevented the completion of the building until 1938. Among its unusual facilities for the time were a library and reading room, a gym and squash court and a hydrotherapy department, including a swimming pool. Fascinatingly, it also offered patients a special magazine, and drama and painting as therapies. Some of the patients' paintings are on display in the museum, together with their case notes. The museum tells the story of the Chrichton family, the history of the hospital and its facilities. There is a cafeteria on the hospital site. Archive material is available to researchers.

BUILDING: Mrs Elizabeth Chrichton had been left a fortune by her husband to use for charitable purposes. She was determined to provide good accommodation and enlightened treatment for the mentally ill. Easterbrook Hall was the result, with its high quality of architecture, stained glass and antique furnishings.

OPENING TIMES: *All year*, Thursday & Friday: 1.30pm–4.30pm. *Easter to October*, plus Saturday: 1.30pm–4.30pm (or by appointment). (Closed Sunday to Wednesday.)

ADMISSION CHARGES: Free

Ⓟ ♿ ⚠ 🎥

DIRECTIONS: Travel south out of Dumfries on the B725. After the traffic lights, cross over a small roundabout where there is a petrol station. After this ignore the turning right to Kingholm Quay and almost immediately afterwards take the left fork to Bankend. Pass the Royal Infirmary on your right. The museum is on your right in Easterbrook Hall.

DUMFRIES
Dumfries and Galloway Aviation Museum ✳

Heathall Industrial Estate, Heathall, Dumfries DG1 3PH

TEL: 01387 251623 or 01387 259546 or 01387 720487 or (schools visit co-ordinator) 01387 256680

E-MAIL: david-reid-50@hotmail.com

WEBSITE: members.xoom.com/dgamuseum/

COLLECTION: The prize exhibit, the Supermarine Spitfire MK2, was recovered from the waters of Loch Doon and is undergoing restoration. The world's first operational jet fighter is represented by the famous Gloster Meteor T7. From the Vietnam War period there is a North American F-100 Super Sabre. Many other aircraft are on display. In addition the control tower contains a large collection of aviation artefacts and memorabilia. A library is available for research, by appointment..

BUILDING: The original three-storey control tower of the former RAF Dumfries, built in late World War II. The top floor is restored to the original layout. There is a picnic area. Due to the layout of the control tower, it is only partially accessible by wheelchair.

Scotland

OPENING TIMES: *Easter to October*, Saturday & Sunday: 10am–5pm. Closed weekdays except for *June, July & August*, Saturday & Sunday plus Wednesday evenings: 6pm–9pm. For other opening times contact the local Tourist Information Centre.

ADMISSION CHARGES: ①

🅿 ♿ 🆆🅲 🛉 ⚠ 📷 👫

DIRECTIONS: From the A75 Dumfries bypass take the A701 to Locharbriggs. At the roundabout, turn right into Tinwald Downs Road towards Dumfries Enterprise Park. Ignore the first and second turning to the right. At the third turning, opposite the playing field, turn right. The museum is on the left.

DUMFRIES
The Robert Burns Centre ❉ ✳

Mill Road, Dumfries DG2 7BE

TEL: 01387 264808

COLLECTION: The final years of Robert Burns's life are covered by this museum. He lived in Dumfries during the 1790s. Original documents and relics of the poet are on display and there is a scale model of Dumfries in the 1790s.

BUILDING: The 18th-century watermill on the west bank of the River Nith.

OPENING TIMES: *April to September*, Monday to Saturday: 10am–8pm, Sunday: 2pm–5pm. *October to March*, Tuesday to Saturday: 10am–1pm, 2pm–5pm. (Closed Sunday & Monday in the winter.)

ADMISSION CHARGES: Free

Ⓟ ♿ 🆆🅲 🛉 ✕ ⚠ 📷 👫

DIRECTIONS: See map.

**Robert Burns
Centre, Dumfries**

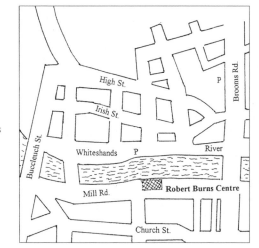

ECCLEFECHAN
Thomas Carlyle's Birthplace ✳

The Arched House, Ecclefechan, by Lockerbie, Dumfriesshire DG11 3DG

TEL: 01576 300666

WEBSITE: (National Trust for Scotland): www.nts.org.uk

COLLECTION: The famous thinker and writer Thomas Carlyle (1795–1881) was born in Ecclefechan but moved on to Edinburgh and London. He returned to Dumfriesshire and wrote most of his books, including *Sartor Resartus*. The museum is furnished mostly with items belonging to Thomas Carlyle and family and objects and letters belonging to Carlyle.

BUILDING: A Victorian house, first opened to the public in 1881. Only the downstairs area is accessible by wheelchair. There are no other facilities for the disabled.

OPENING TIMES: *1 April to 30 September*, daily: 1.30pm–5.30pm. (Last admission 5pm.)

ADMISSION CHARGES: ① (Free for National Trust members.)

P WC ♿

DIRECTIONS: Ecclefechan is four miles south of Lockerbie and two minutes from the M74. The museum is signposted and is in the centre of the village.

KIRKBEAN
John Paul Jones Museum ✳

118 English Street, Dumfries DG1 2DE

TEL: 01387 880613

COLLECTION: Known in the United States as the 'Father of the American Navy', John Paul (he added the Jones later) was born in poverty on the estate of Arbigland in 1747. At the age of 13 he signed up as seaman's apprentice for seven years. After many ships and adventures he became a captain at the age of 21. During the American Revolution he offered his services to the colonists and became first lieutenant in 1777. He raided England and captured ships. In 1781 he advised America on the establishment of its navy. The museum shows aspects of his life, including a reconstruction of his cabin on his ship *Bonhomie Richard*.

BUILDING: The cottage is John Paul Jones's birthplace and is furnished in the style of 1700. There is a picnic site with views of the Solway Firth.

OPENING TIMES: *April to September*, Tuesday to Sunday: 10am–5pm. (Closed Monday.) *July & August*, daily: 10am–5pm.

ADMISSION CHARGES: ①

P ♿ WC ♿ ☕ ♻

DIRECTIONS: The museum is situated in the grounds of Arbigland Estate near Kirkbean, 13 miles south west of Dumfries on the A710.

LANGHOLM
Clan Armstrong Museum ✳

Lodge Walk, Castleholm, Lanhgolm, Dumfriesshire

WEBSITE: www.armstrong.org

COLLECTION: For the Armstrong descendants this is the place to look at genealogical records and learn about the Armstrong clan. The museum also displays the history of the Western Scottish borderland and the part played in that history by the Armstrongs.

BUILDING: An old episcopalian church. The building is accessible by wheelchair but there are no other facilities.

OPENING TIMES: *Easter to mid-October,* Tuesday to Sunday: 1.30–4.30pm. (Closed Monday, except bank holidays.)

ADMISSION CHARGES: ①

Ⓟ ♿ 📷 👫

DIRECTIONS: Off the A7 Carlisle to Hawick road. Langholm is approximately 20 miles from each town. Lodge Walk is off to the left as you travel north, after the turning to Lockerbie. Langholm Castle is also in Lodge Walk.

NEW ABBEY
Shambellie House Museum of Costume ✳

Shambellie House, New Abbey, Dumfries DG2 8HQ

TEL: 01387 850375

WEBSITE: www.nms.ac.uk

COLLECTION: An obsessive collector, Charles Stewart searched through friends' attics, forgotten trunks and market stalls for interesting items of clothing. Many of the costumes and accessories from his collection are on display at Shambellie House. The clothes exhibited would have been worn within a country house setting between 1850 and 1950. Each room shows a different occasion and period. Embroideries and samplers are also to be seen.

BUILDING: Built in 1856 for the Stewart family, Shambellie House was designed by the Scottish architect David Bryce. In 1977 Charles Stewart, the great grandson of the original owner, donated the house and his unique costume collection to the National Museums of Scotland. It is possible to picnic on the lawn and walk through the wooded grounds. The route from the car-park to the house is steep. Use the courtesy telephone in the car-park if you need to bring your car to the front door.

OPENING TIMES: *1 April to 31 October,* daily: 11am–5pm. (Other dates and times by arrangement.)

ADMISSION CHARGES: ①

Ⓟ 🚻 ☕ ♿ 📷 👫

DIRECTIONS: Seven miles south of Dumfries on the A710 Solway Coast Road.

South West

RUTHWELL
Savings Banks Museum ❋ ❀
Ruthwell, Dumfries DG1 4NN
TEL: 01387 870640
E-MAIL: tsbmuseum@btinternet.com
COLLECTION: The dire poverty of his parishioners led Dr Duncan to develop his ideas for a savings bank. He was minister of the parish church in Ruthwell for nearly 50 years, and was determined to save his parishioners from the degradation of the poor rate. In 1810 he opened the world's first commercial savings bank, paying interest on its investors' modest savings. The museum houses a large collection of early home savings boxes, coins and banknotes from around the world. It is now managed by Lloyds TSB Scotland. The museum also has an important archive.
BUILDING: Access is possible by wheelchair with assistance but there are no other facilities.
OPENING TIMES: *Easter to 31 September*, daily: 10am–1pm & 2pm–5pm. *1 October to beginning of Easter*, Tuesday to Saturday: 10am–1pm & 2pm–5pm. (Closed Sunday & Monday.)
ADMISSION CHARGES: Free
Ⓟ Ⓢ 📽
DIRECTIONS: From Carlisle M6 take the A74 to Gretna. Then take the A75 to Annan and then the B724 to Ruthwell.

South East

EYEMOUTH
Eyemouth Museum (fishing) ❀
Auld Kirk, Manse Road, Eyemouth, Berwickshire TD14 5JE
TEL: 018907 50678
COLLECTION: 'Black Friday' for Eyemouth means 14 October 1881, when a terrible storm destroyed almost all of Eyemouth's fishing fleet and 189 fishermen lost their lives. The museum displays objects of industries related to fishing and rural life. A fisherman's cottage is one of the exhibits and so is information on the local fisher-lassies and the disaster of 1881. The museum was created to commemorate that event, and a large tapestry of the disaster hangs in the museum. It was created in 1981. Photography is allowed except of the tapestry.
BUILDING: An old church, the main part of which was built in 1812. The main exhibition area is accessible by wheelchair. There are no other facilities for the disabled.
OPENING TIMES: *Easter to the end of October. April, May, June & October*, Monday to

Saturday: 10am–5pm, Sunday: 12.30pm–2.30pm. *July & August*, Monday to Saturday: 9.30am–5pm, Sunday: 12 noon–5pm. *October*, Monday to Saturday: 10am–4pm. (Closed on Sunday.)

ADMISSION CHARGES: ①

🅿 ⚑ 🛆 ⛟ ⅲ

DIRECTIONS: Eyemouth is off the A1107 Coldingham to Ayton road. The museum is in the centre of Eyemouth in Auld Kirk Square.

SELKIRK
R. Clapperton Daylight Photographic Studio ✳

28 Scott's Place, Selkirk TD7 4DR

TEL: 01750 720523

E-MAIL: ian.w.mitchell@lineone.net

WEBSITE: lineone.net/~ian.w.mitchell/

COLLECTION: Three generations of the Clapperton family ran this photographic studio for over 120 years. The current proprietor is a member of the fourth generation. This is a working museum explaining life in a professional photographer's studio in 1900 and showing how a photograph was taken and printed from the original glass negative. There is also a large photographic archive of Selkirk and the Scottish borders and an ever-changing exhibition of photos.

BUILDING: An original Victorian daylight photographic studio built by Robert Clapperton in 1867.

OPENING TIMES: *May to August*, Friday, Saturday & Sunday: 2pm–4pm. (Closed Monday to Thursday but telephone for appointment at other times on 01750 720523.)

ADMISSION CHARGES: ①

🅿 ⛟

DIRECTIONS: In Selkirk go from the marketplace along the High Street towards the east and Victoria Hall. The studio is on the right after the car-park and police station. Coming from the south on the A7 turn right into the High Street.

SELKIRK
James Hogg Exhibition ✳

Aikwood Tower, Ettrick Valley, Selkirk TD7 5HJ

TEL: 01750 52253 FAX: 01750 52261

E-MAIL: steel@aikwoodscottishborders.com

WEBSITE: www.aikwoodscottishborders.com

COLLECTION: James Hogg (1770-1835) was born and lived most of his life as a shepherd and small farmer in Ettrick Forest. Although he had no formal schooling he became a man of letters, editing and writing for a magazine called *The Spy*, and writing a series of

Jacobite songs and his best-known novel *Confessions of a Justified Sinner.* Memorabilia, letters, first editions and storyboards help to tell James Hogg's story. The James Hogg exhibition will be moving to new premises in 2003.

BUILDING: Part of the 16th-century Aikwood Tower used by Hogg as a location in his prose and poetry.

OPENING TIMES: *May to September,* Tuesday, Thursday & Sunday: 2pm–5pm. (Closed Monday, Wednesday, Friday & Saturday.)

ADMISSION CHARGES: ①

Ⓟ ♿ WC ⚠ 🎦

DIRECTIONS: Four miles south west of Selkirk on the B7009 to Ettrick Bridge. From Selkirk, Aikwood Tower is off the B7009 to the left on Oakwood Farm Road.

WANLOCKHEAD
The Museum of Lead Mining ✳

Wanlockhead, by Biggar, Lanarkshire ML12 6UT

TEL: 01659 74387 FAX: 01659 74481

WEBSITE: www.leadminingmuseum.co.uk

COLLECTION: A number of buildings make up the museum. Three hundred years of gold and lead mining are brought to life through the guided tour of the lead mine, looking at the mining families' cottages, exploring the beam engine and original 17th-century smelt mills, plus panning for gold at the Panning Centre. There are displays of rare minerals relating to the area and a collection of lead-mining tools, lamps, etc. The second oldest workers' subscription library in Britain, established in 1756, with over 3,000 rare books, can also be found at this museum. Research facilities are available by prior appointment.

BUILDING: The miners' library is a Category A listed building. The other buildings formed part of the lead-mining site.

OPENING TIMES: *1 April to 31 October,* daily: 10am–4.30pm (last mine tour 4pm.)

ADMISSION CHARGES: ②

Ⓟ ♿ WC ⛴ ⚠ 🎦 👫

DIRECTIONS: Wanlockhead is on the B797 Menock to Leadhills and Abington road and south of the M74. Leave the M74 by junction 14 for Leadhills going north (there is no exit southbound). Or leave the M74 at junction 13 for Abington and then take the B797.

Edinburgh

Bank of Scotland Museum ✳

Bank of Scotland, The Mound, Bank Street, Edinburgh EH1 1YZ

TEL: (Bank of Scotland switchboard) 0131 529 288

COLLECTION: Banknote forgeries feature among the real notes, plus Scottish coins and a 17th-century bullion chest for putting it all in. To protect the bullion there is a collection of firearms and to illustrate the life and times of old Edinburgh there are maps, watercolours and engravings. The Bank of Scotland was established by the Parliament of Scotland in 1695 and is the oldest commercial bank in the UK still trading under its original name and statutes. Photography is allowed at the museum's discretion.

BUILDING: Opened in 1987, the museum is within the bank. The bank building, at the head of The Mound, was completed in 1806 and has been considerably altered since then but is still the headquarters of the Bank of Scotland.

OPENING TIMES: *Early June to early September*, Monday to Friday: 10am–4.45pm. (Closed Saturday & Sunday.) Group visits can be arranged at other times, contact the Archives number.

ADMISSION CHARGES: Free

🅿 🖾

DIRECTIONS: See map.

One guinea bank-note, Bank of Scotland Museum, Edinburgh

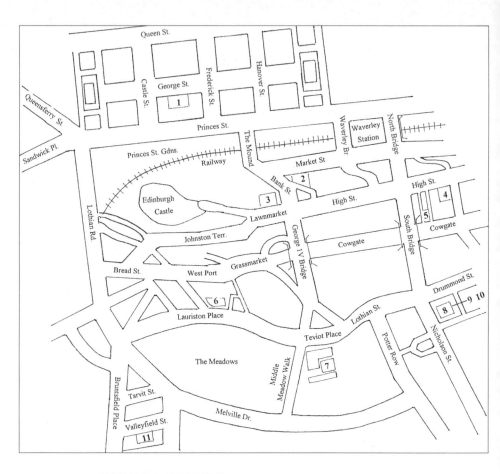

MUSEUMS OF EDINBURGH
Key for map

1. Grand Lodge of Scotland, Museum and Library
2. Bank of Scotland
3. The Writers' Museum
4. Museum of Childhood
5. Russell Collection of Early Keyboard Instruments
6. Museum of Fire
7. Edinburgh University Collection of Historical Musical Instruments
8. The Royal College of Surgeons Museum
9. Sir Jules Thorn Historical Exhibition
10. The Menzies Campbell Dental Museum
11. Edinburgh Scout Museum
12. The Cockburn Museum (see separate map)

Cockburn Museum (geology) ✼ ✱

Department of Geology and Geophysics, University of Edinburgh, Kings
Buildings, West Mains Road, Edinburgh EH9 3JF

TEL: 0131 6508527

E-MAIL: aspen@glg.ed.ac.uk

COLLECTION: This museum is mainly for undergraduate geology teaching and research.
There are about 120,000 specimens and 60 display cases. The museum is not suitable for
children, who will enjoy the Royal Museums of Scotland, just down the road.

BUILDING: The museum dates from about 1915 when geology became a separate dis-
cipline from natural history.

OPENING TIMES: *All year*, Monday to Friday: 9am–5pm. (Closed Saturday & Sunday.)

ADMISSION CHARGES: Free

Ⓟ&ᵂᶜ⊃✕⚠️📷

DIRECTIONS: See map.

**Cockburn Museum,
Edinburgh**

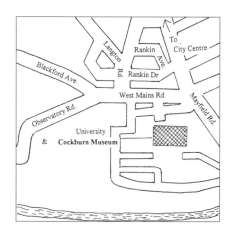

Edinburgh Scout Museum ✼ ✱

7 Valleyfield Street, Edinburgh, Lothian EH3 9LP

TEL: 0131 2293756 FAX: 0131 2219905

COLLECTION: Of the 12,000 items in the collection only about 4,000 are on display.
These consist of photographs, books, uniforms, badges and much more. There is an
exhibition of the history of the Scout movement in Edinburgh and worldwide.

BUILDING: One room in the Scout Headquarters, established in 1973.

OPENING TIMES: *All year*, Monday to Friday: 9.30am–4.30pm, but telephone first before
visiting. (Closed Saturday & Sunday.)

ADMISSION CHARGES: Free

P WC 🎥 ⛴

DIRECTIONS: See map.

Edinburgh University Collection of Historic Musical Instruments ❄ ✳

Reid Concert Hall, Bisto Square, Edinburgh EH8 9AG

TEL: 0131 6502423 FAX: 0131 6502425

E-MAIL: euchmi@ed.ac.uk

WEBSITE: www.music.ed.ac.uk/euchmi/

COLLECTION: Started in 1850 as a teaching collection, it opened as a museum in 1982. Over 1,000 items are on display, stringed, woodwind, brass and percussion instruments from Britain and around the world. The instruments are from the past 400 years. The histories of the instruments of the orchestra, wind band, music in theatre and dance, popular music, brass bands and more are explained. There is a new attraction called 'The Sound Laboratory', which allows a hands-on approach to how musical instruments work, with live sounds, physical models, computer displays and visible effects.

BUILDING: Built in 1859, the collection's galleries still have their original showcases. The museum retains a Victorian atmosphere.

OPENING TIMES: *All year*, Wednesday: 3pm–5pm, Saturday: 10am–1pm. (Closed Sunday to Tuesday & Thursday & Friday.) *During the Edinburgh International Festival*, Monday to Friday: 2pm–5pm in addition to other times.

ADMISSION CHARGES: Free

P WC ♿ 🎥

DIRECTIONS: See map.

Grand Lodge of Scotland Museum and Library ❄ ✳

Freemasons' Hall, 96 George Street, Edinburgh EH2 3DH

TEL: 0131 2255304 FAX: 0131 2253953

COLLECTION: The earliest reference to a Lodge in Edinburgh is 1491. The word 'Lodge' was used for the organisation of specialist builders engaged on cathedrals and castles. After Bannockburn there was little demand for building and the organisation combined with other crafts. It eventually opened its doors to other professions. The museum displays items relevant to Scottish Freemasonry such as glass, pottery, jewellery, manuscripts, regalia and photographs. The Grand Lodge has a substantial library.

BUILDING: Dating from 1912, the building was on the site of the earlier Grand Lodge.

OPENING TIMES: Monday to Friday: 9am–5pm. (Closed Saturday & Sunday.) Open other times by arrangement.

ADMISSION CHARGES: Free

P WC ♿ 🎥

DIRECTIONS: See map.

Museum of Childhood ❄ ☀

42 High Street (Royal Mile), Edinburgh EH1 1TG

TEL: 0131 5294142

COLLECTION: Five galleries display a vast range of toys including push-and-pull toys, dolls' prams, yachts and boats, slot-machines, a Punch and Judy, toy animals and zoos, farms and circuses. There is a large display of dolls and construction toys, a time tunnel and video presentations. Founded in 1955 by an Edinburgh councillor, Patrick Murray, who became its curator, the museum attracted a flood of donations.

BUILDING: An 18th-century tenement. The museum was extended in 1986 and was linked to a building on the west side, which was originally a theatre or music room, built in 1760. A lift was installed for use by the disabled.

OPENING TIMES: *All year*, Monday to Saturday: 10am–5pm. *During the Edinburgh Festival* also Sunday: 2pm–5pm. Otherwise closed on Sunday.

ADMISSION CHARGES: Free

🅿 ♿ 🚾 ⚠ 📹 🚻

DIRECTIONS: See map.

Museum of Fire ❄ ☀

Lothian and Borders Fire Brigade, Brigade Headquarters, Lauriston Place, Edinburgh EH3 9DE

TEL: 0131 2282401 (ask for Community Education)

COLLECTION: Ranged around the floor of the fire station stand horse-drawn and manual fire engines and those that used steam and motorised pumps. These date from the 1800s, but there are fire-related items that go back as far as 1426. The museum tells the story of the oldest municipal fire brigade in the United Kingdom formed in 1824 after a series of disastrous fires in the city of Edinburgh.

BUILDING: A fire station and brigade headquarters.

OPENING TIMES: Telephone in advance to make an appointment to see the museum. Open *all year*, Monday to Friday: 9am–4.30pm. (Closed Saturday & Sunday.) Closed the first two weeks in August for maintenance, and for two weeks over Christmas and New Year. Priority is given to school parties.

ADMISSION CHARGES: Free

🅿 ♿ 🚾 📹 🚻

DIRECTIONS: See map.

The Royal College of Surgeons' Museums ❄ ☀
Sir Jules Thorn Historical Exhibition and The Menzies Campbell Dental Museum

9 Hill Square, Edinburgh EH8 9DW

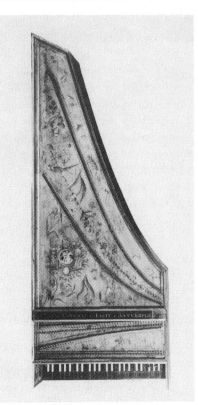

Joannes Couchet
harpsichord, Russell
Collection of Early
Keyboard Instruments,
Edinburgh

TEL: 0131 5271600 FAX: 0131 5576406

COLLECTION: The Royal College of Surgeons in Edinburgh can claim to be one of the oldest surgical corporations in the world. The Town Council granted the barber surgeons their 'Charter of Rights and Privileges' in 1505. The Sir Jules Thorn Exhibition illustrates the scope of modern surgery. The display also describes the history of surgery and Edinburgh's contribution to surgical practice. The Menzies Campbell Dental Museum incorporates the Menzies Campbell collection of dental instruments, artefacts and art. It is one of the largest dental collections in the country and shows the development of dentistry from its early days to modern times.

BUILDING: Designed by William Henry Playfair and completed in 1832, it contains a meeting hall, museum, lecture room and library.

OPENING TIMES: For both museums, Monday to Friday: 2pm–4pm. (Closed Saturday & Sunday.)

ADMISSION CHARGES: Free

🅿 wc

DIRECTIONS: The Dental Museum is on the second floor. The Sir Jules Thorn Exhibition is behind the main building of the college and not immediately visible from the main street. See map for position of Hill Square.

Russell Collection of Early Keyboard Instruments ❄ ✳

St Cecilia's Hall, Niddry Street, Cowgate, Edinburgh EH1 1LJ
TEL: 0131 6502423 FAX: 0131 6502425
WEBSITE: www.music.ed.ac.uk/russell/index/html
COLLECTION: Fifty-one instruments, mostly precursors of the piano, are displayed in galleries next to the Concert Hall. There are harpsichords, spinets and virginals, which produce sound by mechanically plucking the strings. In addition there is the earliest extant English grand piano and a number of small pipe organs. Raymond Russell collected a large number of early keyboard instruments and decided to give his collection to a British university. Edinburgh seized the opportunity and continued to add to the original collection and it is now one of the world's most important collections of early keyboard instruments.
BUILDING: St Cecilia's Hall is the oldest purpose-built concert hall in Scotland. The original building dates from 1763 and is now owned by the University of Edinburgh. The concert hall is a special venue for recitals of early music.
OPENING TIMES: Wednesday & Saturday: 2pm–5pm. (Closed Sunday to Tuesday & Thursday & Friday.) *During the Edinburgh International Festival*, Monday to Saturday: 10.30am–12.30am. (Closed Sunday.)
ADMISSION CHARGES: ①

🅿 wc ♿ 🎥

DIRECTIONS: See map.

The Writers' Museum ❄ ✳

Lady Stair's House, Lady Stair's Close, Lawnmarket, Edinburgh EH1 2PA
TEL: 0131 5294901 FAX: 0131 2205057
COLLECTION: Robert Burns's writing desk and Sir Walter Scott's chessboard, dining table and printing press form part of this collection dedicated to the lives and works of Scotland's great literary figures. The museum concentrates upon Robert Burns (1759–96), Sir Walter Scott (1771-1832) and Robert Louis Stevenson (1850–94). Portraits and manuscripts are also on display, and other writers are featured in a programme of temporary exhibitions.
BUILDING: Lady Stair's House, built in 1622 with some narrow stairs to negotiate. In the Makar's court outside are inscriptions commemorating famous Scottish writers, from the 14th century to today.

OPENING TIMES: *All year*, Monday to Saturday: 10am–5pm. (Closed on Sunday except during August, when it is open Sunday: 2pm–5pm in addition to other times.)

ADMISSION CHARGES: Free

🅿 WC ⒮

DIRECTIONS: See map.

Lothian

LINLITHGOW
Linlithgow Canal Centre ✳

Manse Road Basin, Linlithgow, West Lothian EH49 6AJ

TEL: (answering machine) 01506 671215

E-MAIL: info@lucs.org.uk/index.html

WEBSITE: www.lucs.org.uk

COLLECTION: The whole site is run by Linlithgow Union Canal Society, which is a voluntary organisation. There are canal boats for hire and available for trips. The museum tells the history of the canal, how it is supplied with water and how it has been used for both work and leisure. Photographs and artefacts associated with the canal are exhibited. The museum is suitable for children over the age of 14. A large collection of original boat manifests and waybills is not on display.

BUILDING: The museum is housed in the former canal stable-row houses. There is a small picnic area. Items are for sale at the counter.

OPENING TIMES: *Easter to mid-October*, Saturday & Sunday: approx. 2pm–5pm. (Closed weekdays.)

ADMISSION CHARGES: Free

🅿 ♿ WC ☕ 📷 👫

DIRECTIONS: From Edinburgh on the M9 in the direction of Stirling, exit for Linlithgow (A803). At mini-roundabout turn left and follow signs for the Canal Basin. From Glasgow on the M8 in the direction of Edinburgh, exit for Falkirk (A801), then follow signs for Linlithgow (A706). At T-junction with A803 turn right along the High Street. At mini-roundabout bear right and follow signs for the Canal Basin.

NEWTONGRANGE
Scottish Mining Museum ❅ ✳

Lady Victoria Colliery, Newtongrange, Midlothian EH22 4QN

TEL: 0131 6637519 FAX: 0131 6541618

E-MAIL: enquiries@scottishminingmuseum.com

WEBSITE: www.scottishminingmuseum.com

COLLECTION: Opened in 1890, the new colliery belonging to the Marquess of Lothian was named after his wife, Victoria. The colliery introduced innovative technologies such as steel pit-props and the use of electricity for power as well as light. It was closed in 1981 and the surface buildings were turned into a visitor centre and museum. The story of coal is told and the life of the Scottish coal-mining communities illustrated. There is an extensive collection of mining artefacts. A new Operations Centre allows the visitor to solve the problems faced by miners and a re-created underground roadway and coal-face bring the experience to life. The pithead and the massive winding engine are on view. A research library is available by appointment.

BUILDING: The original colliery buildings of 1890, now a three-storey visitor centre.

OPENING TIMES: *February to November*, daily: 10am–5pm. *December & January*, daily: 10am–4pm. Arrive at least an hour before closing time. Check closing times over the festive period.

ADMISSION CHARGES: ②

Ⓟ ♿ 🚾 ▯△ 🎥 🏃

DIRECTIONS: From the eastern end of Edinburgh city bypass (at Sheriffhall Round-about) follow the signs for Newtongrange and the museum for approximately three miles. From the south, follow the A7 north from Galashiels.

Glasgow and Strathclyde

GLASGOW
Heatherbank Museum of Social Work ❄ ✳

Glasgow Caledonian University, City Campus, Cowcaddens Road,
Glasgow G4 0BA

TEL: 0141 3318637 FAX: 0141 3313005

E-MAIL: A.Ramage@gcal.ac.uk

WEBSITE: www.lib.gcal.ac.uk/heatherbank

COLLECTION: Divided into seven main areas, the museum explains, by means of displays and artefacts, the history of housing, poor houses, church social care, health, childcare, crime and disability. Its aim is to increase public awareness of the social welfare needs of society, particularly those who are disadvantaged. In addition the museum holds a large number of resources, which are available for consultation. There is a book library of 2,000 titles, a picture library of 7,000 prints, slides and negatives, also bound journals, an ephemera library and an audio-visual library, commissioned videos and audio-tapes. These resources are listed on the museum's website.

BUILDING: One room inside the Glasgow Caledonian University buildings, built around 1980. Toilets and disabled toilet, café and shop are available on campus.

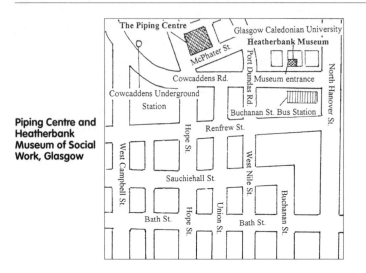

Piping Centre and Heatherbank Museum of Social Work, Glasgow

OPENING TIMES: *All year*, Monday to Friday: 9am–4.30pm. (Closed Saturday & Sunday.)
ADMISSION CHARGES: Free

🅿 ♿ 🎦 🚻

DIRECTIONS: See map.

GLASGOW
Museum of Piping ❋ ✳

30–34 McPhater Street, Cowcaddens, Glasgow G4 0HW
TEL: 0141 3530220 FAX: 0141 3531570
WEBSITE: www.thepipingcentre.co.uk
COLLECTION: The sound of the Great Highland Bagpipe has always evoked the image of the Highlands of Scotland. In a series of glass cases the museum displays a large range of pipes from the smallest to the largest, illustrating how the pipes spread throughout the world. The display is accompanied by a commentary (headsets available in five languages), which gives the fascinating facts and folklore and even the sound of the individual pipes. There is also information on famous pipers and a small audio-visual theatre. Archival material is being collected.
BUILDING: Housed in a Category B listed building, formerly a Free Church of Scotland church and manse before renovation in 1997. As well as the museum, the Piping Centre incorporates facilities for tuition, practice and performance, conferences, banqueting and catering, and it also has a small hotel.
OPENING TIMES: Museum: *March/April to mid-September/October*, daily: 10am–4.30pm. *November to March*, Monday to Saturday: 10am–4.30pm. (Closed Sunday.)

Scotland

ADMISSION CHARGES: ①

🅿 ♿ 🆆🅲 🄿 ✕ Ⓢ 📷 👫

DIRECTIONS: See map.

GLASGOW
Scotland Street School Museum ❄ ✳

225 Scotland Street, Glasgow G5 8QB

TEL: 0141 2870500

COLLECTION: The building was designed by Charles Rennie Mackintosh in 1903–06. In 1872 the Education Act Scotland established a school board in every district in Scotland. In 1903 the Glasgow board decided that the Kingston area needed a school and they commissioned an architect, which was unusual, since the normal practice was for the design to be done by a firm. The interior of the school is restored to reveal classrooms, cookery room, drill hall and cloakrooms. The history of the school from 1906 to 1979 is explained, as is the history of education in Scotland. There is an audio-visual room and there are temporary exhibitions. Photography is allowed only in some areas. Research requests should be made in writing to the curator.

BUILDING: The building has been renovated to the original Mackintosh designs, with impressive leaded glass towers, a magnificent entrance hall and unique stonework. A lift has recently been installed. There is a vending café.

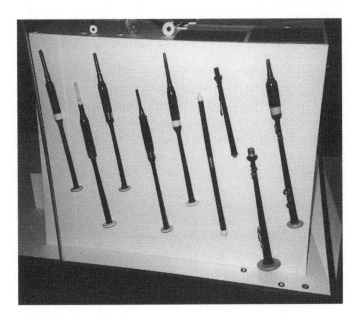

Museum of
Piping,
Glasgow

Glasgow and Strathclyde

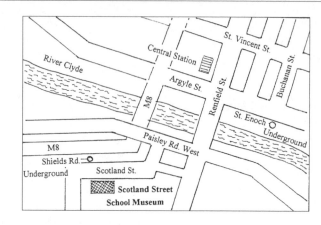

Scotland Street School Museum, Glasgow

OPENING TIMES: *All year*, Monday to Thursday: 10am–5pm, Friday & Sunday: 11am–5pm.

ADMISSION CHARGES: Free

DIRECTIONS: See map.

STRATHCLYDE
Biggar Gasworks Museum ✳

Gasworks Road, Biggar, Lanarkshire ML12

TEL: 01899 221050

E-MAIL: Margaret@bmtrust.freeserve.co.uk

COLLECTION: The process of heating coal in closed containers known as 'retorts' to obtain gas had been discovered during the 18th century. Biggar gasworks began to supply gas in 1839 and was in use for over 160 years. After it had ceased to function the site was selected for preservation and has been developed into a museum of the gas industry to tell the story of gas from its beginnings to the present day. Old gas appliances such as cookers and fires plus gas industry appliances are on display.

BUILDING: The original buildings used as a gasworks. In 1914 the works was virtually rebuilt and new purification equipment was installed.

OPENING TIMES: *June to September*, daily: 2pm–5pm.

ADMISSION CHARGES: ①

DIRECTIONS: Entering Biggar from Glasgow the Cross Keys Hotel is on your left. Go up the lane just before the hotel to the gasworks. It is possible to take the car up to the museum.

CLYDEBANK
Clydebank Museum (sewing machines) ❄ ✳
Town Hall, Dumbarton Road, Clydebank G81 1UE

TEL: 01389 738702 FAX: 0141 9528260

E-MAIL: curator@clybankmuseum.sol.co.uk

COLLECTION: Many sewing machine collectors come from all over the world to see this collection of Singer and non-Singer sewing machines. There is a whole range of machines from different periods and a technical archive from the Singer Manufacturing Company. The museum also has collections on life in past and present Clydebank and wartime Blitz collections. Photography requires permission from Reception.

BUILDING: Situated beside the shipyard where many of the famous liners of the Clyde were built. Café nearby.

OPENING TIMES: *All year*, Monday, Wednesday, Thursday & Friday: 2pm–4.30pm, Tuesday & Saturday: 10am–4.30pm.

ADMISSION CHARGES: Free

ⓟ ♿ wc ⚠ 🎥 ♨

DIRECTIONS: Leave the A82 Dumbarton to Glasgow road at a roundabout and turn south down Kilbowie Road, the A8014, past the Singer railway station to a T-junction. Turn right on to the A814, Dumbarton road. The museum is on the left, not far along the road.

EAST KILBRIDE
Hunter House (story of pioneering medical brothers) ✳
Maxwelton Road, East Kilbride G74 3LW

TEL: 01355 261261

COLLECTION: The story of the Hunter brothers ends with fame and fortune in the world of medicine and science. John and William were raised in the house, now the museum, in the 18th century and made discoveries that still influence modern surgery and anatomy. Their story is told through state-of-the-art interactive technology and computers and on two video screens and a slide screen in the theatre. There is also a display about the story of East Kilbride. Photography is allowed on request. Limited research facilities are available.

BUILDING: Original building in which the Hunter brothers were born. The museum is on two floors. A project room is available for use.

OPENING TIMES: *1 April to 30 September*, Monday to Friday: 12 noon–4pm, Saturday, Sunday & public holidays: 12 noon–5pm.

ADMISSION CHARGES: Free

ⓟ ♿ wc ⛛ ⚠ 🎥 ♨

DIRECTIONS: See map (p. 186).

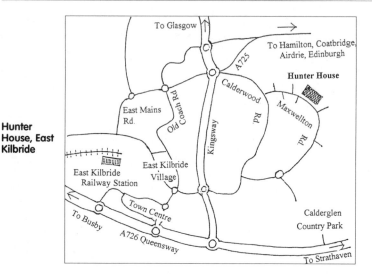

Hunter House, East Kilbride

LANGBANK
The Dolly Mixture ❄ ❉

Finlaystone Country Estate, Langbank, Renfrewshire PA14 6TJ

TEL/FAX: (Finlaystone House) 01475 540285

E-MAIL: info@finlaystone.co.uk

WEBSITE: www.finlaystone.co.uk

COLLECTION: In 1903 Clare Spurgin was given a china doll and her interest in dolls developed as a result of her study of anthropology and extensive travel. Her daughter Jane MacMillan has added to the collection, which now consists of over 700 dolls from around the world. There are dolls of all kinds, including a national character doll with a bisque head from the USA dated around 1896, Chinese mission dolls from the 1920s and an Austrian felt doll from 1932. Research facilities are available by appointment.

BUILDING: The museum is in the converted stable block on the Finlaystone Country Estate, which has a large house, originally 14th century, and gardens and woodlands to explore. An entrance fee has to be paid to enter Finlaystone first. The entrance cost for the museum is minimal. Only the lower half of the museum is accessible by wheelchair.

OPENING TIMES: Museum: *May to September*, daily: 12 noon–4.30pm. *October to April*, Saturday & Sunday: 12 noon–4.30pm. (Closed weekdays in winter.) Finlaystone Country Estate is open all year, daily: 10.30am–5pm.

ADMISSION CHARGES: Museum: ① Finlaystone Estate: ①

Ⓟ ♿ 🚻 ⛲ ✕ Ⓐ 🍴 👪

DIRECTIONS: Finlaystone is on the A8 Langbank to Greenock road, west of Langbank, ten minutes west of Glasgow Airport, 30 minutes from Glasgow. Follow the Scottish Tourist Board signs to the estate.

MILLPORT
University Marine Biological Station Museum ❈ ✳

Millport, Isle of Cumbrae, Strathclyde, KA28 0EG

TEL: 01475 530581   FAX: 01475 530601

E-MAIL: tracy.price@millport.gla.ac.uk

WEBSITE: www.gla.ac.uk/Acad/Marine/

COLLECTION: The displays of simple marine science are still housed within the drawers of a replica of Noah's Ark, from the Robertson collection. There is a comprehensive collection of animal species of the Clyde sea area and a video display on aquaculture.

BUILDING: The museum is in the Marine Biological Station. There is an aquarium in the same building.

OPENING TIMES: *October to May*, Monday to Thursday: 9.30am–12.15pm & 2pm–4.45pm, Friday: 9.30am–1.15pm & 2pm–4.15pm. (Closed Saturday & Sunday.) *June to September*, the above times and dates plus Saturday: 10am–12.15pm & 2pm–4.15pm. (Closed Sunday.)

ADMISSION CHARGES: ①

🅿 ♿ 🆆🅒 ⚠ 🖼 🚻

DIRECTIONS: The Marine Station is on the shores of the Isle of Cumbrae in the Firth of Clyde, one hour's drive from Glasgow.

PAISLEY
Coats Observatory ❈ ✳

49 Oakshaw Street West, Paisley PA1 2DR

TEL: 0141 8892013

COLLECTION: The first equipment, bought for the Observatory in the early 1880s, was a five-inch equatorial telescope. Thomas Coats bought the telescope and had the Observatory built. Other equipment was added. Weather-recording activities were shifted to the Observatory and seismic recorders were added. However, activity at the Observatory slowly dwindled and in 1957, with the retirement of the last curator, the building ceased to function and was offered to Paisley Town Council. After the equipment was overhauled the building was finally re-opened to the public. There are displays of astronomy, meteorology and seismicity.

BUILDING: Designed by John Honeyman and opened in 1883. It was refurbished in the 1970s and a new dome replaced the old one in 1996, built to the original specifications and using original materials. The Observatory is now the major seismic station in south west Scotland.

OPENING TIMES: *All year*, Tuesday to Saturday: 10am–5pm, Sunday: 2pm–5pm (last entry 15 minutes before closing). Closed Monday but open on public holidays.

ADMISSION CHARGES: Free

🅿 🖼

DIRECTIONS: Oakshaw Street West runs parallel to and is north of the High Street. The Observatory is behind the Paisley Museum and Art Gallery.

Highlands and Islands

AUCKENGILL
Northlands Viking Centre ✻

The Old School, Auckengill, Keiss by Wick, Caithness KW1 4XP

TEL: 01955 607776

COLLECTION: Models of a Viking longship and the Viking settlement at Freswick help tell the story of these invaders, who came over the sea from Scandinavia and settled in Shetland, Orkney and Caithness. The museum has genuine examples of currency from the time.

BUILDING: One main room of an old primary school.

OPENING TIMES: *May to September*, daily: 10am–4pm.

ADMISSION CHARGES: ①

🅿 ♿ 🚾 ⚠ 🖼 👫

DIRECTIONS: On the main A9 road about ten miles north of Wick en route to John O' Groats.

CORPACH
Treasures of the Earth ❊ ✻

Main Street, Corpach, Fort William PA33 7JR

TEL: 01397 772283

COLLECTION: A six-foot towering amethyst features amongst some of the world's finest and largest crystals and gemstones. These stones are displayed in a simulation cave, a cavern and mining scenes. Nuggets of gold, silver, aquamarines, garnets, rubies, opals and diamonds are on display.

BUILDING: An old church, converted to be on two levels.

OPENING TIMES: *July, August & September*, daily: 9.30am–7pm. *November to June*, daily: 10am–5pm. Closed 25, 26 December & 3 to 31 January.

ADMISSION CHARGES: ①

🅿 ♿ 🚾 ⚠ 🖼 👫

DIRECTIONS: Corpach is four miles west of Fort William on the A830 to Mallaig.

CROMARTY
Hugh Miller's Cottage ✳

Church Street, Cromarty, Ross-shire IV11 8XA

TEL: 01381 600245 FAX: 01381 600391

E-MAIL: fgostwick@nts.org.uk

WEBSITE: www.hughmiller.org

COLLECTION: A self-taught scientist, a major collector of folklore and a crusading national newspaper editor, Hugh Miller (1802–56) was born in Cromarty and was one of the great Scots of his age. He was the first to discover tropical fossil fish in old red sandstone and many other fossil species. His collection of over 6,000 fossil specimens became the core of the national fossil collection in the Royal Museum in Edinburgh. He also produced a number of books on fossils. The museum is furnished as it would have been in Miller's time and displays some of his works, and there is a geology museum in one of the rooms containing specimens and reconstructions of species he described in his books. Research facilities are available on request.

BUILDING: The cottage was Hugh Miller's birthplace and has been open to the public since 1890. A new building next door is opening soon and will contain more information on Hugh Miller and his fossil finds.

OPENING TIMES: *1 May–30 September*, daily: 1.30pm–5.30pm.

ADMISSION CHARGES: ① (Free to National Trust members.)

🅿 ⛹

DIRECTIONS: Cromarty is on the tip of the Black Isle and north of Fortrose.

EASDALE ISLAND
Easdale Island Folk Museum and Heritage Centre ✳

Heritage Centre, 13A, Ellenabeich, by Oban, Argyll PA34 TB

TEL: 01852 300449/01852 300370 FAX: 01852 300473/01852 300370

E-MAIL: (Heritage Centre) pwithall@sol.co.uk

WEBSITE: (Heritage Centre & Easdale Island) www.slate.org.uk.

COLLECTION: Once a thriving centre of slate-quarrying, Easdale Island is now a unique car-free site that tells the story of this industry. Both inside and outside the museum, the world of slate is everywhere, and there is a walk around the island for the visitor to see the various quarries, the engine and boiler houses and much more. John Campbell, Earl of Breadalbane, who owned vast stretches of Scotland, set up the Marble and Slate Company of Netherlon in 1745 and bought Easdale Island's slate-quarrying industry. The last commercial slate was taken from Easdale quarries in 1911. The museum tells the story of the slate industry and also the life of the people on the island and the Breadalbanes. The Scottish Slate Islands Heritage Centre, which is part of the museum, is situated near to the jetty for the ferry and the car-park. This holds a wider collection of material about the islands. Photography requires permission. Research facilities are available by appointment.

BUILDING: The museum was built about 40 years ago. A restaurant and bar are also on the island in two of the old quarriers' cottages. There is a fish restaurant next to the Heritage Centre. The Centre is in one of the original quarry cottages. Accommodation is available on the island. A five-minute ferry service runs to Easdale Island throughout the day. The ferry operates on call. Getting a wheelchair onto the ferry is a problem at low tide.

OPENING TIMES: Museum: *1 April to mid-October*, daily: 10.30am–5.30pm. Heritage Centre: *March & April*, daily: 9. 30am–5pm. *May to September*, daily: 9.30am–7pm. Limited opening arrangements can be made during October & November by application to the director.

ADMISSION CHARGES: Museum: ① and Heritage Centre: ① (a separate charge for each). A joint admission to both museums, plus the ferry fare, is available.

🅿 ♿ 🆆🅲 🎥 👫

DIRECTIONS: Easdale Island is south west of Oban. From the A816 Oban to Lochgilphead road, take the B844 and continue over Clachan bridge to Seil Island. Continue on the B844 to Balvicar crossroads and turn right for Ellenabeich.

KIRKWALL
Orkney Wireless Museum ✹

Kiln Corner, Kirkwall, Orkney KW15 1LB

TEL: 01856 871400

COLLECTION: Originally a private collection of all things electric owned by the late Jim MacDonald, it is now owned by a charitable trust. Orkney's wartime history is represented in the museum, with transmitters for short-range speech to fighters and long-range Morse to bombers, plus many other items. Early radios are also on display and there are some rare 1920s wireless sets, as well as a stand that traces the history of portable wireless up to the transistor radio.

BUILDING: The museum opened in 1983 and moved to Kirkwall in 1997.

OPENING TIMES: *April to September*, Monday to Saturday: 10am–4.30pm, Sunday: 2.30pm–4.30pm.

ADMISSION CHARGES: ①

🅿 ♿ 🆆🅲 ♿ 🎥 👫

DIRECTIONS: The museum is near the harbour, on the corner of Harbour Street and near the car-park.

'Tuning in',
Orkney
Wireless
Museum,
Kirkwall

PORTMAHOMACK
Tarbat Discovery Centre ❄ ✳

Tarbatness Road, Portmahomack, Tain, Ross-shire IV20 1YA

TEL: 01862 871351 FAX: 01862 871361

E-MAIL: info@tarbat-discovery.co.uk

WEBSITE: www.tarbat-discovery.co.uk

COLLECTION: Excavation at Portmahomack by the University of York has made some exciting discoveries. Wonderful carved Pictish sculpture is now on show, and the workings of the archaeologists are explained. The displays reveal the story of the Picts and also the history of Tarbat through the centuries. Research is possible.

BUILDING: A restored 18th-century Category A listed church, with a long history. The church became redundant in 1980 and was thoroughly excavated before being restored. The discoveries from this research are described inside the building. A lecture room is available. Except for the crypt the building is accessible by wheelchair. There are restaurants locally.

OPENING TIMES: *1 Saturday in March to 1 Saturday in May,* daily: 2pm–5pm. *1 Sunday in May to last Saturday in September,* daily: 10am –5.30pm. *From last Sunday in September until 23 December,* daily: 2pm–5pm. Closed January & February. Groups may visit outside these hours by appointment.

ADMISSION CHARGES: ②

Ⓟ ♿ ⓌⒸ ♿ 🏛

DIRECTIONS: Portmahomack is east of Tain. From the A9 Inverness to Tain road, take the B9165 east to Portmahomack. The Discovery Centre overlooks the village.

ROSEMARKIE
Groam House Museum (Pictish Centre) ❄ ✳

High Street, Rosemarkie, Ross-shire IV10 8UF

TEL: 01381 620961 FAX: 01381 621730

E-MAIL: groamhouse@ecosse.net

COLLECTION: The Picts were a farming people, who adopted Christianity in the 6th century. Although little is known about the people themselves, they left behind intricately carved stones. The museum has a display of these stones found in the village. The magnificent cross-slab is the centrepiece of the collection. The museum exhibits information about other Pictish stones and even has a Pictish harp for the visitor to play. It also holds the George Bain collection of his original Celtic artwork. Upstairs in the mezzanine gallery are temporary exhibitions. Photography for amateur purposes only and no photographs in the upstairs gallery. For research purposes there is a comprehensive collection of photographs of the Pictish stones of Scotland and a local archive for comparing the old Black Isle villages with those of today.

BUILDING: An 18th-century house, named by its previous owner who came from Groam near Beauly. The building was used as a drapers, a grocers, a tea-shop and a private house until 1974, when it was given to the town council. The museum opened in 1980. Only downstairs is accessible by wheelchair. There are no other facilities for the disabled. Toilets are in the car-park near by.

OPENING TIMES: *1 May to 30 September,* Monday to Saturday: 10 am–5pm, Sunday: 2pm–4.30pm. *1 October to 30 April,* Saturday & Sunday: 2pm–4pm. (Closed Monday to Friday.) *Easter week,* daily: 2pm–4.30pm.

ADMISSION CHARGES: ①

🅿 ♿ ⚠ 📹 ♁

DIRECTIONS: Rosemarkie is south of Cromarty on the A832 road to Tore. Groam House is in the High Street near and on the same side of the road as the car-park and the Plough Inn.

STRATHPEFFER
Highland Museum of Childhood ✳

The Old Station, Strathpeffer, Ross and Cromarty IV14 9DH

TEL: 01997 421031

E-MAIL: info@hmoc.freeserve.co.uk

WEBSITE: www.hmoc.freeserve.co.uk

COLLECTION: Home to the Angela Kellie Doll and Toy Collection, the museum has examples of almost every type of doll, from wooden to bisque to wax. There are automata and character and baby dolls. Doll costume is also on display. There is a more serious message as well, for the museum tells of the impact of poor nutrition and disease on family health and explains ancient customs.

BUILDING: A restored Victorian railway station from the 1880s. In fine weather it is possible to eat the coffee-shop food sitting out on the platform under a protective awning. The museum is accessible by wheelchair, but the nearest disabled toilet is 500 metres away in the village.

OPENING TIMES: *April, May, June, September, October,* Monday to Saturday: 10am–5pm, Sunday: 2pm–5pm. *July & August,* Monday to Friday: 10am–7pm, Saturday: 10am–5pm, Sunday: 2pm–5pm. Closed November through to March, but can be opened by appointment.

ADMISSION CHARGES: ①

Ⓟ ♿ 🚾 ☕ ⚠ 📷 👫

DIRECTIONS: Strathpeffer is north of Inverness and west of Dingwall on the A834.

Tayside and Grampian (includes Fife)

ANSTRUTHER
Scottish Fisheries Museum ❄ ✳

St Ayles, Harbourhead, Anstruther, Fife KY10 3AB

TEL/FAX: 01333 310628

E-MAIL: andrew@fisheriesmuseum.freeserve.co.uk

COLLECTION: Fourteen real boats are on display. One of these is the *Reaper*, a fully restored 1901 herring drifter. Visitors can join the crew and see the fishing gear that was used. Skilled craftsmen work in the boatyard. A fisherman's cottage shows the life of a fisher family and there are photographs, paintings and boat models. Photography is allowed by arrangement with the curator. A library is available by appointment only.

BUILDING: A collection of buildings, some listed, some not.

OPENING TIMES: *April to October,* weekdays: 10am–5.30pm, Sunday: 11am–5pm. *November to March,* weekdays: 10am–4.30pm, Sundays: 12 noon–4.30pm.

ADMISSION CHARGES: ②

Ⓟ ♿ 🚾 ☕ ⚠ 📷 👫

DIRECTIONS: Anstruther is south of St Andrews and east of Leven on the A971 coast road. The museum is by the harbour. Follow Shore Street with the sea on your right. There is a car-park on your right. The museum is on your left just after East Green Road to the left.

BURNTISLAND
Burntisland Edwardian Fairground Museum ❋ ✳

102 High Street, Burntisland, Fife.

TEL: (Library) 01592 872781

COLLECTION: Walk through the sights and sounds of the town's fair in 1910. Based on a painting of the scene by local artist Andrew Young, the museum has re-created the fair by means of theatre-set displays, graphic panels, artefacts, rides, stalls and side-shows.

BUILDING: In one room above the library.

OPENING TIMES: Library hours. *All year (except public holidays),* Monday, Wednesday, Friday & Saturday: 10am–1pm & 2pm–5pm, Tuesday & Thursday: 10am–1pm & 2pm–7pm. (Closed Sunday.)

ADMISSION CHARGES: Free

🅿 📵 ⛴ ⛹

DIRECTIONS: Burntisland is south west of Kirkcaldy on the A921 coast road. The museum and library are in the centre of Burntisland in the High Street.

DUNFERMLINE
The Andrew Carnegie Birthplace Museum ✳

Moodie Street, Dunfermline KY12 7PL

TEL: 01383 724302 FAX: 01383 721862

COLLECTION: Born in Dunfermline in 1835, Andrew Carnegie had a most remarkable rise from 'rags to riches'. Eventually selling his steel business in Pittsburgh for $400

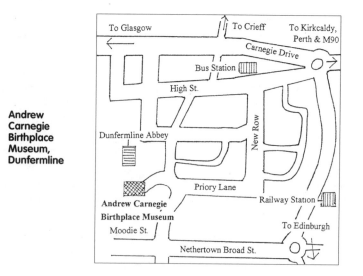

Andrew
Carnegie
Birthplace
Museum,
Dunfermline

million, he retired from business and then proceeded to give away most of his money. By 1919, when he died, he had given $350 million to provide free libraries, church organs, schools and colleges. He also set up several trusts that still function today. The cottage where Carnegie was born tells the story of the family before they emigrated to the United States. The Memorial Hall next door was endowed by Mrs Louise Carnegie to show the rise of her husband's career and the many treasures given to him by grateful towns, cities and institutions throughout the world. Only part of the museum can be photographed.

BUILDING: The cottage was built around 1800 and the Memorial Hall was completed and opened in 1928. Only part of the museum is accessible by wheelchair.

OPENING TIMES: *April to October*, Monday to Saturday: 11am–5pm, Sunday: 2pm–5pm. Closed November to March.

ADMISSION CHARGES: ①

Ⓟ & Ⓦ Ⓒ ⚠ 🎥

DIRECTIONS: Dunfermline is 30 minutes from the centre of Edinburgh across the Forth Bridges. See map for details.

FORDYCE
Fordyce Joiner's Workshop ❊ ✳

Church Street, Fordyce EB45 2SL

TEL: (Aberdeen Council, Recreation) 01771 622906 or (harp-maker, Tim Hoborough) 01261 843322

COLLECTION: The rural carpenter was very important to the local community before mass produced goods. This workshop displays early tools and workshop machinery. The museum is in the machine-shop area. A craftman's workshop occupies the joiner's main working area.

BUILDING: Late 19th-century joiner's workshop. There is a Victorian-style garden. The museum does not have a shop but the harp-maker, who works on the site, does sell various items.

OPENING TIMES: *April to September*, Thursday to Monday: 10 am–6pm. (Closed Tuesday & Wednesday.) *October to March*, Friday to Monday: 10am–6pm (Closed Tuesday, Wednesday & Thursday.)

ADMISSION CHARGES: Free

Ⓟ & Ⓦ Ⓒ 👫

DIRECTIONS: From Banff follow the A98 westwards through Portsoy; turn off left two miles after Portsoy for Fordyce; in centre of Fordyce village, turn left at Fordyce Castle along Church Street; the Joiner's Workshop is 50 metres along the street.

Tayside and Grampian

FRASERBURGH
The Museum of Scottish Lighthouses ✳ ✳
Kinnaird Head, Fraserburgh AB43 9DU

TEL: 01346 511022 FAX: 01346 511033

COLLECTION: The very first lighthouse to be built by the Northern Lighthouse Board, Kinnaird lighthouse was operating in 1787. It was certainly the only lighthouse to be built on top of a fortified castle. The story of Scottish lighthouses is told by the museum, including how they were built and what it was like to be a keeper. Displays include unique glass prism lenses. There is an hourly guided tour to the top of Kinnaird Head lighthouse.

BUILDING: The lighthouse was decommissioned in 1991 and it and the engine room are preserved. The museum is on a split site with interpretation and displays in one building. The lighthouse station is 100 yards away. There are two keepers' cottages.

OPENING TIMES: *April to the end of October*, Monday to Saturday: 10am–6pm, Sunday: 12 noon–6pm. *November to the end of March*, Monday to Saturday: 10am–4pm, Sunday: 12 noon–4pm.

ADMISSION CHARGES: ②

Ⓟ ♿ WC ⏏ ⚠ 📷 ♟

DIRECTIONS: Fraserburgh is north of Peterhead on the A90. The lighthouse is at Kinnaird Head at the west end of Fraserburgh Bay.

KINNESSWOOD
The Michael Bruce Cottage Museum ✳
The Cobbles, Kinnesswood, Kinross-shire, Tayside.

WEBSITE: www.tulbal.demon.co.uk

COLLECTION: Known as 'The Gentle Poet of Lochleven', Michael Bruce was born in 1756 and died at the age of 21 in 1767. In spite of this early death he managed to write over 40 poems and twelve 'Gospel Sonnets'. For over 200 years some of his works were wrongly ascribed to the Reverend John Logan, minister of Leith, who borrowed manuscripts from Bruce's parents and published the work under his own name in 1781. The Michael Bruce Memorial Trust, formed in 1868, bought the cottage in Kinnesswood and worked at righting this wrong. The museum contains Michael Bruce's manuscripts and editions of his works. There is also a display about the parchment and vellum trade and tools. Access to research material on application to the chairman of the Trust.

BUILDING: The birthplace of Michael Bruce. It would have housed a loom on the ground floor, while the family occupied the upper area.

OPENING TIMES: *1 April to 30 September*, daily: 9am–5pm.

ADMISSION CHARGES: By donation

Ⓟ 📷 ♟

DIRECTIONS: Kinnesswood is five miles east of Kinross. It is on the B911 Milnathort to Glenrothes road. Milnathort is off junction 7 of the M90. The museum is in The Cobbles at the centre of the village.

MONTROSE
Montrose Air Station Museum ❄ ✱

Waldon Road, Broomfield, Montrose DD10 9BB

TEL: 01674 674210 or 673107 (mobile at weekends) 07901 592134

E-MAIL: 106212.152@compuserve.com

WEBSITE: ourworld.compuserve.com/homepages/AirspeedNews/

COLLECTION: The first 'Air Station' of twelve planned by the British government in 1912 was at Montrose. The museum tells the history of RAF Montrose from 1913 to 1950. Artefacts, historic photographs, uniforms, memorabilia and archive material are on display. There are aircraft on view on the grass outside. Rallies and events are held on the aerodrome during the summer. Photography is not allowed inside the museum.

BUILDING: Royal Flying Corps Watch Office, three rooms open to the public. The aerodrome is now listed as being of historical importance.

OPENING TIMES: *All year*, Sunday: 12 noon–5pm. (Closed Monday to Saturday.)

ADMISSION CHARGES: ①

Ⓟ [WC] ♿ ⛟ ⛄

DIRECTIONS: Montrose is on the east coast, north of Arbroath on the A92. Go north from the town centre on the A92 Aberdeen road. To your left are two turnings to look out for: Brechin and Borrowfield. On your right is Broomfield. The next road to the right is Waldron Road. Go down that road to the museum.

MONTROSE
Sunnyside Museum (psychiatric museum) ✱

Sunnyside Royal Hospital, Montrose, Angus DD10 7JP

TEL: 01674 830361

E-MAIL: drthompson@angus-nhs.finix.org.uk

COLLECTION: The first of its kind in Scotland, the museum has lantern slides, two audio-visual shows, a strait-jacket, nursing uniforms, photographs and documents. It also shows Victorian pastimes and patients' art.

BUILDING: In the main building of a large Victorian psychiatric hospital. The hospital canteen can be used and is nearby. The museum is accessible by wheelchair but there are no other facilities for the disabled.

OPENING TIMES: *First Wednesday after Easter to end of September*, Wednesday: 2pm–3.30pm.

ADMISSION CHARGES: Free

Ⓟ ♿ [WC] ♿ ⛟

Tayside and Grampian

DIRECTIONS: North of Montrose off the A937. The hospital is in the area of Hillside. Going north from Montrose, turn left into Hospital Road, not long after going under the railway bridge. The hospital is off Hospital Road to the right.

PETERHEAD
Arbuthnot Museum (maritime museum) ❊ ✸

St Peter Street, Peterhead AB42 1QD

TEL: (Aberdeenshire Council, Recreation) 01771 622906

COLLECTION: Peterhead's maritime history is explained in this museum. Models show the development of the Peterhead fishing boats and there is an important collection of Inuit artefacts, plus information on arctic animals and whaling. The museum also holds one of Northern Scotland's largest coin collections. There is an extensive photographic collection.

BUILDING: Built in 1891-93 and opened to the public in November 1893 to house the Arbuthnot museum. This was Adam Arbuthnot's private museum, which had been presented to Peterhead in 1850. The building also houses the public library. The museum is on the first floor.

OPENING TIMES: *All year*, Monday, Tuesday, Thursday, Friday, Saturday: 11am–1pm & 2pm–4.30pm, Wednesday: 11am–1pm. (Closed Sunday.)

ADMISSION CHARGES: Free

🅿 👫

DIRECTIONS: Peterhead is on the east coast, south of Fraserburgh. The museum is in the town centre at St Peter Street and Queen Street junction. The entrance is from St Peter Street.

ST ANDREWS
British Golf Museum ❊ ✸

Bruce Embankment, St Andrews, Fife KY16 9AB

TEL: 01334 478880 FAX: 01334 473306

E-MAIL: kbaker@randage.org WEBSITE: www.britishgolfmuseum.co.uk

COLLECTION: In 1457 there was the first written reference to golf. It began as a Scottish medieval ball game, where a ball was struck with a stick into a hole in the ground. From this humble beginning it spread to the rest of the British Isles and then the world. The museum tells the history of golf through different galleries, explaining famous makers of clubs, showing the personalities of the game, and displaying cups, amateur medals and photographs. The explosion in the interest in golf happened at the end of the 19th century, producing a number of paintings with golfing themes, some of which are exhibited in the museum. There is memorabilia from past and present and a theatre to show films of the famous golf players.

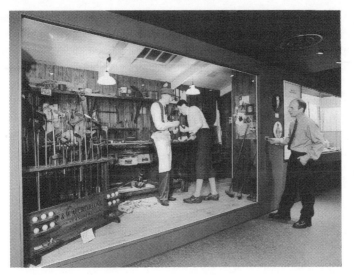

Auchterlonie
workshop
display,
British Golf
Museum, St
Andrews

BUILDING: Specially designed and built as a golfing museum. Opened in June 1990. The museum consists of a number of designed galleries all on the ground floor.
OPENING TIMES: *All year*, daily: 9.30am–5.30pm.
ADMISSION CHARGES: ②

ⓟ ♿ 🚻 ⚠ 📷 👫

DIRECTIONS: The museum is off Golf Place, nearly opposite the R & A Golf Club. There is a car-park just north of the museum, near the sea.

TROYWOOD
Scotland's Secret Bunker ✳

Underground Nuclear Command Centre, Crown Buildings, Troywood, nr. St
Andrews, Fife KY16 8QH
TEL: 01333 310301 FAX: 01333 312040
E-MAIL: mod@secretbunker.co.uk WEBSITE: www.secretbunker.co.uk
COLLECTION: One hundred feet below ground, encased in 15 feet of reinforced concrete, lies the government's nuclear command centre. From here military commanders and central government would have run the country had the UK been attacked and nuclear war broken out. Below ground is 22,000 cubic feet of operations rooms, dormitories, a BBC studio, three cinemas and an audio-visual presentation. A war telephone and original artefacts complete this strange place.
BUILDING: Built in 1951 but taken off the Official Secrets List in 1993. Opened to the public in 1994. It has a function room, which can hold 200 people, and a public house

licence. There is a 1950s-style diner. Although there is a wheelchair available for use, there is limited access for the disabled due to lack of lifts and many stairs.

OPENING TIMES: *April to the end of October*, daily: 10am–5pm.

ADMISSION CHARGES: ③

Ⓟ 🚾 🚻 ✕ ⚠ 📷 🚻

DIRECTIONS: The bunker is on the B940 Cupar to Crail road, heading towards the coast. The bunker is on the right, not long after the crossroads with the B9131 St Andrews to Anstruther road.

9. North West

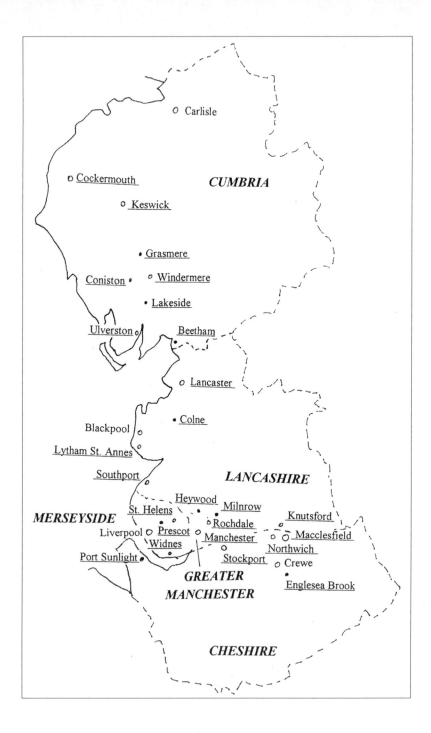

O Carlisle

CUMBRIA

o Cockermouth

o Keswick

• Grasmere

Coniston •   o Windermere

• Lakeside

Ulverston o   Beetham

o Lancaster

• Colne

Blackpool

Lytham St. Annes

Southport

LANCASHIRE

Heywood

St. Helens   Milnrow

MERSEYSIDE   o Rochdale   Knutsford

Liverpool o Prescot   Macclesfield

Widnes   Manchester

Northwich

Port Sunlight   Stockport   o Crewe

GREATER   • Englesea Brook

MANCHESTER

CHESHIRE

Cheshire

ENGLESEA BROOK
Englesea Brook Chapel and Museum (Museum of Primitive Methodism) ✳

Englesea Brook, Crewe, Cheshire CW2 5QW

TEL: 01270 820836

COLLECTION: Known as 'The Ranters', this group of Christians held a large open-air meeting at Mow Cop in 1807. Their aim was to pray and bring the gospel to people outside of church life. To put across their message they tended to hold noisy cottage prayer meetings with loud singing. The museum tells the story of the preachers and displays artefacts related to the movement. There is also a 'chest of drawers' pulpit (1808), the first denominational organ (1828), a printing press from the 1830s and magic lantern slides of around the 1900s. A library is available for research.

BUILDING: A chapel built in 1828 and the museum building, built in 1914, with an extension in 1990. No food is served, just drinks.

OPENING TIMES: *April to November*, Thursday, Friday, Saturday and Bank Holiday Monday: 10.30am–5.15pm, Sunday: 1.30pm–5.15pm. (Closed Monday to Wednesday.)

ADMISSION CHARGES: Free

🅿 🚾 ♿ ♿ 🎥 👫

DIRECTIONS: Leave the M6 at junction 16 and take the B5078 (to Alsager). Turn left on to a minor road to Englesea Brook and Baltersley Heath. Avoid parking in the driveway to the chapel.

KNUTSFORD
The First Penny Farthing Museum ❄ ✳

92 King Street, Knutsford, Cheshire WA16 6ED

TEL: (daytime) 01565 652497 (evenings) 01625 861280

COLLECTION: Learning to ride a penny farthing is, apparently, easy. Getting on and off is another matter. The present custodian of this collection learned to ride on a youth's-size Hillman D.H.F. Realising that this was too small, he bought a Daniel Rudge machine. The Rudge is still in the collection. Other machines featured are the Ariel, the Paragon and the C.M.C. Gentlemans, all built in Coventry. There are many other penny farthings in this largest and definitive collection of English-made ordinaries (as they were known) in the world. Also featured is a range of ephemera, from trophies and medals to bells and sirens.

BUILDING: 16th century. The museum is accessible by wheelchair but there are no other facilities for the disabled.

OPENING TIMES: *All year*, daily: 10am–4pm.

The First Penny Farthing
Museum, Knutsford

ADMISSION CHARGES: Free

🅿 ♿ 🆆🅲 🚻 📹 👫

DIRECTIONS: Knutsford is off the M6, junction 19. The museum is at the rear of 92 King Street. See map.

MACCLESfiELD
Paradise Mill (working silk museum) ❄ ✸

Park Lane, Macclesfield SK11 6TJ

TEL: 01625 618228

COLLECTION: The silk industry in Macclesfield shaped the development of the town. Paradise Mill was a working silk mill until 1981. Now the Jacquard handlooms have been restored and there are knowledgeable guides to explain the production process. Photography requires permission.

BUILDING: The mill complex was built in 1820 and 1860.

OPENING TIMES: *All year*, Tuesday to Sunday: 1pm–5pm. Closed Monday except Bank Holiday Monday (1pm–5pm) and closed on Christmas Eve, Christmas Day, Boxing Day, New Year's Day and Good Friday. (Telephone for winter opening times.)

North West

ADMISSION CHARGES: ① (combined ticket with the Silk Museum ②)

🅿 ⓵ 📷

DIRECTIONS: See map.

MACCLESFIELD
The Silk Museum ❄ ✳

The Heritage Centre, Roe Street, Macclesfield SK11 6UT

TEL: 01625 613210 FAX: 01625 617880

COLLECTION: An audio-visual programme, exhibitions, working models, silk textiles and fashions all help to tell the story of the silk industry. For the education service, contact the education officer. There is a silk manufacturers' pattern archive and a reference library.

BUILDING: Once a non-denominational Sunday school built in 1814 to provide education for the children who worked in the silk mills. It is a Grade II listed building. There is an induction loop in the audio-visual area.

OPENING TIMES: *All year*, Monday to Saturday: 11am–5pm, Sunday and Bank Holiday Mondays: 1pm–5pm. Closed Christmas Day, Boxing Day, New Year's Day and Good Friday.

ADMISSION CHARGES: ① (combined ticket with Paradise Mill ②)

🅿 🆆 🚻 ⓵ 📷

DIRECTIONS: See map.

Silk Museum and Paradise Mill, Macclesfield

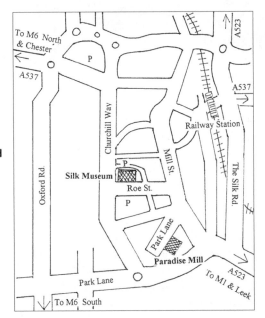

The Silk Museum,
Macclesfield

NORTHWICH
The Lion Salt Works ❄ ✻
Ollershaw Lane, Marston, Northwich, Cheshire CW9 6ES
TEL/FAX: 01606 41823
E-MAIL: afielding@lionsalt.demon.co.uk
WEBSITE: www.lionsaltworkstrust.co.uk
COLLECTION: The first deep rocksalt mine in Northwich was created at Marston at the end of the 18th century. Coal was brought in along the canals and refined salt was taken away. At the site is a horizontal steam engine and 'nodding donkey' brine pump and a 1900s pitch-roofed salt van on its original private siding. To tell the story of the salt industry there are permanent and temporary exhibitions within the former Lion Inn. Demonstrations of open-pan salt evaporation and salt-boiling are held at special events. The site is being restored as a working museum.

North West

BUILDING: Constructed in 1856, the Alliance Works were bought by the Salt Union in 1888. Mooring is available. The Slat Barge pub is opposite the Salt Works. There is a ramp and the exhibits are on the ground floor, but there is no disabled toilet.

OPENING TIMES: *All year.* The site is open Monday to Friday & Sunday (closed Saturday at the moment). Exhibitions and shop open: 1.30pm –4.30pm (telephone to confirm).

ADMISSION CHARGES: ①

Ⓟ ♿ ⓦⓒ ⚠ 🎥 👫

DIRECTIONS: Leave the M56 at junction 10 and take the A559 to Lostock Gralan. The Lion Salt Works is signposted by brown signs from the A559. It is near the Trent and Mersey Canal. From the M6 leave at junction 19 for the A556 to Cuddington and turn right on to the A559 to Warrington.

WIDNESS
Catalyst, The Museum of the Chemical Industry ❄ ✳

Mersey Road, Widness, Cheshire WA8 0DF

TEL: 0151 4201121 FAX: 0151 4952030

E-MAIL: info@catalyst.org.uk

WEBSITE: www.catalyst.org.uk

COLLECTION: Exploring the science and technology behind the chemical industry, the museum offers four interactive galleries. 'The Scientific Gallery' investigates how modern materials and chemicals are made. 'Birth of an Industry' looks at the development of the chemical industry from ancient times to the 1940s. 'Chemicals for Life' explores the role of everyday materials and chemicals in our lives and 'The Observatory' investigates the chemical industry in the neighbourhood. Catalyst offers a complete education service.

BUILDING: The house of Gossages soapworks. There are purpose-built facilities for school parties.

OPENING TIMES: *All year,* Tuesday to Friday: 10am–5pm, Bank Holiday Mondays: 10am–5pm. Saturday & Sunday and most Mondays during school holidays: 11am–5pm. Closed Christmas Eve, Christmas Day, Boxing Day and New Year's Day.

ADMISSION CHARGES: ②

Ⓟ ♿ ⓦⓒ 🚼 ⚠ 👫

DIRECTIONS: Catalyst is in Widnes, just minutes from the Runcorn/Widnes bridge. From the M62 leave at junction 7, take the A557 south. From the M56 leave at junction 12, take the 557 north. Follow the brown tourism signs.

Cumbria

BEETHAM
Museum of Papermaking ✳

Water House Mills, Beetham, Milnthorpe, Cumbria LA7 7AR

TEL: 015395 65027 FAX: 015395 65033

E-MAIL: nt.stobbs@virgin.net

COLLECTION: Paper-making is an important local industry, established over 250 years ago. The process of making paper, both modern and historical, is explained in the museum and various temporary exhibitions show other aspects of the industry and associated trades such as printing. Some 'tools of the trade' are on show, including a number of moulds used in the making of paper by hand, a model 'Calender' and a small 'Hollander'. Various 'Testing' instruments are also on display, plus an ink-mixing machine. There are occasional demonstrations of the hand-making of paper. In the Corn Mill, which is open to the public, there is a gallery devoted to the history of baking. A small archive and library are available for research.

BUILDING: In a restored Carter's barn on the site of the Heron Corn Mill. The mill is 18th century with its machinery still in place. Only parts of the mill and the museum are accessible by wheelchair. There are no other facilities for the disabled.

OPENING TIMES: For the Corn Mill and the museum: *Easter or 1 April to 30 September*, Tuesday to Sunday: 11am–5pm. (Closed Monday.) Open Bank Holiday Mondays.

ADMISSION CHARGES: ①

Ⓟ ♿ WC ⚠ 💺 🚻

DIRECTIONS: Beetham is about one mile south of Milnthorpe and six miles north of Carnforth on the A6. Access from the M6 is by exit 35, then by the M601 to the A6

Scalextric layout, The Cumberland Toy and Model Museum, Cockermouth

northbound. The mill is signposted by brown tourist signs at the entrance of Beetham. Mill Lane is off the west side of the A6 in the village. Care is needed on Mill Lane due to speed ramps. The museum and mill are on the banks of the River Bela.

COCKERMOUTH
The Cumberland Toy and Model Museum ❄ ✳

Banks Court, Market Place, Cockermouth, Cumbria CA13 9NG

TEL: 01900 827606

COLLECTION: Acquired mainly between 1965 and 1980 when many toys were considered junk, this personal collection now fills the four rooms and more toys are in store. There are many visitor operated displays and buttons to press, including 0 and 00 tinplate trains, Scalextric cars, Meccano, Lego models and even a helicopter to fly. There are also prams and dolls' houses and railways. A family quiz and worksheets help keep everyone entertained.

BUILDING: Adjoining, restored 18th-century buildings that used to be a hat factory, a lemonade-bottling plant before 1900 and a joiner's workshop. There are two staircases, making access for the disabled difficult. Objects to touch for the visually handicapped are available. There are many eating places nearby.

OPENING TIMES: *1 February to 30 November*, daily: 10am–5pm. December and January openings vary, telephone for details.

ADMISSION CHARGES: ①

P WC ♿ 🎥 👫

DIRECTIONS: Follow the signs from any car-park in Cockermouth.

COCKERMOUTH
The Printing House Museum ✳

102 Main Street, Cockermouth, Cumbria CA13 9LX

TEL: 01900 824984 FAX: 01900 823124

E-MAIL: Info@printinghouse.co.uk

WEBSITE: www.printinghouse.co.uk

COLLECTION: Visitors can use a printing press to produce cards or keepsakes. A whole range of old printing presses are on display, including iron printing presses (the earliest being an 1820 Cogger), an Imperial Press of 1830, capable of producing newspapers or large posters, and many more. Automated typesetting is represented by a Model 78 and Model 48. Both these machines can be watched in action.

BUILDING: Dates back to the 16th century.

OPENING TIMES: *Easter to just before Christmas*, Monday to Saturday: 10am–4pm. Closed Sunday.

ADMISSION CHARGES: ①

🅿 ♿ ⚠ 📷 ⛹

DIRECTIONS: The Printing House Museum is in the main street, parallel to and south of the River Derwent. It is on the south side of the road.

CONISTON
The Ruskin Museum ✻

The Institute, Yewdale Road, Coniston, Cumbria LA21 8DU

TEL: 015394 41164 FAX: 015394 41132

WEBSITE: www.coniston.org.uk

COLLECTION: Writer, art critic, artist and thinker John Ruskin (1819–1900) lived by Coniston water for the last 30 years of his life. Ruskin is celebrated in this museum in two ways, through his own work and through his enthusiasms and philosophy. The visitor enters a Timeline that goes from the present back to 1819. The earlier galleries explain elements of Coniston such as its history and geology, which interested Ruskin. The latter part of the journey displays Ruskin's watercolours, drawings and personal possessions. Within the Coniston section the museum also looks at Donald Campbell, who died attemping to break the water-speed record on Coniston Water in 1967. Also included in the displays is information on Arthur Ransome's novel *Swallows and Amazons* set in the Lake District. There is an audio-guide in four languages. A virtual tour of Coniston copper mines is available on CD-ROM.

BUILDING: First opened in 1901 and has recently been developed. Many eating places nearby.

OPENING TIMES: *1 April, or Easter (whichever is earlier) to early November*, daily: 10am–5.30pm.

ADMISSION CHARGES: ①

Ⓟ ♿ 🚻 ⚠ 📷 ⛹

DIRECTIONS: In Coniston, going north along the A 593 from Torver, cross the river and take the left fork at the church (the A 593 to Ambleside). The Ruskin Museum is to the left behind some buildings, after a turning to the left.

GRASMERE
The Wordsworth and Grasmere Museum ❄ ✻

The Wordsworth Trust, Dove Cottage, Grasmere, Cumbria LA22 9SH

TEL: 015394 35544 FAX: 015394 35748

E-MAIL: enquiries@wordsworth.org.uk

WEBSITE: www.wordsworth.org.uk

COLLECTION: On a tour of the Lake District with his friend Coleridge, Wordsworth saw Dove Cottage, formerly an inn. By 1799 Wordsworth and his sister, Dorothy, had moved in, and they stayed there until 1808. He wrote some of his finest poetry at the cottage. Today Dove Cottage is preserved and furnished. The museum itself is nearby and houses a unique collection of memorabilia, manuscripts, books and paintings. There is a special major exhibition each year and the Trust runs literary courses and a book festival. A research library is available by appointment.

BUILDING: The former 1850s coach-house for the hotel across the road. Wheelchair access to the ground floor only in Dove Cottage. Assisted wheelchair access in the museum. There is a partially adapted toilet. Also large-print guide, hearing loops and Braille guide.

OPENING TIMES: *All year*, daily: 9.30am–5.30pm (last admission 5pm). Closed 24 & 25 December & the last three weeks in January (check for precise dates of opening).

ADMISSION CHARGES: ①

Ⓟ ♿ 🆆🅒 ⛽ ✗ ♿ ♟

DIRECTIONS: The cottage and museum are south of Grasmere village on the main A591 Kendal to Keswick road.

KESWICK
Cumberland Pencil Museum ❅ ✳

Cumberland Pencil Co., Southet Works, Keswick, Cumbria CA12 5NG

TEL: 017687 73626 FAX: 017687 74679

E-MAIL: museum@acco-uk.co.uk

WEBSITE: www.pencils.co.uk

COLLECTION: Graphite was first discovered in Borrowdale in the 1500s and it was so valuable it had to be kept in a guardhouse. The mine ceased production by 1890 but by that time there was a flourishing pencil industry in Keswick, first as a cottage industry and then after 1832 in a factory. The museum has a replica of Seathwaite Graphite Mine to entertain the visitor and restored machinery to show how a pencil was made. The various stages of pencil production are explained. A precious exhibit is the small collection of wartime pencils (1940–45), which were drilled to hold a map of Germany and a compass and were issued to RAF crew. A worksheet is provided for children.

BUILDING: At the Derwent factory.

OPENING TIMES: *All year*, daily: 9.30am–4pm (4pm is the last admission but it can be extended during peak periods). Closed 25, 26 December & 1 January.

ADMISSION CHARGES: ①

Ⓟ ♿ 🆆🅒 ♿ ☕ ♟

DIRECTIONS: The Cumberland Pencil Factory and Museum is north of Keswick Town Centre on the A66 to Cockermouth. After the bus station on your left and just before the River Greta, turn right to the factory.

**The Wet Dock,
Windermere Steamboat
Museum, Windermere**

NEWBY BRIDGE
Stott Park Bobbin Mill ✳

Newby Bridge, nr. Ulverston, Cumbria LA12 8AX

TEL: 015395 31087

COLLECTION: Entering the mill the visitor steps back 100 years to experience at first hand the conditions in which the bobbin-makers worked. Entire tree-trunks from the Lakeland forests were fashioned, under one roof, into finished bobbins on machines once driven by Lakeland streams. A 45-minute tour explains the role of the mill in the spinning and weaving industry of the 19th century and tells the story of bobbin-making and the people who worked at the mill. There is a working static steam engine, which is operated on Tuesday, Wednesday and Thursday.

BUILDING: The mill was built in 1835 and finally ceased production in 1971. Only the ground floor is accessible by wheelchair. This is an English Heritage property.

OPENING TIMES: *1 April to 30 September*, daily: 10am–6pm (last tour at 5pm). *1 to 31 October*, daily: 10am–5pm (last tour at 4pm).

ADMISSION CHARGES: ①

North West

(P) &. [WC] ⚠ ⛟ 👫

DIRECTIONS: On the Newby Bridge to Hawkshead road, north of Ulverston and half a mile north of Finsthwaite.

ULVERSTON
Laurel and Hardy Museum ❄ ✳

4c Upper Brook Street, Ulverston, Cumbria LA12 7BH

TEL: 01229 582292 or (home) 01229 861614

COLLECTION: Stan Laurel was born in Ulverston in 1890. The founder of the museum, Bill Cubin, devoted his life to collecting material about Laurel and Hardy. There are letters, photographs, personal items and furniture. A small cinema shows films and documentaries all day.

BUILDING: Part 16th century, three rooms on ground level. A large extension has given extra space.

OPENING TIMES: *February to December*, daily: 10am–4.30pm. Closed January.

ADMISSION CHARGES: ①

🅿 &. [WC] ⚠ ⛟ 👫

DIRECTIONS: In the centre of Ulverston. Leave Market Street and go north up King Street and first left into Upper Brook. The museum is on the right.

WINDERMERE
Windermere Steamboat Museum ✳

Rayrigg Road, Windermere, Cumbria LA23 1BN

TEL: 015394 45565 FAX: 015394 48769

WEBSITE: www.steamboat.co.uk

COLLECTION: A unique collection of boats, many with wonderful stories of salvage and loving restoration. The earliest is a 1780 sailing yacht, which was found lying upside down in a field and being used as a hen-house. The 1850 steam launch *Dolly* was raised from Ullswater in 1962. It is the oldest mechanically powered boat in the world. Other boats include the 1869 *Esperance*, the oldest boat on Lloyd's Yacht Register, and many more. A steamboat wet dock accommodates up to 15 boats, mostly still in working order. There are displays of Windermere speed-craft, model boats, Beatrix Potter's rowing boat and exhibitions relating to *Swallows and Amazons*, the children's novel set in the Lake District, written by Arthur Ransome.

BUILDING: On a former sand wharf site, where barges used to unload gravel dredged from the bed of the lake. When this operation ceased in 1975, the Windermere Nautical Trust acquired the use of the site and the museum was built in 1977.

OPENING TIMES: *Mid-March to the end of October*, daily: 10am–5pm. Open in winter by appointment only.

Cumbria

ADMISSION CHARGES: ②

ⓟ ♿ 🚾 🅿 ⚠ 🎥 ⅲ

DIRECTIONS: The Steamboat Museum is on the A592 from Bowness on Windermere to Ambleside. It is on the shore.

Lancashire

COLNE
The British in India Museum ✻

1 Newtown Street, Colne, Lancashire BB8 0JJ

TEL: 01282 613129 FAX: 01282 870215

COLLECTION: Britain's long association with India began with the forming of the East India Company in 1600. A fascinating collection of all kinds of material associated with the British in India is on display at the museum. The collection was built up over 30 years by Colne businessman Henry Nelson and includes E. M. Forster's Indian clothes worn when he was staying with the Maharaja of Dewas Senior, the last Union Jack lowered at Lucknow before Indian independence, and models of soldiers fighting on stilts for the Rao of Kutch (he could not afford the upkeep of elephants, so soldiers on stilts were the next best thing). There are dioramas, postage stamps, picture postcards, photographs, paintings and military uniforms. The library can be visited upon written request.

BUILDING: A former sweet factory, probably built around 1900. It was once occupied by Thomas Veevers & Co., sweet manufacturers from 1889 to 1969. There are two steps and no facilities for the disabled.

OPENING TIMES: *May to September,* Monday & Wednesday to Friday: 1pm–5pm. (Closed Tuesday.) Saturday: 11am–5pm. (Closed Sunday.) Before May and after September telephone 0976 665320 for opening times.

ADMISSION CHARGES: ①

🅿 🎥 ⅲ

DIRECTIONS: Colne is on the main road (A56–A6068) from Burnley (six miles) to Keighley (twelve miles). The M65 ends at Colne (junction 14). Skipton is twelve miles away, British Rail Colne station one mile.

LANCASTER
Maritime Museum ❄ ✻

Custom House, St George's Quay, Lancaster LA1 1RB

TEL: 01524 64637 FAX: 01524 841692

E-MAIL: awhite@lancaster.gov.uk

WEBSITE: www.lancaster.gov.uk/council/museums

COLLECTION: Using sound, smells, reconstructions and audio-visuals, the museum tells the story of the port of Lancaster, the Lancaster Canal, fishing and the ecology of Morecambe Bay. There are also four preserved boats.

BUILDING: The museum opened in 1985 and occupies the former custom house of 1764, designed by Richard Gillow, and an adjacent warehouse.

OPENING TIMES: *All year. Easter to October,* daily: 11am–5pm. *November to Easter,* daily: 12.30pm–4pm. (Closed Christmas and New Year.)

ADMISSION CHARGES: ①

Ⓟ ♿ 🚾 ⛴ ⚠ 📷 ♛

DIRECTIONS: The museum is on St George's Quay by the River Lune, north of the castle. There is a footpath from near the castle to the museum and the museum is signposted from the city centre.

LYTHAM ST ANNES
Lifeboat Museum ✳

East Beach (next to the Windmill), Lytham St Annes, Lancashire

TEL: 01253 730155 or (Tourist Office) 01253 725610

COLLECTION: One of the main exhibits in the museum is the Mexico Disaster, which took place on the night of 9 December 1886. Three lifeboats went out to help the *Mexico of Hamburg,* which was caught in a fierce storm. The Lytham lifeboat returned safely with the crew of the *Mexico,* but of the other two lifeboats, one was lost with all its crew and only two crew of the other boat survived. This loss of 27 men was the greatest disaster in the lifeboat service. The museum also has displays and materials showing the work for the Royal National Lifeboat Institution from the past to the present. The Lytham Windmill is next door and offers displays on the history of windmills and milling, with a small amount of original machinery in place.

BUILDING: Original lifeboat house built in 1861. Toilets, including a disabled toilet, are nearby. The Windmill was built in 1805. It acts as the Tourist Information Point during the season.

OPENING TIMES: *Two weeks at Easter & then from near end of May to end of September,* Tuesday, Thursday, Saturday & Sunday and bank holidays: 10.30am–4.30pm. (Closed Monday, Wednesday & Fridays.) *July & August,* open Wednesday as well: 1.30pm–4.30pm. The Windmill opening times are about the same as the museum. Telephone the Tourist Department if in need of further information.

ADMISSION CHARGES: Free

🅿 ♿ ⚠ 📷 ♛

DIRECTIONS: Lytham is south of Blackpool. The museum and the windmill are on East Beach, Lytham.

SOUTHPORT
British Lawnmower Museum ❄ ✳

106-114 Shakespeare Street, Southport, Lancashire PR8 5AJ

TEL: 01704 501336 FAX: 01704 500564

WEBSITE: www.lawnmowerworld.co.uk

COLLECTION: Invented in 1830 by Edward Budding of Gloucester, the lanwnmower was based on the machine designed to trim the nap from cloth. The cylinder machine has not really changed since then. The museum houses a private collection of over 200 exhibits, part of 400, built up over 50 years. It is a tribute to the garden machinery industry of the past 170 years. Many of the machines have been rescued from scrap and restored. There are some of the fastest lawnmowers in the world, the unique Cordless Electric Ride-on lawnmower, the water-cooled 'Egg Boiler' lawnmower and a genuine two-inch lawnmower, plus many more. There is also the largest collection of vintage toy lawn-mowers and games in the world. A guided tour and lectures are available.

BUILDING: Built in 1890.

OPENING TIMES: *All year*, Monday to Saturday: 9am–5.30pm. (Closed Sunday & bank holidays.)

ADMISSION CHARGES: ①

🅿 ⚠ 📷 ♨

DIRECTIONS: Southport is by the sea, south of Lytham and north of Formby. From Lord Street go south along Duke Street, over the railway line. There is a car-park on the left and the museum is on the corner of Duke Street and Shakespeare Street.

Manchester and Greater Manchester

MANCHESTER
Gallery of Costume ❄ ✳

Platt Hall, Rusholme, Manchester M14 5LL

TEL: 0161 224 217 FAX: 0161 2563278

WEBSITE: www.cityartgalleries.org.uk

COLLECTION: Dr C. Willett Cunnington was one of the first serious students of the history of dress. He formed a substantial costume collection that first opened to the public at Platt Hall in 1947. Manchester Corporation bought the collection, and more costumes are being acquired. Although it is a very large collection, only part of it can be on display. Everyday dress is rarely preserved, so the woollen shawls and wooden clogs of Lancashire mill-workers are highly prized. There are also Victorian male and female costumes and outfits by designers such as Paul Smith and Vivienne Westwood, bringing the collection up to date. Accessories are on display too, including handbags, fans, umbrellas, even

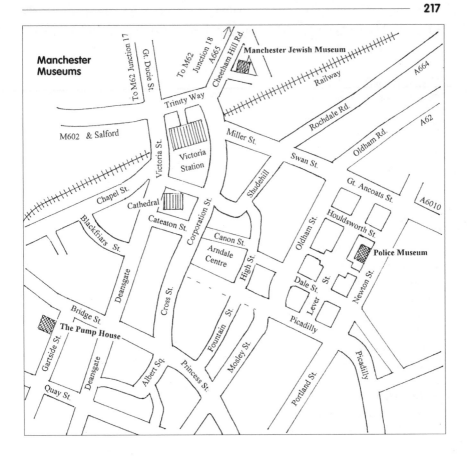

**Manchester
Museums**

toothpicks, curling-tongs and wigs. The exhibitions change frequently. Photography is allowed but not the use of a flash. Research facilities are available for the stored collections and a substantial library may be viewed by appointment.

BUILDING: Platt Hall is a neo-Palladian house built in 1762–64 to the designs of Timothy Lightoller. The dining room on the first floor has been restored to its 1764 decorative scheme. Only the ground floor is accessible by wheelchair, but there is a video of displays on other floors for those who cannot visit them.

OPENING TIMES: *March to October*, daily: 10am–5.30pm. *November to February*, daily: 10am–4pm.

ADMISSION CHARGES: Free

DIRECTIONS: From Manchester take the Wilmslow Road (B5117) south. The road becomes Oxford Road. First suburb is Rusholme. Platfield Park is on the right and the museum is in the park.

MANCHESTER
Greater Manchester Police Museum ❄ ❉
Newton Street, Manchester M1 1ES
TEL: 0161 8563287 FAX: 0161 8563286
COLLECTION: In the police station's original cells, the wooden 'pillows' still remain as a reminder of the severity of cell conditions. The Charge Office is there too and upstairs the history of policing in the Manchester region is traced from the first 'Peeler' of 1839 to the present day. Also illustrated are changes in uniforms, equipment and transport. The museum has extensive archive and photographic collections, which may be viewed by appointment. Check with staff before taking photographs.
BUILDING: The old Newton Street Police Station, built in 1879. It was operational for 99 years. The museum was established in 1981. Parking space for orange badge holders only outside the museum. Only the ground floor is accessible by wheelchair.
OPENING TIMES: *All year*, Tuesday: 10.30am–3.30pm. Open other weekdays by appointment. Closed Saturday & Sunday and public holidays.
ADMISSION CHARGES: Free

🅿 ♿ WC 🎥 ♦
DIRECTIONS: See map.

MANCHESTER
Manchester Jewish Museum ❄ ❉
190 Cheetham Hill Road, Manchester M8 8LW
TEL: 0161 8349879 FAX: 0161 8349801
COLLECTION: The history of Manchester's Jewish community, now over 250 years old, is brought to life in this museum. A kitchen with the table set for the Sabbath meal, a waterproof garment-makers' factory and the office of an early Zionist, Joseph Massel, are all re-created in detail to show the lives of ordinary people. There are recorded recollections of older members of the community and photographs, documents and objects of all kinds. Photographers must sign a form to say that photographs are for private use only. The museum has an extensive education programme.
BUILDING: A Grade II listed building, a former Spanish and Portuguese synagogue. Completed in 1874, the building has splendid stained-glass windows and cast-iron fitments. It has been completely restored since it ceased to be a synagogue and opened as a museum in 1984. Access to downstairs only by wheelchair.
OPENING TIMES: *All year*, Monday to Thursday: 10.30am–4pm, Sunday: 10.30am–5pm. Closed Friday but group appointments can be made. Closed Saturday and Jewish holidays

(telephone for dates if not known). Also closed over Christmas and New Year and Pass-over in April.

ADMISSION CHARGES: ②

🅿 ♿ 🚾 ⚠ 🎥 🚻

DIRECTIONS: See map.

MANCHESTER
The Pumphouse People's History Museum ❄ ✳

Left Bank, Bridge Street, Manchester M3 3ER

TEL: 0161 8396061 FAX: 0161 8396027

E-MAIL: pumphouse@nmlhweb.org WEBSITE: www.nmlhweb.org

COLLECTION: The only national museum in Britain dedicated to people's history. It focuses on the organisations, such as trade unions or political parties, that people set up to bring about change. The unpaid work done at home is also shown. The displays begin with the cotton industry in Manchester and include the Co-op shop and football. There is a renowned collection of historic banners and a number of different exhibitions and events. The museum runs an Archive and Study Centre, which holds important collections, including the Labour History Archive and the Communist Party Archive. Photographers have to fill in a permission form.

BUILDING: Manchester's only remaining hydraulic pumping station. Opened in 1909 it provided power for the cotton-bailing and packing warehouses. Limited disabled parking available at the museum (telephone ahead). There is a ramp at the main entrance and lifts to all floors. Large-print information.

OPENING TIMES: *All year*, Tuesday to Sunday: 11am–4.30pm. (Closed Monday except Bank Holiday Mondays.)

ADMISSION CHARGES: ①

🅿 ♿ 🚾 🚻 ⚠ 🎥 🚻

DIRECTIONS: See map.

HEYWOOD
Corgi Heritage Centre ❄ ✳

53 York Sreet, Heywood, Rochdale, Greater Manchester OL10 4NR

TEL: 01706 365812 FAX: 01706 627811

E-MAIL: sales@corgi-heritage.co.uk

WEBSITE: www.corgi-heritage.co.uk

COLLECTION: Originally called Mettoy and set up just before World War II, the company changed its name to Corgi in the mid-1950s. Examples of all the vintage Corgi models are here: cars, buses, helicopters and a whole host more. There is an archive of Corgi catalogues and historical display material.

Rochdale
Pioneers
Museum,
Rochdale

BUILDING: The museum is behind the shop. There are two floors. The main exhibits are accessible by wheelchair. There is a café next door.

OPENING TIMES: *All year*, Monday to Friday: 9am–5.30pm, Saturday: 9am–5pm.

ADMISSION CHARGES: Free

Ⓟ ♿ ⚠ 🎥 ♯♯♯

DIRECTIONS: Heywood is on the A58 Bury to Rochdale road. Leave the M62 at junctions 19 and 20 or the M66 at junction 2. The collection is in one of the main streets and near Market Hall.

MILNROW
Ellenroad Engine House ✳

Elizabethan Way, Milnrow, Rochdale, Greater Manchester OL16 4LG

TEL: 01706 881952 (there is a recorded message for events)

E-MAIL: r.unwin@virgin.net

COLLECTION: In 1916 a fire broke out, destroying the whole of the cotton mill that had been producing fine cotton yarn using mule-spinning since 1892. The mill was rebuilt installing ring spinning frames that needed more power. The engine was upgraded to become a twin tandem compound engine. In 1921 the mill re-opened. Electricity was used for the mill in 1975. By 1985 the mill had closed and everything except the Engine and Boiler House and the chimney was demolished. The Ellenroad Trust took over the Engine House in 1985. One of the 1921 coal-fired boilers was preserved and a Whitelees beam engine was bought. Other small items of steam mill equipment have been bought and are displayed at the mill.

BUILDING: Engine House and Boiler of the former cotton mill built in 1892 on the banks of the River Beal. It is now a listed Grade II scheduled monument. There is a picnic area by the river.

OPENING TIMES: *April to October (inclusive)*, every Sunday: 12noon– 4pm. (Closed Monday to Saturday.) Only in steam on the first Sunday in the month.

ADMISSION CHARGES: ① (reduced rates on when engine not in steam)

Ⓟ ⓌⒸ ⇗ ⚠ 📹 ♟

DIRECTIONS: Ellenroad Engine House is beside junction 21 of the M62 motorway at Milnrow. Leave by the slip-road and turn under the motorway bridge. The Engine House entrance is 200 yards on your right. There is a train station at Newhey, a few minutes' walk away.

ROCHDALE
Rochdale Pioneers Museum (Co-operative movement) ❄ ✳

31 Toad Lane, Rochdale, Manchester OL2 0NV

TEL: 01706 524920

E-MAIL: co-operativearchive@co-opcollege.zee.web.co.uk

WEBSITE: www.co-op.ac.uk/toad-lane.htm

COLLECTION: The 1840s have been called 'the hungry forties'. Many working people were very poor and had virtually no food. A group of 28 working men in Rochdale formed the Co-operative Society in 1844, raising capital in shares of £1 each to establish a store for the sale of provisions and clothing. Other main aims were providing housing, employment and land for cultivation. The shop was opened in December 1844. The museum, in the original building, has laid out the premises as it used to be, showing the rather sparse provisions on sale at the beginning. In the back storeroom is the history of Robert Owen (1771-1858), whose ideas inspired the pioneers in Rochdale, and the story of the Pioneers themselves. Upstairs are more displays. The museum is linked to the Co-operative archive at Co-operative College, Stanford Hall, Loughborough, Leicestershire LE12 5QR.

BUILDING: Originally a warehouse built in 1790 and then the Co-operative shop from 1844. It became a museum in 1931. Only the ground floor is accessible by wheelchair. Some exhibits can be handled by the visually handicapped.

OPENING TIMES: *All year*, Tuesday to Saturday: 10am–4pm, Sunday: 2pm–4pm. (Closed Monday.)

ADMISSION CHARGES: ①

Ⓟ ♿ ⓌⒸ ⚠ 📹 ♟

DIRECTIONS: In the centre of Rochdale at the rear of the Exchange Shopping precinct on Hunters Lane.

STOCKPORT
Hat Works ✣ ✹

Wellington Mill, Wellington Road South, Stockport SK3 0EU

TEL: 0161 3557770

WEBSITE: www.stockportmbc.gov.uk/heritage/hatworks.htm

COLLECTION: The only museum in Britain dedicated to the world of hats and hat-making. Hats have been made in Stockport from at least the 16th century. The trade declined after World War II. Hats from many centuries are displayed, from fine fur felt hats of the early 1800s to fashion hats of today. There are miniature hats made by apprentices and the world's tallest topper. A resident milliner and textile designer are available to talk about their work. There are two audio-visual theatres, an early hatting workshop and a hatter's cottage. For photography a consent form must be signed. Research facilities are available.

BUILDING: Built in 1830 as a cotton mill, it is now a Grade II listed building. It has eight storeys, and the museum is on the lower three floors. There are craft studios.

OPENING TIMES: *All year*, Monday to Saturday: 10am–5pm, Sunday: 11am–5pm. Closed Christmas Day and Boxing Day.

ADMISSION CHARGES: ②

🅿️ ♿ 🚾 ⟁ ⚠️ 🎥 ♨️

DIRECTIONS: The M60 runs near Stockport and the A6 goes through the town. Wellington Mill's landmark chimney is visible from all the main routes into Stockport. The mill is on the A6 Wellington Road South, opposite the bus station and close to the railway station. It is only two minutes' walk from Merseyway Shopping Centre and other town centre shops.

Merseyside

PORT SUNLIGHT
Heritage Centre ✣ ✹

95 Greendale Road, Port Sunlight, Wirral CH62 4XE

TEL: 0151 6444800 FAX: 0151 6458973

COLLECTION: The picturesque village of Port Sunlight was built in the 19th century by William Hesketh Lever for his soap factory workers and named after his famous Sunlight soap. Lever employed 30 different architects to create Port Sunlight's unique style. The Heritage Centre tells the story of the village and its community by means of a scale model of the village and copies of the original plans, plus old photographs and early film footage. Displays of packaging and advertising of Lever's soap products show his use of marketing. There are walking guides of the village available and guided tours on

Sundays from April to September (check times and dates). The village and centre are now owned by the Port Sunlight Village Trust. Research facilities are available by appointment. Photography is not allowed in the Heritage Centre, but exterior photography of the centre and the village is fine.

BUILDING: Built in 1896, the centre was a girls' hostel and later the library.

OPENING TIMES: *April to October*, daily: 10am–4pm, *November to March*, Monday to Friday: 10am–4pm, Saturday & Sunday: 11am–4pm. Closed Christmas week.

ADMISSION CHARGES: ①

🅿 ♿ 🚾 △ 📷 ᐧᵻᵻᵻ

DIRECTIONS: Port Sunlight is north west of Chester. The Heritage Centre is near the Port Sunlight railway station.

PRESCOT
Prescot Museum (watchmaking) ❄ ✳

34 Church Street, Prescot, Knowsley, Merseyside L34 3LA

TEL: 0151 4307787

COLLECTION: A small settlement of religious dissenters set up watchmaking in the Toxteth area of Liverpool during the early 1600s. They formed close connections with watchmakers in London and developed a range of specialist manufacturing industries, supplying watchmaking, clockmaking and precision tools. During the 1700s these horological industries became concentrated in Prescot and the surrounding villages and by 1800 Prescot had become the principal UK centre for the production of watch movements, watch and clock components and horological and precision tools. The industry declined in the late 19th century due to its failure to innovate and the competition from USA and Switzerland. During the 1960s and 1970s, clock, watch and toolmaking equipment was collected by Alan Smith of Liverpool City Museum. A declaration form must be completed before photography is allowed. Research facilities are available on request.

BUILDING: Once a 1770 town house and later the National Westminster Bank until the Bank moved out in 1979. The museum was opened in 1982. Toilets available on request. Only the ground floor is accessible by wheelchair. There is no disabled toilet.

OPENING TIMES: *All year*, Tuesday to Saturday: 10am–1pm & 2pm–5pm. (Closed Sunday & Monday.)

ADMISSION CHARGES: Free

🅿 ♿ △ 📷 ᐧᵻᵻᵻ

DIRECTIONS: Prescot is on the A57, which runs from junction 2 of the M57 to junction 7 of the M62. The museum is on the corner of the High Street (the A57) and Church Street, opposite the library. There are frequent rail services from Wigan and Liverpool Lime Street. Prescot station is just ten minutes' walk away.

Merseyside

ST HELENS
The World of Glass ❅ ✳

Chalon Way East, St Helens, Merseyside WA10 1BX

TEL: Enquiries: 08707 444777 or 01744 22766 FAX: 01744 616966

E-MAIL: info@worldofglass.com

WEBSITE: www.worldofglass.com

COLLECTION: The Pilkington Glass Museum has been transformed into this new and exciting experience. How glass is made and the evolution of the techniques are displayed, aided by the latest multi-media technology. The story of St Helens is also displayed. Glass-blowing can be watched and the past, present and future of glass is explored in Exhibition Hall 2. The Cone House, a Victorian glass furnace, is on the other side of the canal and is reached via a bridge. In here is the story of flat glass manufacture.

BUILDING: The Cone House is a Grade II listed building. The World of Glass is in a new building opened in 2000 and built to show off the qualities of glass. The entrance area has a glazed roof based on a 19th-century glass-house and there are glazed walls. Lifts, wheelchair access and adapted toilets are provided.

OPENING TIMES: *All year*, daily: 10am–5pm. Closed Christmas Day, Boxing Day & New Year's Day.

ADMISSION CHARGES: ②

Ⓟ ♿ 🅆🅒 ☕ ⚠ 🎥 ††††

DIRECTIONS: St Helens is east of Liverpool and north of the M62. For the World of Glass, see map.

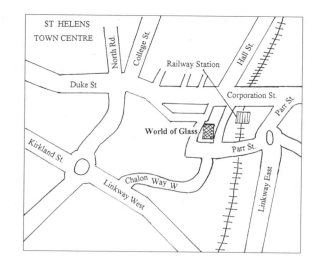

World of Glass, St Helens

10. West Central

Gloucestershire

BERKELEY
Edward Jenner Museum ✳

Church Lane, Berkeley, Gloucestershire GL13 9BH

TEL: (information) 01453 811690 (office) 01453 810631 FAX: 01453 811690

E-MAIL: jennermuseum@berkeley19.freeserve.co.uk

WEBSITE: www.dursley-cotswold-uk.com

COLLECTION: Edward Jenner (1749-1823) made one of the most important discoveries of modern medicine: immunology. Intrigued by the country lore that said that milkmaids who caught the mild disease cowpox could not catch smallpox, he experimented and produced a vaccine against smallpox. The disease was finally eradicated in 1980. The museum was Jenner's home for 38 years, while he worked as the local doctor in Berkeley. His study remains as it was when he died. His many other interests are explained and an exhibition on modern immunology, using models, computers and CD-ROMs, helps to explain the importance of the discovery and its development.

BUILDING: A Grade II listed building, once a chantry, dating from 1378 and rebuilt in

Dr Edward Jenner,
Edward Jenner
Museum, Berkeley

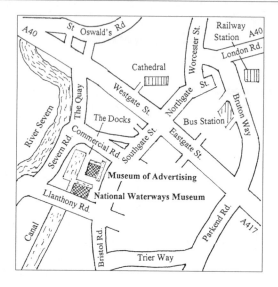

Museum of Advertising & Packaging, and National Waterways Museum

the Georgian style in 1702 and extended by Jenner. Only the ground floor and gardens are accessible by wheelchair (70 per cent of the museum).

OPENING TIMES: *April to September,* Tuesday to Saturday: 12.30pm–5.30pm, Sunday: 1pm–5.30pm. Closed Monday, except Bank Holiday Mondays. *October,* Sunday only: 1pm–5.30pm.

ADMISSION CHARGES: ①

Ⓟ ♿ 🚻 ⚠ ♟

DIRECTIONS: Berkeley is off the A38 Gloucester to Bristol road, which runs parallel to the M5. Follow the brown signs from the A35 at Berkeley turnings. In Berkeley, from the A38, go straight ahead at a roundabout into Canonburg Street (the B4066) and take the second left, which is the High Street, the B4059. The museum is off to the left. The first turning left is to Berkeley Castle. There is a footpath from the castle and its car-park to the museum.

GLOUCESTER
Museum of Advertising and Packaging ❋ ✳

The Albert Warehouse, Gloucester Docks, Gloucestershire GL1 2EH

TEL: 01452 302309 FAX: 01452 308507

COLLECTION: All the memories of the larder are to be found in this museum. Robert Opie's collection of packaging now numbers about 300,000 items. There are the old favourites of Saxa salt and Vim, Marmite, Camp coffee and Huntley & Palmer's biscuits and many other fascinating packages from Victorian times, which once filled the shelves of Britain's grocers, confectioners, chemists, tobacconists, pubs and the earliest super-markets. There is also a section devoted to old posters and television advertising. Photography is limited, so check with the reception desk.

BUILDING: The Albert Warehouse was built in 1851 to cater for the corn trade. Disabled toilets are within 200 yards of the museum.

OPENING TIMES: *March to September*, daily: 10am–6pm. *October to February*, Tuesday to Sunday: 10am–5pm. (Closed Monday.) Open all bank holidays but closed on Christmas Day and Boxing Day.

ADMISSION CHARGES: ②

Ⓟ ♿ 🚾 ▽ ⚠ ☕ 👫

DIRECTIONS: See map.

GLOUCESTER
The National Waterways Museum ❊ ✳

Llanthony Warehouse, Gloucester Docks, Gloucestershire GL1 2EH

TEL: 01452 318054 FAX: 01452 318066

E-MAIL: info@nwm.demon.co.uk

WEBSITE: www.nwm.org.uk

COLLECTION: The canals formed a vital network for the transport of goods throughout Britain and the museum traces the changing fortunes of canals over the last 250 years. It introduces Thomas Telford, the navvies and the leggers and explains how canals were created. There are touch-screen videos and computers to bring history to life and hands-on displays. A blacksmith is on site most weekdays working in the traditional forge. There

The National
Waterways
Museum,
Gloucester

Gloucestershire

are floating historic boats, small objects and archive material dating from the mid-18th century. Research facilities are available by appointment, and 45-minute boat trips can be booked.

BUILDING: A listed Victorian warehouse, dating from 1879. Lifts to all floors. No access by wheelchair to the floating exhibits.

OPENING TIMES: *All year*, daily: 10am–5pm. (Closed Christmas Day.) Last admission one hour before closing.

ADMISSION CHARGES: ②

🅿 ♿ 🆆🅲 ⛴ ✖ ⚠ 📷 ⛹

DIRECTIONS: See map.

GOTHERINGTON
The Bugatti Trust ❄ ✳

Prescott Hill, Gotherington, Cheltenham, Gloucestershire GL52 4RD

TEL: 01242 677201 FAX: 01242 674191

E-MAIL: trust@bugatti.co.uk

COLLECTION: Ettore Bugatti (1881–1947) is most famous for his racing cars of the 1920s and 1930s but he also designed luxury limousines and engines, machine tools, railway rolling stock and many other examples of 20th-century industrial design. All his work is marked by an uncompromising design integrity. The collection was gathered by Hugh Conway (1914-89), who was an expert on Bugatti history. On display are items that tell aspects of the Bugatti story: photographs, models, diagrams, mechanical components and complete cars. Photography is allowed but not of the archive material. There is a photograph and document archive and a library, which forms one of the most important collections of material on the work of Bugatti. It is available for academic research by appointment only.

BUILDING: The sale of one of Hugh Conway's Bugattis funded the building in which the collection is housed.

OPENING TIMES: *All year*, Monday to Friday: 10.30am–3.30pm. (Closed Saturday & Sunday.) Open at other times by arrangement.

ADMISSION CHARGES: Free

🅿 ♿ 🆆🅲 📷 ⛹

DIRECTIONS: Gotherington is north of Cheltenham off the A435 Cheltenham to Evesham road. Turn off on to the Gotherington to Winchcombe road. The Bugatti Trust is beyond Gotherington on the way to Gretton. It is on the right-hand side after Gotherington, about half-way between the two villages.

NORTHLEACH
Keith Harding's World of Mechanical Music ❄ ✳

The Oak House, High Street, Northleach, Gloucestershire GL54 3ET

TEL: 01451 860181 FAX: 01451 861133

E-MAIL: Keith@mechanicalmusic.co.uk

WEBSITE: www.mechanicalmusic.co.uk

COLLECTION: From a tiny singing bird concealed in a snuff-box to a Steinway, a marine chronometer to the great tower clock by Vulliamy, a whole range of mechanical clocks, musical boxes and automata are on display. Even a Maharajah's musical box is to be found, reputed to have been a present from Queen Victoria. Everything in the museum has been restored to the most perfect possible condition by Keith Harding and Cliff Burnett. There are guided tours where instruments are played and also a re-creation of a Victorian music room.

BUILDING: Two houses, joined and modified in 1947 for use by the Northleach Rural District Council, then becoming a factory. The Oak House, parts of which are more than 300 years old, was formerly a wool house, a pub and a youth hostel. Next door Westwoods Grammar School opened in 1589 and continued until 1902.

OPENING TIMES: *All year*, daily: 10am–6pm. Closed Christmas Day. Last tour 5pm.

ADMISSION CHARGES: ②

Ⓟ ♿ WC ⚠ 🎥 👨‍👩‍👧

DIRECTIONS: Northleach is south west of Cheltenham, off the A40 Cheltenham to Oxford road. Also off the A429 Cirencester to Stow-on-the-Wold road. The museum is in the High Street, near the marketplace and opposite the Green. The car-park is off the road to Farmington.

STOW-ON-THE-WOLD
Toy Museum ❄ ✳

8 Park Street, Stow-on-the-Wold, Gloucestershire GL54 1AQ

TEL: 01451 830159

COLLECTION: The collection began with just one doll and from then on George and Barbara Sutton began to gather together Victorian and Edwardian toys, also adding interesting ones from the 20th century. Dolls, teddy bears, trains, boats, planes, lead soldiers and even Action Man crowd in lit glass cases either side of a dark corridor that winds behind the Suttons' shop.

BUILDING: An old building with narrow corridors.

OPENING TIMES: *April to September*, Wednesday to Saturday & Monday: 10am–4.30pm, Sunday: 11am–4.30pm. (Closed Tuesday.) Closed for the month of May. *October to March*, Wednesday to Monday: 11am–4pm. (Closed Tuesday.) (Confirm opening times before travelling long distances to the museum.)

ADMISSION CHARGES: ①

🅿♿⚠🎥🚻

DIRECTIONS: Stow-on-the-Wold is on the A429 Moreton in the Marsh to Cirencester road. From the Square walk south west down Digbeth Street into Park Street. The Toy Museum is on the left before you reach the Bull Inn. There is a car-park south of the Bull.

TETBURY
Tetbury Police Museum ❋ ✳

The Old Courthouse, 63 Long Street, Tetbury, Gloucestershire GL8 8AA

TEL: 01666 504670

COLLECTION: The people of Gloucestershire raised a petition against the formation of a police force in 1839. In spite of their wishes, the police force started operation and is the second oldest police force in the country. Wiltshire's was established a month earlier. The museum is in the cells of the old police station and there are early police batons, helmets, gas-masks and a plate camera, plus Fred, the prisoner (a model). The story of police work is also told. The museum is more suitable for older children.

BUILDING: The old Victorian police station, which was bought by Tetbury Town Council when the police moved to another building. The cells contain the museum and an old police office. Coffee-shops and toilets are available in the town. Only part of the museum is accessible by wheelchair.

OPENING TIMES: *All year*, Monday to Friday: 10am–3pm. Closed on Saturday & Sunday and bank holidays.

ADMISSION CHARGES: Donation of 20p for leaflet.

🅿♿🚻

DIRECTIONS: Tetbury is on the A433 Cirencester to Chipping Sodbury road. From the marketplace walk along Long Street. The museum is on the right at the crossroads.

WINCHCOMBE
Winchcombe Folk and Police Museum ✳

Old Town Hall, High Street, Winchcombe, Gloucestershire GL54 5LJ

TEL: 01242 609151

COLLECTION: Pictures, historic items and documents and displays make up the folk section, which covers the heritage and history of Winchcombe. There is information on local history and family histories. International police uniforms, caps, helmets, badges, truncheons and a rare 1835 'Peeler' in his tall stovepipe hat make up the collection on the police. The police material, known as the Simms Collection, was donated by a local resident, a renowned expert on police uniforms.

BUILDING: Winchcombe Town Hall, 1853-71. The museum is on the upper floor and includes the old courtroom.

OPENING TIMES: *April to October*, Monday to Saturday: 10am–4.30pm. (Closed Sunday.)

ADMISSION CHARGES: ①

🅿 WC ♿ ♣♣♣

DIRECTIONS: Winchcombe is north east of Cheltenham on the B4632 to Broadway. The museum is in the centre of Winchcombe above the Tourist Information Centre, in the old town hall.

Herefordshire

HEREFORD
Churchill House Museum (costume) ✳

Venns Lane, Aylestone Hill, Hereford HR1 1DE

TEL: 01432 260693

COLLECTION: Hereford City Council bought the house in1965 and moved its large collection of costumes there from the Broad Street Museum. Many of the costumes were donated in the 1930s and the museum contains a range of clothes and accessories, including needlepoint lace of the late 16th century and a cavalry officer's hat with plume dating from 1910. There is also the Hatton Gallery dedicated to the work of local artist Brian Hatton, who was killed in World War II. Permission must be requested for photography. Research facilities are available by appointment.

BUILDING: Built around 1834 by the Reverend John Evans and originally known as Penn Grove House. Only the ground floor is accessible by wheelchair.

OPENING TIMES: *April to September*, Wednesday to Friday, Sunday and bank holidays. (Closed Monday, Tuesday & Saturday.)

ADMISSION CHARGES: Free

🅟 ♿ WC ♿ 🎥 ♣♣♣

DIRECTIONS: The museum is off the A4103, Commercial Road, which goes north east towards Malvern and Worcester. Cross the railway line and take the fourth road to the left.

HEREFORD
The Cider Museum ✳ ✳

21 Ryelands Street, Hereford HR4 0LW

TEL: 01432 354207 FAX: 01432 371641

WEBSITE: www.cidermuseum.co.uk

COLLECTION: H.P. Bulmer Ltd is the largest cider-maker in the world. It was due to the efforts of the retiring chairman, Bertram Bulmer, that the museum was created and opened in 1981. It is the only registered museum devoted entirely to cider- and perry-making. The whole cider-making industry, from its earliest beginnings to the mass production methods of today, is explored. Cider-making machinery, equipment, advertising material, photographs and newspaper cuttings from 1760 are on display. A reconstructed farm cider-house contains a complete set of a travelling cider-maker's tack. There is a working distillery, which produces cider brandy and other products. The archives are available for research by appointment.

BUILDING: Percy Bulmer's original cider mill.

OPENING TIMES: *April to October*, daily: 10am–5.30pm. *November to December*, daily: 11am–3pm. *January to March*, Tuesday to Sunday: 11am–3pm. (Closed Monday.) Tea-room open April to October and in winter by arrangement. Only the ground floor is accessible by wheelchair. There are no other facilities for the disabled.

ADMISSION CHARGES: ①

Ⓟ ♿ 🚾 ◭ ⚠ ♨

DIRECTIONS: The museum is west of Hereford off the A438 Hereford to Brecon road. Eign Street becomes Whitecross Road and the museum is off to the left if heading west.

HEREFORD
Waterworks Museum ✳

Broomy Hill, Hereford HR4 0JS

TEL: (museum coordinator) 01432 356653 or 01600 890118 or 01432 359915

COLLECTION: A 100-year time-capsule of working machinery and social history, the museum tells the story of water supplies in Wales and the Marches. There is a unique range of engines and pumps on display and some machines are the last examples of their kind working anywhere in the world. The treasure of the collection is the oldest working triple-expansion steam engine in the UK, which stands two floors high. The historic water-pumping station from Leominster, which saved that town from typhoid in the 1860s, has been rebuilt on the museum site. The archives of the museum are available for research on application.

BUILDING: The Victorian water-pumping station for the city of Hereford. It is a scheduled ancient monument and listed Grade II building. Picnic tables are available. Next door is a water-treatment plant, which can be visited as well as the museum, with good prior notice.

OPENING TIMES: *Easter to the end of September*, last Sunday in the month for public open days in-steam, all engines working: 2pm–5pm. *June to end of September*, plus second Sunday in the month and also on Easter Monday, Spring Holiday Monday and August Holiday Monday. *April to end of September*, not in-steam, but with at least one engine working every Tuesday: 11am–4pm. (Telephone for details of all times and dates if travelling any distance to the museum.)

The Waterworks
Museum, Hereford

ADMISSION CHARGES: ①

ⓟ ♿ 🚾 🚼 ⚠ 📷 👫

DIRECTIONS: By the River Wye in Hereford, about two-thirds of a mile from the cathedral. Follow brown heritage signs from the A49 through-route in Hereford. There are brown signs at the Wye bridge. Also a riverside walk to the museum, signposted from the city centre.

WORMELOW
Violette Szabo G.C. Museum ✳

'Cartref', Wormelow, Hereford HR2 3HN

TEL: 01981 540477

E-MAIL: rosemaryerigbymbe@violetteszabogcmuseum.org

WEBSITE: www.violetteszabogcmuseum.org

COLLECTION: Daughter of an English father and French mother and brought up in Brixton, Violette Bushell became a heroine. She met and married a French officer of the French Foreign Legion, Etienne Szabo. She had a daughter but her husband was killed in 1942. She spoke fluent French, and the authorities contacted her to become a British secret agent in France. Her role was to contact the French Resistance Movement. In an effort to save others she was captured and tortured, but remained silent. Finally she was shot. She was posthumously awarded the George Cross. Her life was told in a book and the film *Carve Her Name With Pride*. Panels of written work and photos tell her life and there are other items of interest, such as her letters. The collection was put together by Rosemary Rigby, who spent years tracing documents and photographs. Research facilities are available.

BUILDING: A small purpose-built building of Herefordshire stone.

OPENING TIMES: *April to October*, Wednesday: 11am–1pm & 2pm–4pm.

ADMISSION CHARGES: Free

Ⓟ ♿ 🚾 ♨

DIRECTIONS: Wormelow is south of Hereford. From there take the A49 towards Ross-on-Wye. At the Pilgrim Hotel at Much Birch, turn right for Wormelow. 'Cartef' is the first house on the left.

Oxfordshire

HENLEY
River and Rowing Museum ❄ ✳

Mill Meadows, Henley-on-Thames, Oxfordshire RG9 1BF

TEL: 01491 415610 FAX: 01491 415601

E-MAIL: museum@rrm.co.uk   WEBSITE: www.rrm.co.uk

COLLECTION: From the Greek Trireme to modern Olympic rowing boats, the museum explores rowing in all its forms. It is the only museum in the world with galleries dedicated to rowing and the quest for speed. The history of the River Thames is displayed and the riverside town of Henley is featured during the Royal Regatta.

BUILDING: An award-winning building designed as a museum by David Chipperfield.

OPENING TIMES: *Easter to 30 September*, Monday to Friday: 10am–6pm, Saturday & Sunday: 10.30am–6pm. *1 October to Easter*, Monday to Friday: 10am–5pm, Saturday & Sunday: 10.30am–5pm. Closed Christmas Eve, Christmas Day, New Year's Eve and New Year's Day.

ADMISSION CHARGES: ②

Ⓟ ♿ 🚾 ☕ ☂ ♨

DIRECTIONS: By car follow signs for Mill Meadows off the A4130 Oxford to Maidenhead Road in Henley. To walk follow the fingerpost signs around the town centre. Meadow Road is off Station Road and Mill Meadows is a continuation of Meadow Road.

KELMSCOTT
Kelmscott Manor (William Morris) ✳

Kelmscott, nr. Lechlade, Oxfordshire GL7 3HJ

Kelmscott
Manor,
Kelmscott

TEL: (enquiries) 01367 252486 (administration) 01367 253348

FAX: 01367 253754

COLLECTION: Known as the founder of the Arts and Crafts movement, William Morris (1834–96) lived in Kelmscott Manor from 1871 until his death. He spent a lot of his time in London overseeing the production of furniture, textiles, wallpapers and stained glass. The manor is full of Morris's possessions and his products, including furniture, textiles, carpets, ceramics and drawings. Images of the gardens and the local countryside pervade his textile and wallpaper designs. A charming house and garden.

BUILDING: The original Elizabethan building of Kelmscott Manor was built around 1570, probably by Richard Turner, a local farmer, and extended by his great-grandson in the 17th century. Parking in a rough grass field.

OPENING TIMES: *1 April to 30 September*, every Wednesday: 11am–1pm & 2pm–5pm. *April, May, June & September*, Wednesday plus every third Saturday: 2pm–5pm. *July & August*, above days & times plus every first Saturday: 2pm–5pm. Private visits, minimum of 15 people, can be arranged on Thursdays and Fridays from April to September.

ADMISSION CHARGES: ②

Ⓟ ⒲ⓒ ▽ ♿

DIRECTIONS: Kelmscott is off the A417 Cirencester to Farringdon road. After Lechdale turn left at the fork on to the B4449. Kelmscott is on the right. The village and the Manor are signposted from the road.

OXFORD
Bate Collection of Musical Instruments ❆ ✺

Faculty of Music, St Aldgate's Street, Oxford OX1 1DB

TEL: 01865 286261 FAX: 01865 276128

E-MAIL: bate.collection@music.ox.ac.uk

WEBSITE: www.ashmol.ox.ac.uk/BCMIPage.html

COLLECTION: A fascinating collection of over 1,000 historic woodwind, brass and per-cussion instruments. There are twelve historic keyboards, including Handel's harpsichord, a fine collection of bows and a unique bow-maker's workshop. The Bate Collection runs workshops to introduce instruments, such as the viol to beginners and also offers to teach bow-making. Photography is allowed only for research purposes out of hours and by appointment with the curator. Research facilities, a library and archive are available by appointment.

BUILDING: Housed in the Faculty of Music. There are two galleries. Only partially accessible by wheelchair.

OPENING TIMES: *All year*, Monday to Friday: 2pm–5pm, Saturday (during Oxford full term only): 10am–12noon. (Closed Sunday.) Visits at other times by appointment.

ADMISSION CHARGES: Free

🅿 ♿ 🅆🅒 ♿ 👪

DIRECTIONS: It is easier to use the Park & Ride car-parks. For Collection see map.

OXFORD
Museum of the History of Science ❆ ✺

Broad Street, Oxford OX1 3AZ

TEL: 01865 277280

E-MAIL: museum@mhs.ox.ac.uk

WEBSITE: www.mhs.ox.ac.uk

COLLECTION: All kinds of scientific instruments are on display, including astrolabes, telescopes, microscopes, sundials and clocks. The displays also cover all aspects of the history of science from antiquity to the early 20th century. There are early mathematical

Flutes, Bate
Collection
of Musical
Instruments,
Oxford

West Central

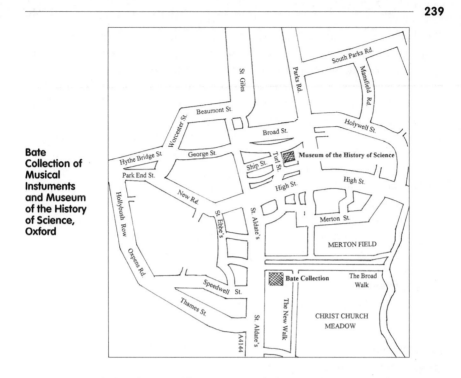

**Bate
Collection of
Musical
Instuments
and Museum
of the History
of Science,
Oxford**

instruments, including those used for surveying, calculating and astronomy. The apparatus associated with chemistry is also exhibited. The museum is of interest to older children from about twelve years of age. There is a unique reference library. Photography is allowed but not the use of a tripod.

BUILDING: The Old Ashmolean, built in 1683, is the oldest surviving purpose-built museum.

OPENING TIMES: *All year*, Tuesday to Saturday: 12 noon–4pm. (Closed Sunday & Monday.) Closed Christmas week and bank holidays.

ADMISSION CHARGES: Free

DIRECTIONS: See map.

UFFINGTON
Tom Brown's School Museum ❋

Uffington, Oxfordshire SN7 7RA

TEL: 01367 820259

E-MAIL: museum@uffington.net WEBSITE: www.uffington.net/museum

COLLECTION: John Little, a great collector of editions of the novel *Tom Brown's School*

Days by Thomas Hughes, had the idea of starting the museum, which was opened in 1984. The museum building is actually the school that Thomas Hughes refers to in the opening chapters of his book. It now holds John Little's collection of editions of the book and has displays about Hughes and information on Victorian schools. It is also a showcase for items of local history and documents the lives of some of Uffington's famous residents, including Sir John Betjeman.

BUILDING: Built in 1617 by Thomas Saunders, a merchant of Woolstone for the education of twelve poor boys of Uffington and Woolstone. It was subsequently endowed with land and a house to provide for a schoolmaster in perpetuity. When a new village school was built in the 1850s the old schoolroom became the village reading room. It now has Grade I listed building status. Only partly accessible by wheelchair.

OPENING TIMES: *Easter Sunday to last full weekend in October*, Saturday, Sunday and Bank Holiday Mondays: 2pm–5pm. (Closed Monday to Friday.) Open other times for school parties, etc. by arrangement with the curator.

ADMISSION CHARGES: ①

DIRECTIONS: Uffington is signposted from the B4507 Swindon to Wantage road and the A420 Swindon to Oxford road.

WATERPERRY
Garden Antiques Museum ❄ ✺

Waterperry House and Gardens, Waterperry, nr. Wheatley, Oxfordshire OX33 1JZ

TEL: (main office for Waterperry Gardens) 01844 339226
FAX: 01844 339883
WEBSITE: (for Waterperry Gardens) www.waterperrygardens.co.uk

COLLECTION: An 1882 apple-peeler that can peel an apple in less than three seconds, leaving the peel in one long strip, is just one of the intriguing antique gadgets in this museum. Victor Hawes donated a large collection of garden tools to Gordon Dempster, the curator of the museum, in 1993. Gordon began collecting himself and now the little museum room is full of such strange items as the six-spiked mole-trap, an early food-processor, boots for horses and a spiral weeder for those impossible weeds. There are many more recognisable things such as horse brasses and one-handed shears. The Waterperry Gardens themselves are well worth visiting and are open daily: 9am–5pm.

BUILDING: The museum was opened in July 2000 and consists of one room in an old barn in the Waterperry complex of buildings. Toilets and a café are part of the Waterperry Garden facilities.

OPENING TIMES: *All year*, Thursday to Sunday: 2pm–5pm. Closed Monday to Wednesday. (Check times as the museum might be open for more days.) During the Art in Action

Festival for four days in July (check for dates), the gardens and museum are closed to non-festival visitors.

ADMISSION CHARGES: Free

Ⓟ ♿ 🄫 ↻ ⚠ 🖭 ᴟᴟᴟ

DIRECTIONS: From junction 8 on the M40, take the A418 to Thame. Not long after joining the A418 take a turning to Waterstock and Waterperry to your left. At the fork go left to Waterperry House and village. The museum is in the complex of buildings at Waterperry House, which includes the Art in Action Gallery and the Granary.

Shropshire

IRONBRIDGE
The Ironbridge Gorge Museums ❄ ✳

Ironbridge, Telford, Shropshire TF8 7AW

TEL: 01952 432166 (group bookings) 01952 433522 FAX: 01952 432204

E-MAIL: info@ironbridge.org.uk WEBSITE: www.ironbridge.org.uk

COLLECTION: Ironbridge Gorge is now known as the 'birthplace of the Industrial Revolution'. It is the site of five small museums, Rosehill House, a 'Victorian town' and, of course, the Ironbridge itself, and has been designated a World Heritage Site.

The Museum of the Gorge features a 40-foot model of the Gorge as it was in 1796. *The Museum of Iron* contains the original iron-smelting furnace of Abraham Darby I and illustrates the history of iron-making and the story of the Coalbrookdale Company. In the 18th century the valley was the most important iron-making centre in the world. *Rosehill House* is the restored home of Abraham Darby I's son-in-law and displays the possessions and the way of life of a Quaker ironmaster during the first half of the 19th century.

Jackfield Tile Museum A century ago, Jackfield was home to two of the largest decorative tile-works in the world. The museum displays decorative tiles and ceramics in gaslit galleries. Modern tile-making is demonstrated and there is a shop.

Coalport China Museum The remains of the old china-works form part of the museum, which also includes galleries, demonstration workshops and a shop. A café is next door. From the museum there is a walk along the canal to the Tar Tunnel. *The Tollhouse* at the south end of the bridge contains an exhibition about the bridge.

Broseley Pipeworks Museum on the south side of the river is a preserved 'time-capsule' of the ancient local industry of clay tobacco pipe-making. It is a few miles from Ironbridge and has limited opening hours. The Long Warehouse, next to the Museum of Iron, houses the Museum Library and the Elton Collection. This is a collection of industrial art, photographs, prints and drawings. The Library and Archives Department is available by written appointment only. There are some restrictions on photography depending on the individual sites.

BUILDING: The buildings are original. Some museums are less wheelchair-accessible than others. There is a special free guide for visitors with special needs.

OPENING TIMES: The site is open *all year*, daily: 10am–5pm. However, some museums close from November to March. The Broseley Pipeworks is open 1pm–5pm in the main season. All museums are closed on 24 & 25 December and New Year's Day. The Tourist Information Centre in Ironbridge is open daily: weekdays at 9am & weekends at 10am. Telephone on the numbers above to check opening times in winter, or check the website.

ADMISSION CHARGES: For a passport for all the attractions: ③
Individual museums have separate and quite reasonable charges. The passport is more economical for visiting all the attractions.

Ⓟ ♿ 🚾 ⛱ ⚠ 🎥 🏢

DIRECTIONS: Ironbridge is on the River Severn, five miles south of Telford. Take junction 4 from the M54 and the brown signs take you straight to Blists Hill Victorian Town. Or follow the signs to Telford and start at the Iron Bridge Tollhouse, The Museum of the Gorge or the Tourist Information Centre.

OSWESTRY
The Cambrian (trains, bicycles, motorcycles) ❄ ✳

Oswald Road, Oswestry, Shropshire SY11 1RE

TEL: 01691 671749

COLLECTION: Oswestry was once the headquarters of the Cambrian Railways Company until amalgamation with the Great Western Railway Company in 1922. Locomotives, carriages and wagons were built and repaired in the town. The Cambrian Railway Society is restoring and operating trains on part of the old Cambrian narrow-gauge railway. In the museum there is a collection of railway memorabilia, steam locomotives and rail wagons, plus 45 old bicycles and twelve motorcycles.

BUILDING: A former Cambrian Railway grain-shed. One large room. There are two steps up into the museum, otherwise the museum itself is accessible by wheelchair. There is a café only on special open days.

OPENING TIMES: *All year, Easter to mid-September*, daily: 10am–4pm. *Mid-September to Easter*, daily: 10am–3pm. Closed Christmas Day. The museum is staffed by volunteers and opening hours may be changed. Telephone if travelling any distance.

ADMISSION CHARGES: ①

Ⓟ ♿ 🚾 ⚠ 🎥 🏢

DIRECTIONS: Oswestry is north west of Shrewsbury off the A5. The museum is in the town centre next to the disused railway station.

Staffordshire

LEEK
Brindley Mill ✳

Mill Street, Leek, Staffordshire ST13 8ET

TEL: (Leek Tourist Information Office) 01538 483741

COLLECTION: This working water-powered corn mill was built by James Brindley (1716–72). He became an important engineer and canal-builder. He was brought up as a millwright, and his work as an architect is seen in the mill and in a special display illustrating his life and work. There are also displays on the history of milling. Traditional tools associated with milling are on show and so are some of Brindley's own possessions, his notebooks and his surveyor's level.

BUILDING: The mill was built in 1752 and restored in 1974. It operates to demonstrate corn-milling. It is on three floors. There is a riverside garden.

OPENING TIMES: *Easter Saturday to the end of September*, Saturday & Sunday and bank holidays: 2pm–5pm. (Closed weekdays.) *July to the end of August*, also open on Monday, Tuesday & Wednesday: 2pm–5pm.

ADMISSION CHARGES: ①

🅿 ⚠ 🚻 ♿

DIRECTIONS: The mill is on the A523, north west out of Leek to Bosley and Maccles-field. Once you are on the edge of Leek the mill is on the right-hand side.

LONGTON
Gladstone Pottery Museum ❄ ✳

Uttoxeter Road, Longton, Stoke-on-Trent ST3 1PQ

TEL: 01782 319232 FAX: 01782 598640

E-MAIL: gladstone@stoke.gov.uk

WEBSITE: www.stoke.gov.uk/gladstone

COLLECTION: The museum is the only complete Victorian pottery factory from the days when coal-burning ovens made the world's first bone china. The most important features are the four original bottle ovens and an enamel kiln. There is also a ceramic tile collection and the chance to make your own pot and a bone china flower. Demon-strations of a potter at work are given.

BUILDING: Built in the 1770s, the works had a series of owners. The ovens last fired at the Gladstone works in 1960. The site was saved from demolition by a group of interested people and bought by Derek Johnson, a tile manufacturer. It was handed over to the Staffordshire Pottery Industry Preservation Trust and opened as a museum in 1974. The

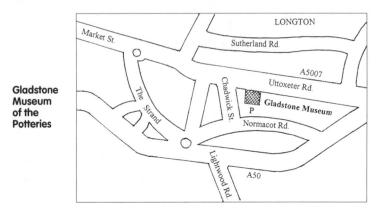

Gladstone
Museum
of the
Potteries

museum plans new developments, such as a restored doctor's house and surgery, plus the opening of the Museum of the Toilet.

OPENING TIMES: *All year*, daily: 10am–5pm. Two hours are recommended for a visit. Last admission 4pm. Closed Christmas week.

ADMISSION CHARGES: ②

Ⓟ ♿ WC 🚻 ⚠ 📹 👫

DIRECTIONS: From the M6, junction 15, follow the A500 and take the A50 to Longton. For museum see map.

STOKE-ON-TRENT
The World of Spode ❄ ✳

Spode, Church Street, Stoke-on-Trent, Staffordshire ST4 1BX

TEL: 01782 744011 FAX: 01782 572526

E-MAIL: spodemuseum@easynet.co.uk

WEBSITE: www.spode.co.uk

COLLECTION: When the East India Company began to reduce its imports of chinaware, Josiah Spode (1733-97) perfected the process of blue underglaze printing on earthenware from hand-engraved copper plates. These reproductions of the blue Chinese porcelain designs and later original patterns were enough to secure his reputation. He went on to discover how to make bone china as well. All this is celebrated in the museum, which features a priceless collection of blue-and-white pieces dating back to the 1770s. There are also Copeland ceramics. Factory tours are available by pre-booking and there is a demonstration area. Photography is allowed, but only with prior permission from the museum office. An archive of patterns from the late 18th century is available for research by appointment.

BUILDING: Spode is the English pottery company still operating on the same historic

Three items of
antique blue and
white Spode,
The World of
Spode,
Stoke-on-Trent

site. Part of the original Spode factory from the 1700s is still there, with developments through the last 200 years. Due to the nature of the buildings access is limited by wheel-chair and for the disabled.

OPENING TIMES: *All year,* Monday to Saturday: 9am–4pm, Sunday: 10am–4pm.

ADMISSION CHARGES: Free

Ⓟ ⓦ ✕ ⚠ 📷 🚻

DIRECTIONS: See map.

**Spode
Museum,
Stoke-on-
Trent**

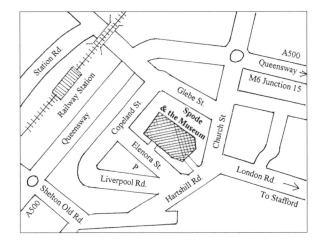

Staffordshire

Warwickshire

RUGBY
James Gilbert Rugby Football Museum ❋ ✳

5 St Matthews Street, Rugby CV21 3BY

TEL: 01788 333889 FAX: 01788 540795

E-MAIL: museum@james-gilbert.com

WEBSITE: www.rugby-museum.com

COLLECTION: Rugby memorabilia from around the world, such as early photographs, programmes and caps, help to tell the story of the game of rugby from its early beginnings to the present day. The making of rugby balls is explained and there is often a demonstration of this craft. There is a ten-minute audio-visual show about rugby.

BUILDING: The site where Gilbert footballs have been made since 1842. The original shop-front from which Gilbert traded is still there. The museum is accessible by wheelchair but there are no other facilities for the disabled.

OPENING TIMES: *All year*, Monday to Friday: 9am–5.15pm, Saturday: 9am–5pm. (Closed Sunday.)

ADMISSION CHARGES: Free

DIRECTIONS: See map.

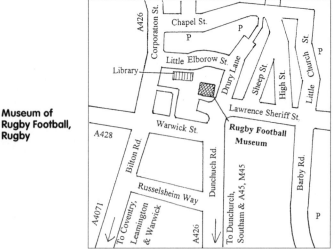

Museum of Rugby Football, Rugby

STRATFORD-UPON-AVON
Royal Shakespeare Company Collection ❊ ❋

Royal Shakespeare Theatre, Stratford-upon-Avon, Warwickshire CV37 6BB

TEL: 01789 296655   FAX: 01789 294810

WEBSITE: www.rsc.org.uk

COLLECTION: This is a unique theatre collection owned by the RSC. It consists of paintings, sculptures, drawings, costumes, stage properties, production designs and memorabilia. There are costumes worn by Sir John Gielgud and Sir Laurence Olivier and many more, plus the famous Flower Portrait of Shakespeare and portraits of actors. The collection was founded in 1881 as an integral part of the Shakespeare Memorial Theatre and temporary exhibitions of selected material from the collection are housed in the original Picture Gallery. There are research facilities. Apply in writing to the curator.

BUILDING: Within the RSC building. Café, restaurant and toilets are available within the theatre.

OPENING TIMES: *All year*, Monday to Saturday: 12.30pm–6pm, Sunday: 12 noon–4pm. Closed Christmas Day.

ADMISSION CHARGES: ①

Ⓟ ⓦⓒ ⛱ ✕ ⚠ 📹 ♀♂

DIRECTIONS: See map (on p. 248).

STRATFORD-UPON-AVON
The Teddy Bear Museum ❊ ❋

19 Greenhill Street, Stratford-upon-Avon, Warwickshire CV37 6LF

TEL: 01789 293160

WEBSITE: www.theteddybearmuseum.com

COLLECTION: Hundreds of bears from around the world are arranged in different rooms, the bedroom, music room and library. There is a rare Steiff bear, a Bavarian wooden cut-out bear that dances and far less rare but much-loved examples of teddy bears whose fur has almost disappeared through constant hugging. There are bears of the famous and hand-made dressed teddy bears. All these bears are named 'Teddy' after the American President Theodore 'Teddy' Roosevelt, who in 1902 refused to kill a bear that had been tied up especially for him to shoot. He let the bear go and a shopkeeper in Brooklyn, hearing of the event, sought his permission to manufacture a small toy bear-cub called 'Teddy's bear'. From such ideas do museums of teddy bears grow! Photography is allowed only in the shop.

BUILDING: Once an Elizabethan farmhouse. Restored 400 years later to its former glory.

OPENING TIMES: *All year*, daily: 9am–6pm (5pm in January and February). Closed 25 & 26 December.

ADMISSION CHARGES: ①

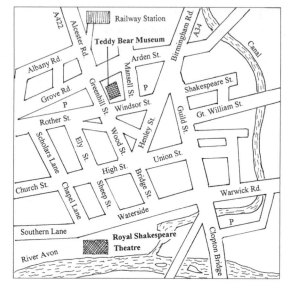

The Teddy Bear Museum and Royal Shakespeare Museum, Stratford-upon-Avon

DIRECTIONS: See map.

WARWICK
The Doll Museum ❄ ✹

Oaken's House, Castle Street, Warwick CV34 4BP

TEL: 01926 495546 or 01926 412500

COLLECTION: Mechanical toys, a German 'Revalo' doll of the 1920s, plus hundreds of dolls, teddy bears and toys from the 18th century to the present day. The workings of the mechanical toys are explained on video. There is a book corner and a chance to have a go at hopscotch or spinning tops. The doll collection was once privately owned and was bought by the Warwickshire Museum service in the late 1980s. Photography is allowed with permission.

BUILDING: A small half-timbered 16th-century house with six small rooms.

OPENING TIMES: *Easter to October*, Monday to Saturday: 10am–5pm. Sunday: 11am–5pm. *November to Easter*, Saturday only: 10am to dusk. (Closed Sunday to Friday in winter.)

ADMISSION CHARGES: ①

DIRECTIONS: Parking nearby is not easy. The museum is off the High Street, down Castle Street, towards Warwick Castle. The museum is on the right in Castle Street.

WELLESBOURNE
Wellesbourne Wartime Museum ❄ ✺

Wellesbourne Airfield, Control Tower Entrance, Wellesbourne, Warwickshire CV35 9EU

TEL: 01926 855031

COLLECTION: The Wellesbourne Aviation Group decided to set up a museum in 1986, at the airfield, to house its growing collection of aircraft archaeology and wartime memorabilia. It now has a few static aircraft as well, such as a Vampire T11 XK590 and the nose of a Sea Vixen XJ575. It also has a Roll of Honour of the 316 airmen and women who died while serving at Wellesbourne from 1941 to 1945, 243 of whom were from the Royal Canadian Air Force.

BUILDING: Created in 1941, the Wellesbourne airfield was a base for an Operational Training Unit until 1945. It was bombed four times. The underground section of the museum is not accessible by wheelchair.

OPENING TIMES: *All year*, Sunday and bank holidays: 10am–4pm. Closed Monday to Saturday and Christmas Day, Boxing Day and New Year's Day.

ADMISSION CHARGES: ①

Ⓟ ♿ Ⓐ ▣ 👫

DIRECTIONS: The museum and airport are between the B4086 Stanford to Wellesbourne road and the A422 Stratford to Banbury road. It is north of Loxley.

Museum of the Jewellery Quarter, Birmingham

Warwickshire

West Midlands

BIRMINGHAM
Museum of the Jewellery Quarter ❄ ✳

75–79 Vyse Street, Hockley, Birmingham B18 6HA

TEL: 0121 554 3598

WEBSITE: www.birmingham.gov.uk/bmag (Quote reference JQ99)

COLLECTION: This is a jewellery factory just as it used to be. The business was begun by Smith & Pepper in 1899 and the firm made gold bangles, brooches, cufflinks, lockets and crosses. When it ceased operation in 1981 everything was left in place. The museum has re-created the factory, including all the work-benches, machines and even the original jars of Marmite that were to go on the daily toast made in the workshop. Displays tell the story of the jewellery-making area and the raw material of the trade. Videos explain jewellery-making through the ages and the techniques used. Jewellers now work at the special bench as they used to when the factory was operating. Obtain a permission form for photography.

BUILDING: The factory was built at Vyse Street in 1914. In 1990 its contents were emptied and catalogued. The derelict house next door was rebuilt to provide visitor facilities, and finally everything was put back in its place inside the restored factory.

OPENING TIMES: *All year*, Monday to Friday: 10am–4pm, Saturday: 11am–5pm. Closed Sunday. Open bank holidays, except Christmas and New Year.

**Museum of
the Jewellery
Quarter,
Birmingham**

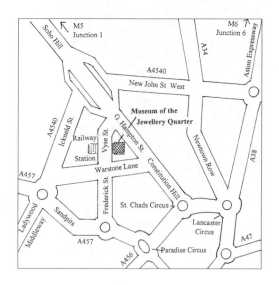

Sappho cameo
glass plaque,
Broadfield House
Glass Museum,
Kingswinford

ADMISSION CHARGES: ①

P 🚻 WC 🚼 ⚠ 🍴 🚻

DIRECTIONS: See map.

KINGSWINFORD
Broadfield House Glass Museum ❄ ❋

Compton Drive, Kingswinford, West Midlands DY6 9NS

TEL: 01384 812745 FAX: 01384 812746

WEBSITE: www.dudley.gov.uk

COLLECTION: Featuring the very best of British glass, much of which was made locally, the collection begins with the 18th century. It moves from this elegant glass right through to contemporary work. There are Regency cut decanters, Victorian cameo vases and Art

Deco clocks. Glassblowers and engravers are at work. Holiday workshops are run. The museum library is available by appointment.

BUILDING: A late Georgian mansion, with an award-winning all-glass extension. Hot drinks are available. The ground floor galleries, glass-making studio and shop are accessible by wheelchair.

OPENING TIMES: *All year*, Tuesday to Sunday: 2pm–5pm. Closed Monday but open on bank holidays: 10am–5pm. Glassblowing studio open Wednesday to Sunday: 2pm–5pm. Museum and studio closed Christmas Day, Boxing Day and New Year's Eve. Telephone to check Christmas and New Year opening.

ADMISSION CHARGES: Free

Ⓟ ♿ 🚻 ♿ 🍴 🚻

DIRECTIONS: Twelve miles from M5 junction 2 (Dudley), or junction 4 (Stourbridge). Compton Drive and the museum are off the A491 Stourbridge to Wolverhampton road to the west in Kingswinford.

WALSALL
Walsall Leather Museum ❋ ✳

Littleton Street West, Walsall, West Midlands WS2 8EQ

TEL: 01922 721153 FAX: 01922 725827

E-MAIL: leathermuseum@walsall.gov.uk

COLLECTION: The peak of the leather industry in Walsall was around 1900, when 10,000 people were engaged in the leather industry and making saddlery and harness. After a

Walsall Leather Museum

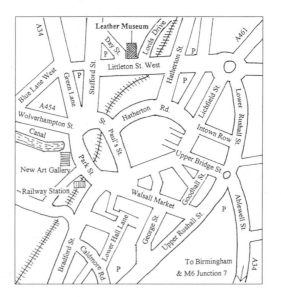

dip, the saddlery business is back in demand and there are about 60 saddlery firms in the area. Featuring examples of local craftsmanship, past and present, the museum's collection includes saddles made for the royal family and exciting contemporary designs. In the workshops skilled leatherworkers make wallets and purses and the visitor can have a go. Displays tell the story of the Walsall trades. There is a library.

BUILDING: Built in 1891 as a leather and metalwork factory. The museum was opened in 1988 and has landscaped gardens and picnic areas.

OPENING TIMES: *All year*, Tuesday to Saturday: 10am–5pm, Sunday: 12 noon–5pm. (Closed Monday.) November to March closed at 4pm. Leather demonstrations from Tuesday to Saturday.

ADMISSION CHARGES: Free

🅿 ♿ 🆆🅲 🛆 🎥 ♨

DIRECTIONS: See map.

WILLENHALL
The Lock Museum ❄ ✳

54/56 New Road, Willenhall, West Midlands WV13 2DA

TEL/FAX: 01902 634542

WEBSITE: members.tripod.co.uk/lockmuseum

COLLECTION: Since the reign of Elizabeth I, Willenhall has been the centre of lock-making. The buildings of the Lock Museum were owned by the Hodson family, who had made locks in Willenhall since 1792. Their descendants, John and Sarah Hodson, moved to 54 New Road in 1904. Locks were then made by hand but now they are mass-produced by machine. After World War I the two Hodson sisters, Edith and Flora, daughters of John and Sarah, ran a draper's shop in the front downstairs room and locks continued to be made in the workshop. The draper's shop and the living quarters are on display, as are the workshops and varnish room, where the locks were protected against rust. There is also a collection of unusual locks.

BUILDING: Built in the 1840s and home to the Hodson family from 1904. Ground floor access by wheelchair. There are disabled toilets.

OPENING TIMES: *All year*, Tuesday, Wednesday, Thursday & Saturday: 11am–5pm (last admission 4pm). (Closed Friday, Sunday & Monday.) Open bank holidays except Christmas. Evening bookings by arrangement and advance booking for parties.

ADMISSION CHARGES: Free

🅿 ♿ 🆆🅲 🛆 🎥 ♨

DIRECTIONS: Willenhall is west of Walsall on the A454 Wolverhampton to Walsall road. From Wolverhampton as you come into Willenhall take the left turning at the roundabout, which is the B4464, Somerford Place. At the next roundabout take the third turning (straight on) into New Road. The museum is on the left.

Worcestershire

REDDITCH
Forge Mill Needle Museum ❄ ✳

Needle Mill Lane, Riverside, Redditch B98 8HY

TEL: 01527 62509

E-MAIL: museum@redditchbc.gov.uk

COLLECTION: Illustrations of how needles were made in the 19th century and the story of the Redditch needle industry are featured in the museum. Needles, needle machinery and tools, fishing tackle and photographs are on display. It has also become a leading centre for textile lovers, with exhibitions by top textile artists and a competition. The museum shop specialises in unusual needles and sewing accessories. There is archive material available for research. Bordesley Abbey Visitor Centre is nearby and features finds from the excavations at the adjacent Cistercian abbey site.

BUILDING: An early 19th-century industrial building with a working water wheel. There is a picnic area. The upper floor is not accessible by wheelchair. There is a disabled toilet and picnic table for wheelchairs.

OPENING TIMES: *Easter to September*, Monday to Friday: 11am–4.30pm, Saturday & Sunday: 2pm–5pm. *February to Easter & October & November*, Monday to Thursday: 11am–4pm, Sunday: 2pm–5pm. (Closed Friday & Saturday.) Closed December & January.

ADMISSION CHARGES: For both the museum and the visitor centre: ②

Ⓟ ♿ [WC] ⚠ 🎥 👪

The Nelson
teapot,
The Museum
of Worcester
Porcelain,
Worcester

West Central

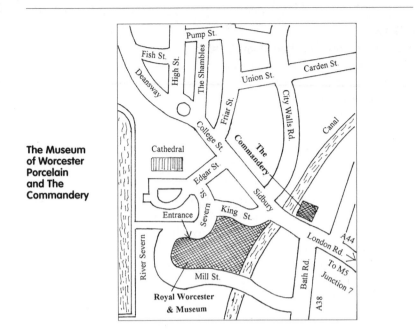

The Museum of Worcester Porcelain and The Commandery

DIRECTIONS: Junction 2 on the M42, on to the A441 for Stratford. The museum is off the A441, to the east of the road in Redditch.

WORCESTER
The Commandery (Cavaliers and Roundheads) ❄ ✳

Sidbury, Worcester WR1 2HU

TEL: 01905 361821

COLLECTION: At the Battle of Worcester in 1651, the Commandery was used as the Royalist Headquarters. It is now the country's only museum devoted to the story of England's Civil War. There are permanent displays and objects that help explain the events of the war and a video re-enactment of the last battle of the war. There are also a number of exhibitions and events throughout the year.

BUILDING: A complex of buildings from the medieval to the Georgian period.

OPENING TIMES: *All year*, Monday to Saturday: 10am–5pm, Sunday: 1.30pm–5pm. Closed Christmas Day, Boxing Day & New Year's Day.

ADMISSION CHARGES: ②

🅿 🚾 ↻ ♿ 📷 👫

DIRECTIONS: Junction 7 of the M5. The museum is right in the heart of Worcester just three minutes' walk from the Cathedral. See map.

Worcestershire

WORCESTER
The Museum of Worcester Porcelain ❄ ✺

Royal Worcester, Severn Street, Worcester WR1 2NE

TEL: 01905 23221   FAX: 01905 617807

E-MAIL: museum@royal-worcester.co.uk

WEBSITE: www.royal-worcester.co.uk (museum section)

COLLECTION: Porcelain manufacture began in Worcester in 1751. First of all shapes and patterns were copied from the Far East, but by the Victorian period Royal Worcester were producing original pieces of great craftsmanship. The museum displays the world's largest collection of Worcester porcelain in its three galleries. There are also panels explaining historical information and room settings, shopfronts and period scenes to display the porcelain. There is a new exhibition hall that hosts a programme of exhibitions and a search room open to the public. Tours of the factory can be arranged Monday to Friday.

BUILDING: A Victorian two-storey building.

OPENING TIMES: *All year*, Monday to Saturday: 1am–5.30pm, Sunday: 11am–5pm.

ADMISSION CHARGES: ①

Ⓟ ♿ 🚾 🚻 ✗ ⚠ 👪

DIRECTIONS: See map (on p. 255).

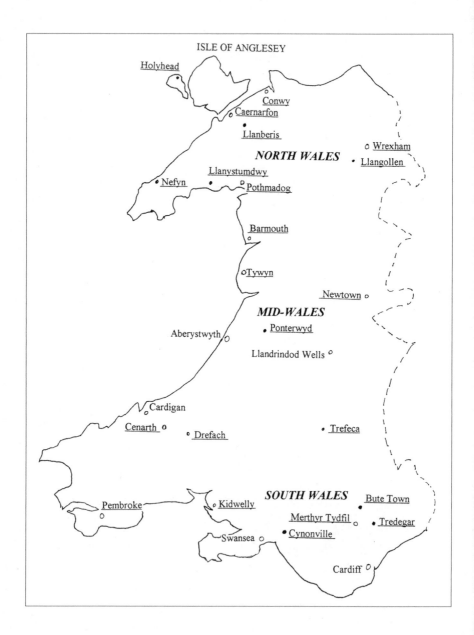

ISLE OF ANGLESEY

Holyhead

Conwy
Caernarfon

Llanberis

NORTH WALES

Wrexham
Llangollen

Llanystumdwy
Nefyn
Pothmadog

Barmouth

Tywyn

Newtown

MID-WALES

Ponterwyd
Aberystwyth

Llandrindod Wells

Cardigan
Cenarth
Drefach

Trefeca

SOUTH WALES
Bute Town

Pembroke
Kidwelly
Merthyr Tydfil
Tredegar
Cynonville
Swansea

Cardiff

North Wales

BARMOUTH
Barmouth RNLI Museum (lifeboat) ✸
The Quay, Barmouth, Gwynedd, Wales LL42 1HB

TEL: 01341 280940

COLLECTION: Photographs and exhibits of Barmouth lifeboat.

BUILDING: Upper floor of the original lifeboat house, 1828.

OPENING TIMES: *Easter to the end of September,* daily: 10.30am–4pm.

ADMISSION CHARGES: Free

🅿️ ♿ 🎁 ♟️

DIRECTIONS: Barmouth is south of Harlech on the A496 Harlech to Llanelltyd road. The museum is on Barmouth Harbour.

BEAUMARIS
Museum of Childhood Memories ✸
1 Castle Street, Beaumaris, Isle of Anglesey, Wales LL58 8AP

TEL: 01248 712498

WEBSITE: www.nwi.co.uk/museumofchildhood

COLLECTION: Toy money-boxes are one of Bob Brown's specialist areas. He first developed this interest in America. When he retired he realised that he had amassed a large collection of old toys, games, dolls and puzzles plus the money-boxes. This collection

Museum of
Childhood
Memories,
Beaumaris

forms the basis of the museum, which now houses about 2,000 items. A fully furnished Victorian dolls' house, rocking-horses and a large toy theatre complete with cut-out figures and decorative scenery are on display. In show cases are early dolls, tin toys and railway models including a rare British made cast-iron locomotive.

BUILDING: A Class II Georgian building with an extension building at the back. Only the ground floor is accessible by wheelchair, but admission is free.

OPENING TIMES: *Easter to 31 October*, Monday to Saturday: 10.30am–5.30pm, Sunday: 12 noon–5pm. Last admission half an hour before closing.

ADMISSION CHARGES: ①

🅿 ♿ Ⓦⓒ ⚠ 🍴 ♟

DIRECTIONS: Beaumaris is on the A545 from the north side of Menai Bridge. The museum is opposite the 13th-century Beaumaris Castle.

CAERNARFON
Caernarfon Maritime Museum ✳

Victoria Dock, Caernarfon, North Wales

TEL: 01286 675269

COLLECTION: Maps, ship models, navigational instruments and photographs help to illustrate the maritime and industrial history of the port and town of Caernarfon. There are items made and used by seamen. A new display demonstrating the operation of the dredger *Seiont II* re-creates the bridge and engine room, and there are also buoys and anchors.

BUILDING: Once the town mortuary, it is a whitewashed building on the dockside. Toilets and cafés are nearby.

OPENING TIMES: *Spring Bank Holiday to mid-September*, daily: 11am–4pm.

ADMISSION CHARGES: ①

🅿 ♿ ⚠ 🍴 ♟

DIRECTIONS: At Victoria Dock in Caernarfon, outside the town wall.

CONWY
Conwy Teapot Museum and Teapot World ✳

25 Castle Street, Conwy, North Wales LL32 8AY

TEL/FAX: 01492 593429 or 596533

E-MAIL: christine@teapotworld.co.uk

WEBSITE: www.teapotworld.co.uk

COLLECTION: A teapot looking like a wigwam, designed by Clarice Cliff around 1930, a Wedgwood teapot in the shape of a cauliflower and even a teapot of the top half of a man, his arms forming spout and handle, made by Worcester in 1880 are all on display.

These curious items are part of a collection that contains antique, novelty and humorous teapots and spans three centuries. Many of the teapots are extremely rare.

BUILDING: A look-out tower, part of Conwy Castle. The museum is looking for new premises, so do telephone if travelling some distance.

OPENING TIMES: *Easter to October,* Monday to Saturday: 10am–5.30pm, Sunday: 11am–5.30pm.

ADMISSION CHARGES: ①

🅿 ⚠ ♁

DIRECTIONS: The museum is 50 yards down from the castle in the main street of Conwy.

HOLYHEAD
Holyhead Maritime Museum ✳

Newry Beach, Beach Road, Anglesey, Holyhead, North Wales LL65 1ES

TEL: 01407 769745

COLLECTION: When the many layers of paint were removed from a figure-head painted to represent a white woman, the features of a black woman emerged. There are three other figure-heads in this museum plus ship models, photographs and artefacts relating to the maritime history of the town and port of Holyhead.

BUILDING: Said to be the oldest lifeboat house in Wales, it was built around 1857/58.

OPENING TIMES: *Week before Easter to end of September,* Monday to Sunday: 1pm–5pm. (Closed Saturday.)

ADMISSION CHARGES: ①

Ⓟ ♿ 🆆🅲 ⛢ ⚠ ♁

DIRECTIONS: Holyhead is on the north west corner of Wales, off the Isle of Anglesey. The museum is on Newry Beach, off Prince of Wales Road.

LLANBERIS
Welsh Slate Museum ❄ ✳

Gilfach Ddu, Padarn Country Park, Llanberis, Gwynedd, Wales LL55 4TY

TEL: 01286 870630 FAX: 01286 871906

E-MAIL: wampost@btconnect.com WEBSITE: www.nmgw.ac.uk

COLLECTION: Slate has been quarried in Wales since Roman times but it was not until the 1780s that the Welsh slate-mines and quarries began to develop. By the late 19th century Welsh counties produced over four-fifths of the total UK slate. This is a working museum with most of the machinery on display still usable and demonstrations of slate-splitting taking place daily. The different rooms are around a central courtyard and give a feeling of this once busy and noisy place. The iron brass foundry is a high building full of machines and objects. Up some stairs is the giant working water wheel, this can now also be reached by a lift. A re-erected and refurbished terrace of quarrymen's houses and

North Wales

the chief engineer's house are also within the complex of buildings. The museum has the only working example of a slate-carrying incline, used to carry slate down from the quarry. There is a 3D audio-visual show.

BUILDING: At the foot of Snowdon, the museum is located within the former repair and maintenance workshops of the Dinorwig slate quarry and was in use until 1969, when the quarry closed. The museum opened in 1972.

OPENING TIMES: *April to October*, daily: 10am–5pm. *November to March*, Sunday to Friday: 10am–4pm. (Closed Saturday.) Last admission one hour before closing.

ADMISSION CHARGES: ②

Ⓟ ♿ ⓦⓒ ☕ ⚠ 🎥 ⚇

DIRECTIONS: The museum is near the Llanberis Lake Railway in Llanberis.

LLANGOLLEN
Llangollen Motor Museum ❄ ✹

Pentrefelin, Llangollen, Wales LL20 8EE

TEL: 01978 860324

COLLECTION: A 1950s village garage with all its tools is on display, plus the living room next to the garage. There are more than 30 cars and motorbikes from the 1920s to the 1970s and motoring memorabilia. An additional exhibition depicts the history of the canal network. The shop is full of parts for older vehicles. There is a Motoring Reference Library.

BUILDING: An old slate-dressing works of around 1830, stone-built. There are no special facilities for the disabled. Teas and ices are sold.

OPENING TIMES: *April to October*, Tuesday to Sunday: 10am–5pm (closed Monday). *October to December & February to March*, Wednesday to Sunday: 11am–4pm (closed Monday & Tuesday). Closed for January.

ADMISSION CHARGES: ①

Ⓟ ♿ ⓦⓒ ⚠ 🎥 ⚇

DIRECTIONS: 1¼ miles from Llangollen bridge towards the Horshoe Pass. The museum is between the canal and the river.

LLANYSTUMDWY
The Lloyd George Museum ✹

Llanystumdwy, Criccieth, Gwynedd, Wales LL52 0SH

TEL/FAX: 01766 522071

E-MAIL: amgueddfeydd-museums@gwynedd.gov.uk

COLLECTION: David Lloyd George (1863–1945), although born in Manchester, was brought up in Wales and lived at Highgate, his boyhood home, from 1864 to 1880. He became a successful reforming Liberal MP and was prime minister from 1916 to 1922.

He introduced the pension, founded the welfare state, gave women the vote and tackled the Irish question. He also 'won the Great War'. The museum has re-created Lloyd George's uncle's shoemaking workshop and a Victorian schoolroom. There is a selection of memorabilia and a unique collection of about 25 caskets that were given to Lloyd George as offerings of the 'Freedom of the City' to recognise his work over the years. A film tells the story of Lloyd George's life. There are library facilities.

BUILDING: Highgate is 17th century or earlier. The museum building was designed by Clough Williams Ellis and opened in 1960. Only the first floor of the cottage is not accessible by wheelchair.

OPENING TIMES: *Easter*, daily: 10.30am–5pm. *April & May*, Monday to Friday: 10.30am–5pm (closed Saturday & Sunday). *June, July & September*, Monday to Saturday: 10.30am – 5pm (closed Sunday). *August*, daily: 10.30am–5pm. *October*, Monday to Friday: 11am–4pm (closed weekends). Closed November to Easter or beginning of April, whichever comes first. Open every bank holiday weekend. Open other times by appointment.

ADMISSION CHARGES: ①

DIRECTIONS: The museum is on the south side of the A497 between Pwllheli and Criccieth.

NEFYN
Lleyn Historical and Maritime Museum ✳
Old St Mary's Church, Church Street, Nefyn, Gwynedd, Wales LL53 6LB

TEL: 01758 720270

COLLECTION: Paintings, photographs and artefacts show the local maritime history. Details of shipbuilding, coasting vessels, the herring industry and everyday life at the turn of the 19th century are on display.

BUILDING: An old church on the site of a 6th-century Celtic church. On the tower is a weather-vane shaped as a full rigged ship.

OPENING TIMES: *Beginning of July to mid-September*, Monday to Saturday: 10.30am–4.30pm, Sunday: 2pm–4pm.

ADMISSION CHARGES: Free

DIRECTIONS: Nefyn is north of Aberdaron on the B4417 to Llanaelhaern. From the centre of the village, go north up Church Street. The museum is on the right in Old St Mary's Church. There is a field to park in.

PORTHMADOG
Maritime Museum ✳
Oakley Wharf, Porthmadog, North Wales

Welsh
Highland
Railway,
Porthmadog

TEL: 01766 513736 or 512864

COLLECTION: A display of shipbuilding tools, charts and navigational aids, plus paintings, photographs and models, all help to explain the maritime history of Porthmadog. The story of the world famous 'topsail' schooners and of other vessels is told, and there is information on the men who sailed in them.

BUILDING: An old slate shed on the wharf.

OPENING TIMES: *Easter week and then May Bank Holiday to the end of September*, daily: 11am–5pm.

ADMISSION CHARGES: ①

P &. WC ⑤ ♦♦♦

DIRECTIONS: Porthmadog is west of Ffestyniog on the A487 to Pwllheli. The museum is on the harbour wharf by the bridge, opposite Ffestyniog railway harbour's station.

PORTHMADOG
Welsh Highland Railway ❋
Tremadog Road, Porthmadog, North Wales LL49 9DY

TEL: 01766 513402 or 01766 514040

WEBSITE: www. whr.co.uk

COLLECTION: Starting life in 1872 as the North Wales Narrow Gauge Railway, it was extended and re-named in 1923 but finally closed in 1937. Today, original and replica stock runs on a ¾-mile section of track and this should soon be extended. Passengers can also look around the sheds and see a fine collection of locomotives, carriages and wagons and other artefacts from the original railway. It is possible to climb aboard several of the unused locomotives. There are steam and diesel locomotives. The museum is still in development.

BUILDING: Railway carriage shed.

OPENING TIMES: *April to October*, Saturday & Sunday, Easter week, some days in the week during *May, June & July, September and October*. Open all of *August*. (If travelling any distance, telephone for opening times and dates.) Train times beginning at 10.30am, then approximately every hour. Last train at 4pm.

ADMISSION CHARGES: ①

Ⓟ ♿ 🚾 🖤 ⚠ 📷 🏃

DIRECTIONS: Just off the High Street in Porthmadog.

TYWYN
The Narrow-Gauge Railway Museum ✳

Talyllyn Railway, Wharf Station, Tywyn, Gwynedd, Wales LL36 9EY

TEL: 01654 710472   FAX: 01654 711755

WEBSITE: www.talyllyn.co.uk/ngrm/

COLLECTION: Narrow-gauge railways were designed to suit the area and so are highly individual. The collection includes six steam locomotives and a large number of other items from the British and Irish narrow-gauge lines including wagons, signals, signs and brassware. A special exhibition tells the story of the Talyllyn Railway Preservation Society, the first volunteer group in the world to run a public railway. From Tywyn Wharf steam locomotives run on the narrow-gauge line to Nant Gwernol, and much of the railway is in the Snowdonia National Park.

BUILDING: The main terminal station. Most of the museum is accessible by wheelchair.

OPENING TIMES: *Easter to November*, daily: 10am–5pm, plus Boxing Day to New Year.

ADMISSION CHARGES: ①

🅿 ♿ 🚾 🖤 ⚠ 📷 🏃

DIRECTIONS: Tywyn is north of Aberdovey, on the A493 from Aberdovey to Dolgellau.

Mid-Wales

LLANDRINDOD WELLS
National Cycle Collection ✳ ❄

The Automobile Palace, Temple Street, Llandrindod Wells, Powys, Mid-Wales
LD1 5DL

TEL/FAX: 01597 825531

COLLECTION: Over 250 cycles are on display and there are a similar number in store. This is now one of the largest collections of cycles open to the public in Britain. Penny

'Ordinary
Penny Farthing',
National Cycle
Collection,
Llandrindod
Wells

farthings, hobby horses and boneshakers all date from 1818 and the display takes the viewer right up to date with modern Raleigh cycles. A journey through 180 years of cycle history includes drawings by cycle magazine illustrator Frank Patterson, modern fine art prints, photographs and memorabilia. The National Cycle Archive is kept at Warwick University. Researchers should contact university staff at the Modern Records Centre.

BUILDING: A Grade II listed Art Deco building, built in 1911.

OPENING TIMES: *All year*, daily: 10am–4pm.

ADMISSION CHARGES: ①

Ⓟ ♿ 🅦🅒 🛗 ⚠ 🎥 👪

DIRECTIONS: Llandrindod Wells is on the A483 Builth Wells to Newtown road. There are AA signs to the museum.

NEWTOWN
Newtown Textile Museum ❋ ✳

5–7 Commercial Street, Newtown, Powys, Wales SY16 2BL

TEL: (during opening hours) 01686 622024 (outside opening hours) 01938 554656

COLLECTION: Telling the story of the woollen and flannel industry in Newtown from 1790 to the beginning of the 20th century, the museum looks at the process from sheep to yarn. It investigates the qualities of Welsh wool and the effect of the industry on the people in the town. On display are spinning-wheels and other items associated with the industry. There is also an exhibition about the tanning and clog-making industries and a re-created worker's cottage.

BUILDING: An early 19th-century weaving shop, two floors of six, now three, back-to-back cottages and two large rooms on the third and fourth floors running the full length of the building. The workers would have lived in the cottages and worked upstairs in the weaving shop as handloom weavers or on associated tasks.

OPENING TIMES: *All year*, Tuesday to Saturday: 2pm–5pm. (Closed Sunday & Monday.) Open Bank Holiday Mondays, except Easter: 2pm–5pm.

ADMISSION CHARGES: Free

P WC ☕ ♁

DIRECTIONS: See map (on p. 268).

NEWTOWN
Robert Owen Museum ❄ ☀

The Cross, Broad Street, Newtown, Wales SY16 2BB

TEL: 01686 626345

E-MAIL: hojnd@robert-owen.midwales.com

WEBSITE: robert-owen.midwales.com/

COLLECTION: Born in Newtown, Robert Owen (1771–1858) became a reformer, a philanthropist and one of the first socialist theorists. Managing the New Lanark cotton-mills in Scotland from 1800, he developed into one of the greatest cotton manufacturers of his time, establishing a model factory village, reducing the hours of children's employment and creating an educational system. He was the inspirer of the Co-operative movement. The museum tells Robert Owen's story and displays items associated with him, his family and followers, including portraits and books and his life mask. Unusual items are a 'Silent Monitor' from New Lanark and labour notes denominated in hours. Research facilities are available by appointment. Photography requires permission.

BUILDING: Built in 1902 to provide a free library and reading room. It is a Grade II listed building. The Co-operative movement donated part of the cost in memory of Robert Owen. There are three steps at the entrance but a stair-climber is available.

OPENING TIMES: *All year*, Monday to Friday: 9.30am–12 noon & 2pm–3.30pm, Saturday: 9.30am–11.30am. (Closed Sunday.) Closed Christmas week and Good Friday.

ADMISSION CHARGES: Free

P ♿ ⚠ ☕ ♁

DIRECTIONS: See map (on p. 268).

NEWTOWN
W.H. Smith Museum ❄ ☀

24 High Street, Newtown, Powys, Wales SY16 2NP

TEL: 01686 626280

COLLECTION: From a humble paper round (or paper walk), started by Henry Walton Smith and Anna Smith in 1792, the business grew to today's household name, W.H. Smith.

Textile, W.H. Smith and Robert Owen Museums, Newtown

The museum documents this story with displays, models and memorabilia. A restored handcart was used from the early 1900s until the 1950s for the early-morning collection of newspaper parcels from the railway station. The firm used horses and bicycles to distribute papers and introduced a motorvan in 1932. Models of the bookstalls started on railway stations by W.H. Smith are reminders of the fact that the firm set up the first one at Euston Station in London. The firm also began circulating libraries in 1858, closing them down in 1961. There is a reserve collection of photographs, printed materials, etc., which may be viewed by appointment.

BUILDING: The first floor of the shop was once used as a circulating library and all the furniture in the museum comes from other W.H. Smith libraries. The shop has been restored to its original condition when it was first opened in 1927.

OPENING TIMES: Open during the shop's business hours, Monday to Saturday: 9am–5.30pm (closed Sunday). Closed bank holidays.

ADMISSION CHARGES: Free

P ⛟ ⛹

DIRECTIONS: See map.

PONTERWYD
Llywernog Silver-Lead Mine Museum ✳

Ponterwyd, nr. Aberystwyth, Dyfed, Wales SY23 3AB
TEL: 01970 890620 FAX: 01545 570823
E-MAIL: silver-mine@cs.com

COLLECTION: For nearly 2,000 years the mining of silver-rich lead ore was a major rural industry in mid-Wales. The mines reached their peak between the 1850s and 1870s, but then came a slump and most of the mines were abandoned. The museum has an underground guided tour, with a chance to do your own gold-panning. There are mine artefacts such as tools, working water wheels, mining machinery and photographs and documents.

BUILDING: Llywernog mine was briefly reopened in 1907 as a zinc prospect. In 1973, the mine was saved from dereliction by the late Dr Stephen Harvey and his son. There are several 19th-century buildings, some original, some replica. The mine buildings are Grade II listed. There are some limitations to wheelchair access.

OPENING TIMES: *Easter to the end of October*, Tuesday to Sunday: 10am–6pm (closed Monday). Open over Easter and bank holidays. *July & August*, daily: 10am–6pm, or later. Open for pre-booked groups of 20 or more during the winter.

ADMISSION CHARGES: ②

Ⓟ ♿ 🚾 🚻 ⚠ 🎥 ⅋⅋

DIRECTIONS: 11½ miles east of Aberystwyth on the A44.

South Wales

BUTE TOWN
Drenewydd Museum ✳

26–27 Lower Row, Bute Town, Rhymney, Wales NP2 5QH

TEL/FAX: 01685 843039

COLLECTION: In one of the two terraced cottages is a re-creation of the everyday events of a busy ironworker's household. There is a two-cell 'cellar dwelling', a kitchen, parlour, two bedrooms and an attic room. Each room has been furnished and decorated to represent the household in 1870. In each room is a 'set piece' tableau, with static, costumed figures.

BUILDING: Three rows of terraced cottages, of which the museum is part, appear to have been built very differently from the usual workers' housing of the time. The houses are well-built, spacious, well-lit and ventilated. The cottages in Lower Row had cellars, which formed separate dwellings. Outside the museum is a re-created Victorian garden. There is a picnic area. For those who have difficulty with stairs access is limited to the ground floor and gardens.

OPENING TIMES: *Easter to October*, Saturday, Sunday and bank holidays: 2pm–5pm (closed Monday to Friday). School and group bookings taken all year round.

ADMISSION CHARGES: ①

Ⓟ 🚾 ⚠ 🎥 ⅋⅋

DIRECTIONS: Just off the A465 (Heads of the Valleys Road) on the A469. Signposted Rhymney. (See New Tredegar for Eliot Colliery, which is very near.)

CENARTH FALLS
National Coracle Centre ✳

Cenarth Falls, Carmarthenshire, Wales SA38 9JL

TEL/FAX: 01239 710980

E-MAIL: martinfowler@btconnect.com

WEBSITE: www.coraclecentre.co.uk

COLLECTION: Coracles are small, hide-covered, circular, dish-shaped boats, which probably date back to the Ice Age. Cenarth was the centre of coracle fishing in Wales, and there is a workshop where the ancient craft of coracle-making is shown. On display are coracles from all over the world, including Tibet, India, Iraq, Vietnam and North America. There is a 17th-century flour mill next door.

BUILDING: Converted outbuildings, part of the mill's grounds. There is a café next door. Toilets are in the village.

OPENING TIMES: *Easter to end of October*, Sunday to Friday: 10.30am–5.30pm (closed Saturday). Other times by appointment.

ADMISSION CHARGES: ①

🅿 ♿ ⚠ 🎥 ⅏

DIRECTIONS: In Cenarth Falls walk up the road, opposite the post office, towards the Mill. The river is on your left. The Coracle Centre is part of the mill grounds.

CYNONVILLE
Miners Museum ✱ ✳

Afan Argoed Countryside Centre, Cynonville, Port Talbot, West Glamorgan, Wales SA13 3HG

TEL: 01639 850564 FAX: 01639 850446

COLLECTION: Photographs, displays, mining tools and lamps and some mining equipment all help to portray life in a Welsh mining community. The Countryside Centre has a hands-on exhibition demonstrating the landscape and history of the Afan Valley. Photography requires permission.

BUILDING: Attached to the Countryside Centre.

OPENING TIMES: *April to September*, daily: 10.30am–6pm. *October to March*, 10.30am–5pm.

ADMISSION CHARGES: ①

🅿 ♿ 🚻 ☕ ⚠ 🎥 ⅏

DIRECTIONS: Leave the M4 at junction 40 on the A4107 north. Turn right staying on the A4107 to Croeserw. Cynonville is half-way along.

DRE-FACH FELINDRE
Museum of the Welsh Woollen Industry ✱ ✳

Dre-fach Felindre, Llandysul, Ceredigion, Wales SA44 5UP

Coracles on the River Teifi, National Coracle Centre, Cenarth Falls

TEL: 01559 370929 FAX: 01559 371592
WEBSITE: www.nmgw.ac.uk.co
COLLECTION: The village was the centre of the woollen industry in the first half of the 20th century. In the museum, centuries-old techniques, such as hand carding, spinning, hand-loom and powered weaving, are demonstrated. There are also exhibitions tracing the wool from fleece to fabric and telling the story of the community that was dependent on spinning and weaving. All this is alongside a working woollen-mill, still producing for the modern market. Enquire about permission to take photographs.
BUILDING: The museum occupies the site of the former Cambrian Mills built between 1902 and 1912. Wheelchair access is possible on the ground floor and in the grounds.
OPENING TIMES: *April to September*, Monday to Saturday: 10am–5pm (closed Sunday). *October to March*, Monday to Friday: 10am–5pm (closed weekends). Opening times may vary, ring to confirm.
ADMISSION CHARGES: Free

DIRECTIONS: Dre-fach Felindre is four miles east of Newcastle Emlyn and 16 miles north west of Carmarthen off the A484.

KIDWELLY

Kidwelly Industrial Museum ✸

Kidwelly, Carmanthenshire, Wales SA17 4LW
TEL: 01554 891078 or 891084
COLLECTION: The site of the second oldest tinplate works in Britain became a museum

in 1980. Tinplate consists of iron or steel rolled to a wafer-thin thickness and then coated with molten tin. Many large buildings, housing industrial machinery, remain on the site and the process of producing tinplate can be followed through such places as the pickling area, the annealing area and the tinning house. The Hot Rolling Mill is where the metal bars were rolled and re-rolled. The Cold Rolls and Engine House is where the metal plates received their final rolling. In addition there are steam locomotives and a steam-powered crane to view.

BUILDING: Tinplate production started at Kidwelly in 1737 and carried on almost continuously until the works finally shut down in 1941. There are picnic areas. Light refreshments are served in the shop/reception area. Access by wheelchair is better on dry days, as not all the paths have tarred surfaces.

OPENING TIMES: *Easter, Bank Holiday May Day and Spring Holiday. Then June to August,* Monday to Friday: 10am–5pm, Saturday & Sunday: 2pm–5pm.

ADMISSION CHARGES: Free

Ⓟ ♿ 🅆🅒 ⚠ 🎥 🏃

DIRECTIONS: The museum is off the ring road for Kidwelly, between the north and south roundabouts. Coming from the south and nearly opposite Priory Street, turn right into Mynddygarreg and then left into Llangadog Road. The museum is off to the left on the river.

MERTHYR TYDFIL
Joseph Parry's Ironworkers Cottage ✻

4 Chapel Row, Merthyr Tydfil, South Wales CF48 1BN

TEL: 01685 383704 or 721858

COLLECTION: The composer Joseph Parry (1841–1903) lived in the cottage as a child. The cottage has been restored to show living conditions of the 1840s. The upstairs rooms have an exhibition of Parry's life and work. Professor of music at University College, Aberystwyth from 1873 to 1879, Parry composed five operas and three oratorios, as well as cantatas and hymn tunes.

BUILDING: Built in 1825, two-up two-down cottage. It is a typical example of a skilled ironworker's dwelling house. Only the ground floor is accessible by wheelchair and there is no disabled toilet.

OPENING TIMES: *April to September,* Thursday to Sunday: 2pm–5pm. (Closed Monday to Wednesday.)

ADMISSION CHARGES: ①

Ⓟ ♿ 🅆🅒 ⚠ 🎥 🏃

DIRECTIONS: Follow the brown signs from the A465 or the A470.

NEW TREDEGAR
Elliot Colliery ✳

White Rose Way, New Tredegar, Wales NP34 6DF

TEL/FAX: 01443 822666/winter: 01443 864225 or 029 2088 001

E-MAIL: museums@caerphilly.gov.uk WEBSITE: www.caerphilly.gov.uk

COLLECTION: Once one of Powell Duffryn Steam and Coal Company's most productive collieries, the colliery now displays a steam winding engine, the only one of its kind remaining in South Wales. There is the winding house to see and the original Thornhill and Warham steam engine, which has been restored to working order. The story of the coal industry in the area is explained.

BUILDING: Producing coal for nearly 80 years, Elliot Colliery finally closed in 1967.

OPENING TIMES: *Easter to October*, Saturday, Sunday and bank holidays: 2pm–5pm. (Closed Monday to Friday.)

ADMISSION CHARGES: ①

Ⓟ ♿ WC ⚠ 🖼 ♟

DIRECTIONS: From the A465 (Heads of the Valleys Road), turn into the A469, signposted Rymney. Follow the road on to New Tredegar.

PEMBROKE
Museum of the Home ✳

7 Westgate Hill, Pembroke, Pembrokeshire, Wales SA71 4LB

TEL: 01646 681200

COLLECTION: Grouped according to its use, there are over 3,500 items of home equipment on display from cleaning things to lighting devices and the paraphernalia of eating and drinking. They cover the last 400 years. Judy and St John Stimson began collecting in the 1950s, and the museum is the result of their enthusiasm. In the first room are dairy and garden objects. Then comes the 'Home Medicine and Child Care' section. In the kitchen are all the items for cooking and food storage. Tobacco and snuff-taking are not forgotten, and there are needlework tools. The largest room has an extensive collection of games and toys, from a Roman dice to a Rubik's Cube. There is also a display of Welsh love spoons. Help is offered from an extensive library when requested.

BUILDING: An Edwardian renovation of a Georgian house on a medieval basement. Three domestic-sized rooms open to the public. Not accessible by wheelchair but personal attention will be given to suit disability.

OPENING TIMES: *1 May to 30 September*, Monday to Thursday: 11am to 5pm. (Closed Friday to Sunday.) *Children under 5 years are not admitted.*

ADMISSION CHARGES: ①

Ⓟ 🖼 ♟

DIRECTIONS: Just across the road from Pembroke Castle, which is well signposted.

TREFECA
Amgueddfa Howell Harris Museum (18th-century Methodist preacher) ❄ ✹

Trefeca, Aberhonddu, Brecon, Powys, Wales LD3 0PP

TEL/FAX: 01874 711423

E-MAIL: trefeca@surfaid.org

WEBSITE: www.ebcpcw.org.uk/pcwtrefeca.htm

COLLECTION: There was a religious community here in the 18th century and there is a re-created 18th-century room, displaying items of furniture made by the resident religious community from 1752. A re-created 18th-century preaching scene uses figures and a sermon of the Methodist preacher Howell Harris. Harris's swords and guns, scientific instruments and other items are on display, as are photos and information on the history of the Methodist revival in Wales and the subsequent history of Trefeca. A specialist library is available by appointment.

BUILDING: Howell Harris's 'castellated monastery', built to house his religious community. It is now a retreat, conference and lay training centre. Not accessible by wheelchair but suitable for ambulent disabled. Next door the Conference Centre is fully equipped for the disabled.

OPENING TIMES: *All year*, Monday to Friday: 9am–4pm (closed Saturday & Sunday). Closed Good Friday to Easter Tuesday & 24 to 26 December. Appointments preferred but they will try to accommodate casual visitors. Open at other times only by appointment. Refreshments by prior arrangement.

ADMISSION CHARGES: Free

ⓟ WC ⚠ 📷 ⛟

DIRECTIONS: Talgarth is on the A479 Abergavenny to Bronllys road. Caleg Trefeca is just south of Talgarth on the B4560 from Bwlch (which is on the A40). The museum is on the right as you drive towards Talgarth.

Index of Museums

Index of Museums

Index of Place Names